MILITARISM IN ARAB SOCIETY

MILITARISM IN ARAB SOCIETY

An Historiographical and Bibliographical Sourcebook

John Walter Jandora

Robin Higham, Advisory Editor

GREENWOOD PRESS
Westport, Connecticut • London

Library of Congress Cataloging-in-Publication Data

Jandora, John Walter.
Militarism in Arab society : an historiographical and bibliographical sourcebook / John Walter Jandora.
p. cm.
Includes bibliographical references and index.
ISBN 0-313-29370-8 (alk. paper)
1. Arab countries—History, Military. I. Title.
DS37.8.J36 1997
355'.00917'4927—dc20 96-35019

British Library Cataloguing in Publication Data is available.

Library of Congress Catalog Card Number: 96-35019
ISBN: 0-313-29370-8

First published in 1997

Greenwood Press, 88 Post Road West, Westport, CT 06881
An imprint of Greenwood Publishing Group, Inc.

Printed in the United States of America

The paper used in this book complies with the Permanent Paper Standard issued by the National Information Standards Organization (Z39.48-1984).

10 9 8 7 6 5 4 3 2 1

Contents

Illustrations

MAPS

TABLES

PHOTOGRAPHIC PLATES

Preface

This sourcebook offers a framework for the historical and comparative study of the military culture of Arab society. Through an extensive glossary and a series of essays, arranged as chapters, it introduces key events, institutions, and issues and discusses their historiographic treatment from both internal and external perspectives. Topical bibliographic lists follow the background essays in each chapter. The purpose of this work is to provide a much-needed reference aid for use by both academic and national defense communities. It is written primarily for the following potential users: professors and students of comparative military history, national and service intelligence analysts, and students of Arab-Islamic or Middle Eastern history. However, my hope is that generalist historians will also find it useful.

For the existence of this work, I am much indebted to Dr. Robin Higham, who sponsored and encouraged the project. I would also like to thank Dr. David Nicolle, who was kind enough to review and critique the entire draft typescript, and Mr. Robert Vreeland, who assisted with the production of maps. Finally, I wish to commend anonymous staff members of the Research Center of the Marine Corps University, the Marquat Memorial Library of the John F. Kennedy Special Warfare Center and School, and the Library of Congress, where most of my source hunting was accomplished. They all deserve some credit for this publication; however, I alone am responsible for whatever flaws exist in it.

Given the wide scope of this work, it was not practicable to find and cite every relevant source. I undoubtedly made some inadvertent omissions, and I apologize to those authors whose works deserve mention. On the other hand, I did make a conscious effort to limit the bibliographies in three ways. First, in view of the target readership, I opted not to cite Arabic works that have not been translated inasmuch as their use would not be feasible for most researchers. Second, I omitted certain works on the Crusades and the Arab-Israeli wars because of their indifference toward, if not bias against, the Muslim and Arab causes. There is virtually nothing to learn where one side has been shallowly depicted as "the enemy." Third, I omitted citation of works that purport to be "political-military histories" yet neglect coverage of military matters. Conversely, when parts of works seemed to be particularly relevant, I included them with chapter or page references.

Aside from source selection, other inevitable decisions concerned the rendering of proper names. Given the number of cultures pertinent to this study (Byzantine, Arabic, Perso-Turkish, Latin-Crusader, and others), one has to cope with a multiplicity of conventions for designating people and sites and transliterating foreign names. The problem with Middle Eastern site names (toponyms) in historical studies is that most have pre-Classical, Classical, Islamic, and modern variants. In this sourcebook, the English version is cited for those place names that are more commonly known in the West. Less familiar ones are rendered as transliterations of Arabic. Relevant variants are provided in parentheses. As for personal, dynastic, and other related names, this work generally follows the conventions used by the *Cambridge History of Islam*, again with variants in parentheses. Transliterations from Arabic are rendered in the International Phonetic Alphabet. The background discussions in chapters 1 and 2 contain some translations from Arabic sources. These are my own. The researcher will see that they vary somewhat from the versions found in the fully translated works, which are cited in the bibliographies.

As naming conventions cannot be taken for granted, neither can the use of dates. For the modern era of the Middle East (which begins with Napoleon Bonaparte's invasion of Egypt in 1798), historians almost always use the Gregorian calendar. For earlier periods, this is not the case. Thus, dates are indicated in this sourcebook with the Gregorian year first, followed by the Islamic (or Hijrī) year. It should be further noted that, in some cases, dates are only close approximations. The Islamic year is eleven days shorter than the Gregorian year. So, depending on relative chronology, a Gregorian year may include most of one Islamic year, variant proportions of two Islamic years, or roughly half of one year and half of another. Similar asymmetries pertain if one takes the Islamic calendar as the chronologic base. In comparing sources, the researcher will probably detect small variances in the dating of some events. Such disparity comes from one or both of the following: scholars erred in correlating the two calendar systems, or they were unable to resolve inconsistencies among "original" source documents. (Within the medieval Christian context, some dating inconsistency inevitably results from the reckoning of 25 March as New Year's Day.) Such problems of chronology are especially characteristic of the study of earlier historical periods.

Turning from historiographic to bibliographic concerns, the internal referencing conventions used in this sourcebook also require some comment. The bibliographic references are listed by chapter (i.e., main topic) and then by subtopics, which are numbered. The more comprehensive sources are listed where they have the most relevance. It is exceptional that the same work is cited in more than one bibliographic listing. The listings are introduced via background discussions. The reader should note that my internal referencing conventions rely on the above-mentioned bibliographic arrangement. The background essay usually refers to sources listed within the same chapter; however, it sometimes refers to sources listed in other chapters. In the first case, contextual references cite the author's name, short title, and publication date; footnotes cite author's name, publication date (or other means of differentiating works by the same author), and bibliographic list number (e.g., Bibliog. 4). In the second case, the footnote citation includes author's name, short title, and chapter and bibliographic list number (e.g., Chap. 1, Bibliog. 3). In the rare case that the background essay refers to a work that is not a bibliographic source, a full footnote format is used.

Finally, there remains to explain the chapter lead-ins, that is, the background essays. Their primary purpose is to assist those researchers who may not be familiar with the general outline of Arab or Islamic history or with the thematic bent of Arabic history writing. Some may be astonished to learn that Arabic historiography has no genre that is comparable to the military history of the Classical and Western worlds. In premodern Arabic historiography, military events have significance mainly insofar as they reflect on divine providence, group honor, or Sunni (orthodox Muslim) resurgence against infidels and sectarians. An understanding of this cultural contrast allows the researcher to understand better the apparent limitations of the source material.

The background essays attempt to focus research on relevant topics without being drawn into scholarly argumentation. For a study of this scope, there are many actual and potential issues of debate—largely because Arab-Islamic military terms and institutions have yet to be studied in a comprehensive way that accounts for continuity and change from one time period to another. In this work, I seek to present a consensual view but resort to my own where other scholarship lacks the necessary military perspective. Some among our academic readership may dislike this matter-of-fact approach. I can only encourage them to publish their own findings and help elucidate the relevant issue. Along the same line, I call attention in the essays to various subtopics that are particularly worthy of further study.

Bibliographic Abbreviations

AIUON	*Annali dell'Instituto Universitario Orientale di Napoli*
BSOAS	*Bulletin of the School of Oriental and African Studies*
C&S	*Crusade and Settlement*. Edited by Peter W. Edbury (Cardiff, Wales: University College Cardiff Press, 1985)
EI	*Encyclopedia of Islam*
IAA	*Islamic Arms and Armour*. Edited by Robert Elgood (London: Scholar Press, 1979)
IFAOC	L'Institut Français d'Archéologie Orientale du Caire
JRAS	*Journal of the Royal Asiatic Society*
JSAI	*Jerusalem Studies in Arabic and Islam*
RHC, Hist. Or.	*Recueil des Historiens des Croisades*, Historiens Orientaux
RUSI	Royal Uniformed Services Institute
WTS	*War, Technology, and Society in the Middle East*. Edited by V. J. Parry and M. E. Yapp (London: Oxford University Press, 1975)

Introduction

As the Vietnam War faded in Americans' consciousness, the study of military history eventually gained wide acceptance within American academia. Interest in military history has been further stimulated by the fiftieth anniversary of World War II. Yet, the field of study has been virtually restricted to Western military history and, particularly, the phenomena of the 19th and 20th centuries. Military historians have seen the need to expand their discipline. We in the West accept that our civilization evolved from Classical civilization in competition and conflict with other civilizations. We, therefore, cannot accept that Western ways of war evolved in isolation. This consideration notwithstanding, the comparative study of military history has not progressed very far. It has been hampered by the lack of primary and secondary source material and shortfalls in identification, translation, and interpretation of primary sources. Some recent worthy efforts have been made concerning source interpretation for Classical warfare.[1] Similar efforts have been made for Arab-Islamic warfare.[2] Disparity in outcome was inevitable, however, because the Arabs never wrote campaign histories like those of the Greeks and Romans.

The present volume grew out of an effort to establish a framework and define the limits for a study of war in the Arab East. It is generally known that Arab armies and, later, forces of Arab-led regimes threatened the Mediterranean lands of Europe in early and "high" medieval times. Thus, it is safe to assume that the Arabs have military traditions. However, it is not safe to assume that the Arabs have military history, particularly as it is written in the West. They do not. Consequently, for premodern times, we can generally reconstruct the *what* but not the *how* of the Arabs' military achievements. We can also reconstruct their perception of these achievements. For the modern period, the availability of Western sources compensates for the lack of native ones, which is due in part to censorship and the secrecy of military operations and in part to scholarly disinterest in military affairs. Because of the nature of the relevant sources, it is not possible to develop the theme of military history. Nonetheless, it is possible to develop related themes.

Over the past fifty years, we have seen the Arab world as the scene of military coups, arms races, and armed conflicts. Regional conflicts have included the many Arab-Israeli wars, the Egyptian intervention in Yemen, the Lebanese civil war, the Iran-Iraq War, the Gulf War, and the Yemeni civil war. Throughout this same period, we have seen the leaders of regional states and organizations making public appearances in military uniform. From such evidence we can deduce that contemporary Arab society is in some sense militaristic. Moreover, contemporary Arabic historiography idealizes the great Arab-Islamic conquests of early medieval times. Thus, for lack of a better term, the topic of militarism suggests itself as a unifying theme for this survey of the historical military culture of Arab society.

According to dictionary definitions, militarism is a complex concept that entails predominance of the military in governmental affairs, glorification of the ideals of the military class, and a policy of aggressive military preparedness. To that, I would add glorification of past military achievements and martial feats in literature, art, song, official propaganda, and other media. All four of these tendencies exist in the Arab world, particularly in the Arab lands of the Middle East. In this work, my view of Arab society has that limited scope. It does not encompass the entire Arab world but rather the eastern part only. This area, the "Arab East," consists of the lower Nile Valley (Egypt), the Levant (eastern Mediterranean littoral lands), Mesopotamia (Iraq), and the Arabian Peninsula. The Arab East is taken as an integral unit of historical analysis for three reasons. First, this territory formed the core of the early Islamic empire. Second, its modern-day inhabitants have a common cultural and historical heritage, which is somewhat different from that of Arab North Africa. Third, they face similar political problems, which derive from the collapse of the Ottoman Empire during World War I.

Finally, regarding definition, there remains to explain the historical significance of the word *Arab* as it has evolved through different cultural and chronologic contexts. From the internal perspective of Arabic historiography, the association of common origin, destiny, and name has been a late occurrence. In pre-Islamic times, the native people of the land that

Map I
The Eastern Arab World

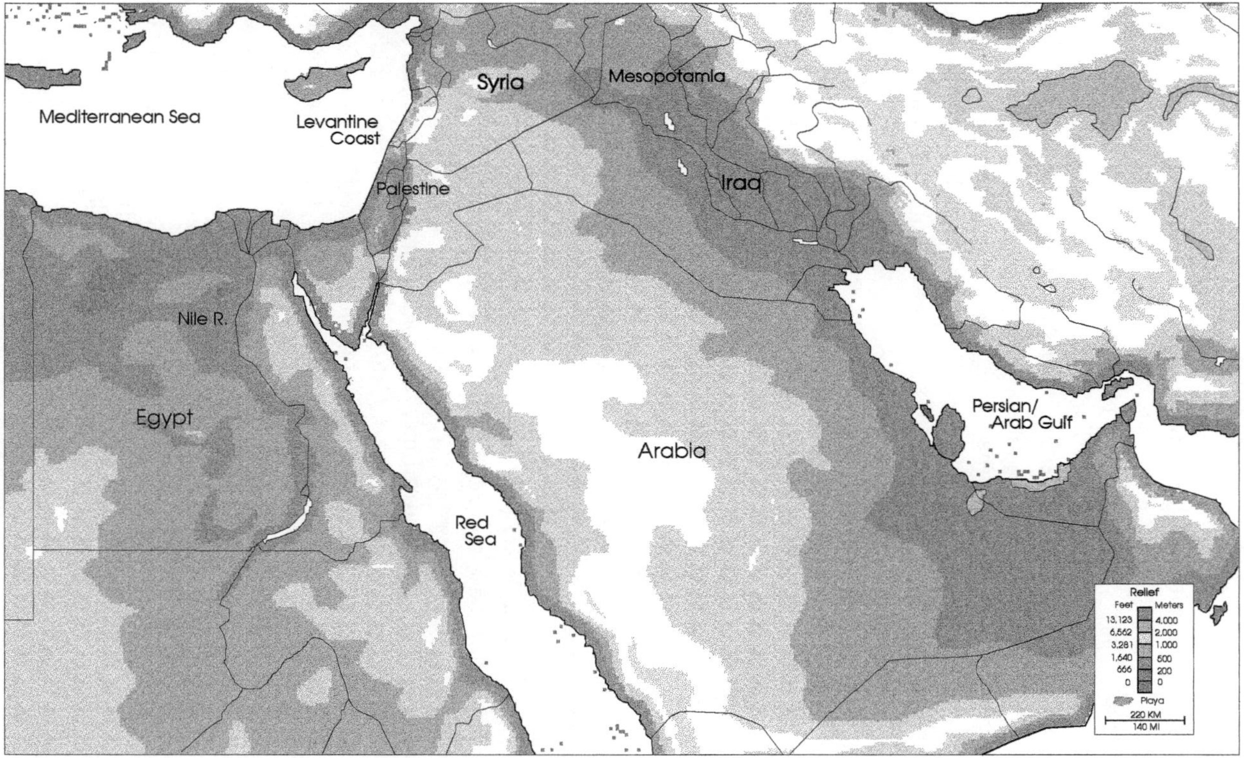

we call Arabia had some sense of common ethnicity but no grand epic work to define it. They identified with their clan or tribe, calling themselves the sons (*banū*, *banī*) of some eponymous ancestor. Among the more prominent tribes or tribal confederacies were Thamūd, Azd, Kinda, and Ghassān.

Under Islamic leadership in the 7th–8th/1st–2d centuries, the Arab people, calling themselves Muslimūn (Muslims), conquered much of the known world of Classical antiquity. As the Muslim Arabs merged with or assimilated indigenous populations, their scholars reverted to the older practice of distinguishing between sedentary and nonsedentary people. They reserved the name Arab for the Arabic-speaking, nomadic and seminomadic people of the desert and steppe areas of the Islamic world. They referred to the settled Arabs and Arabized people by various conventions, for example, the name of their religious sect or political-military faction. Adherents of mainline, orthodox Islam (Sunnism) referred to themselves as *Ahl al-Sunna wa al-Jamāʿa*, meaning People of the Tradition (of the Prophet) and of the Community (of True Believers).

When the Near East became exposed to the ideas of 19th-century European nationalism, Arabic-speaking intellectuals stimulated an Arab consciousness movement within their circles of influence. They initially chose the figurative term *Abnā' al-ʿArab* (sons of the Arabs) to express their ethnicity, since *ʿArab* itself still denoted nomads or bedouins. Eventually, *Abnā' al-ʿArab* gave way to the simpler *ʿArab* (sing., *ʿArabī*), which caught hold in popular usage. As a modern historical term then, *Arab* designates the people who conquered much of the Classical world and also the descendants of those people, by blood or cultural assimilation.

In the external perspective of Western historiography, the notion of *Arab* similarly varied over time. It derived from sources for late antiquity, the Crusading era, the period of Ottoman decline, and the modern Middle East. In late antiquity, the civilized nations of the Hellenistic East knew the Arabs as the oasis-dwellers and nomadic or seminomadic tribes that inhabited the borders of Syria-Mesopotamia and the peninsula to the south. Various histories relate that Arabs served in standing units of the Roman army and also joined in campaigns as allies of either the Romans or Persians. As the balance of power changed consequent to the Arab-Islamic conquests (633–715/11–96), so too did the designation of ethnicity. To denote Muslim Arab, the late Roman (i.e., Byzantine) historians increasingly used the word *Saracen*, which originally designated a specific tribe in Syria.

Historiographers of the Crusading era usually referred to the enemies in the Levant as Saracens, although Muslim forces then consisted of ethnic Arabs, Turks, Kurds, and other people. Crusader sources, if they differentiated the Arabs at all, usually did so by their language and customs, not by their livelihoods (nomadic versus sedentary). Still, there was not much reflection on the history of this particular ethnic group. The rise of the Mamluks at Cairo (mid-13th/7th century) brought an end to the Western military presence in the Near East. They and their successors, the Ottoman Turks, shielded the region from the Western world for nearly five centuries. Western forces returned to the Near East in the late 18th century and eventually dispossessed the Ottomans of Egypt and much of "Arabistan" (the Arab Near East). During that era, Western observers again distinguished the Arabs by language and customs, at first viewing them as subjects of the Turks and then as aspirants for independence.

For the first half of the 20th century, the external and internal historiographic notions of *Arab* merged. Afterward, they parted again. Faced with their countries' socioeconomic stagnation and military defeat in the first Arab-Israeli wars, many Arab intellectuals turned away from the unpleasantness of the present. They preferred to consider their race as being the heirs of past glory. Western observers, in contrast, saw the Arabs as lagging behind on the road to technological and sociopolitical modernization.

Taking from both contexts and reconciling differences in ethnographic designation, one can put together a fairly consistent general history of the Arab people. Such was achieved by Philip K. Hitti with his famous *History of the Arabs*. This work comprehensively records what the contemporary Arabs have learned about their history from both indigenous and foreign sources. The same general outline is reflected in the works of various other authors—both Muslim and Christian Arabs as well as Westerners. The main historical themes are as follows.

The disparate tribes and peoples of Arabia were forcefully united under Islam during the period 624–633/2–12. The Islamic momentum continued as a great conquest movement, whereby Muslim Arab arms quickly overran the Byzantine Near East and the whole Sassanid realm—in all, Syria, Palestine, Egypt, Armenia, Mesopotamia, and Iran. The political and religious leadership of Islam became embodied in the position of caliph (Arabic *khalīfa*, denoting successor of the Prophet). Consequent to the first Islamic civil war (656–660/35–40), the caliphate was changed from an elective office to a hereditary one. The Umayyads, who prevailed over the Alids (kinsmen of the Prophet), became the first dynasts of Islam. Under the House of Umayya, Arab arms pushed the frontiers of Islam across North Africa into Spain and beyond Iran into Central Asia and northern India. The Islamic establishment assimilated many different people, and some of these joined with Arab dissidents to overthrow the Umayyads in 750/132.

The rise of the Abbasid dynasty coincided with the rise of the ulema class (Arabic *'ulamā'*, religious scholars). During the Abbasid era (750–1258/132–656), significant advances were made in Islamic religious studies and Arabic literary culture in general. Concurrently, there was a catastrophic decline in Arab military and political power. Alien troops replaced Arabs in the elite units of the Islamic armies, and Muslim potentates of alien origin eventually subverted the temporal power of the Arab caliphate. Still, the Abbasids, at least the early ones, have retained high respect in the eyes of later generations. The ulema, many of whom wrote histories, rather subjectively represented them as being righteous and pious in contrast to their unholy Umayyad predecessors. The Abbasid dynasty also reclaimed some power and prestige during the late 12th/6th–early 13th/7th century. At this time, the tide of war was turning against the Crusader forces in the Levant.

Although the Crusades did not appear as catastrophic events to contemporary Muslim Arab observers, they gain preeminence in the works of modern Arab nationalists and Islamic activists.[3] They are now seen as precursive of later Western aggression against the Arab East. The Muslim counter-Crusading heroes, although ethnically non-Arabs, have become the saviors of both Arab culture and Islamic civilization in the Near East. The deeds of the Ayyubid and Mamluk sultans, particularly Saladin and Baybars, are included among the great achievements of the Arab people. In this case, the historiographic aggrandizement of non-Arab dynasties is seemingly based on the fact that they ruled from Cairo over a largely Arab dominion. This relationship between rulers and ruled changed when the Ottoman Turks conquered the Mamluk realm in 1517/922. The Arab East was thereby included in a larger, more ethnically diverse empire, which was ruled from Istanbul (formerly Constantinople). It was also wholly insulated from the struggle against Christian Europe and partially insulated from the struggle against Shiite Persia. Under Ottoman rule, however, the culture and economy of the region declined considerably. Thus, the Ottoman centuries have been viewed as "dark ages" for the Arab East.

With the gradual demise of the Ottoman regime, the Arabs started to gain a new consciousness of their role in history. Some saw the Wahhabi sectarian challenge in Arabia as a reminder of the religious primacy of the Arabs within Islam. Others saw the rise of the Muḥammad ʿAlī regime in Egypt (early 1800s) as a restoration of the Ayyubid-Mamluk dominion, which protected and promoted the interests of the Arab East. Arab hopes for autonomy were dashed when the Western powers shored up Ottoman authority in numerous crises during the 19th century. Yet, those hopes were revived in the following century. When the Ottomans joined the Axis powers at the onset of World War I in 1914, Britain and France reversed their policies and abetted the fledgling Arab drive for independence. As events transpired, however, the activists' goal of unifying the Arab East as one kingdom was never realized. Full autonomy was delayed for most of the Arab people, who had first to endure the rule of Western mandate and protectorate regimes. When independence finally came, its potential benefits were negated by the weakness of the existing political and economic institutions and the conflict with Israel over Palestine, which began in 1948 and lingered on for decades.

This historical outline obviously has considerable chronologic gaps—between the early Abbasid and counter-Crusading eras and the Ottoman conquest (of the Mamluk realm) and late Ottoman eras. However, these gaps are inevitable when one distinguishes the Arabs from the Islamic people in general. They reflect the fact that the period of Arab political dominance at the onset of Islamic civilization was relatively short. Still, the Arab (and Arabized) people remained the majority population of the central Islamic lands. As a conventional practice, Arab historians credited the governing regime and its troops, regardless of their ethnic origin, with protecting society from internal and external threats. They very seldom commented on those Arabs who served the regime as auxiliary forces or fought it as rebels. It is such low-profile experiences, though, which reflect continuity in Arab culture.

As noted above, the emergence of the Arabs in history coincides with the emergence of Islam in Arabia. Nonetheless, Arab culture has both Islamic and ethnic elements, and this dichotomy accounts for divergent themes of militarism. The Islamic myth of origin is militaristic; the Arab myths of origin are not. The divergence of themes can perhaps be best explained in terms of the literary-historical image, which is largely a courtier perspective, of three kinds of men at arms: bedouin tribal warriors, militias of sedentary communities, and professional troops (in standing units). Before taking up that task, however, it would do well to define each fighting force in generic terms.

The bedouins, who are known as the "sons of glory," are the nomads of the Arabian steppe. Their self-identity is based on tribal, or extended kinship, groups. Their livelihood largely depends on the breeding and herding of camels, which provide means of subsistence, travel, transport, and barter. The larger a tribe's herd, the greater is its wealth and prestige. The bedouins live apart from, but in symbiosis with, settled society. They constantly move with their camel herds between and within traditional grazing areas. They uphold their own laws, based on custom, and carry arms to protect themselves and their interests.

Historically, the stronger tribes had an ample supply of weapons, war horses, and transport and riding camels. They were quickly able to mass hundreds, if not thousands, of fighting men. In adverse circumstances, these warriors could just as quickly disperse. Most of the bedouins lived beyond the control of regional states. Those tribes that encountered state authority had the option of accommodating or defying it. In the first case, the bedouins might be employed, at minimal cost, as frontier defense forces or as auxiliary light cavalry in field operations against a common enemy. In the second case, they could pose a short- or long-term threat to settled society by attacking small, isolated garrisons and raiding poorly defended settlements.

The militias are the popular defense forces of both urban and rural, agrarian communities. They are often organized along clan or tribal lines, particularly in rural areas. They generally lack the mobility and harsh conditioning of the bedouins and, in some cases, may be less experienced in the use of weapons. The militias' armament and skill with weaponry are commensurate with the state's willingness to arm them or allow them to retain their own arms. From the perspective of state power, the militias, like the bedouin warriors, are sometimes auxiliaries and sometimes adversaries, depending on relations between the government and the populace. In mountainous regions, the people have a better chance of defying governmental authority because their militias can employ the difficult and broken terrain to their advantage.

The professional troops are the full-time soldiers who receive pay, provisions, lodging, and other compensation for their service. Thus, the size and armament of the standing formations are determined by the financial capacity of the state. The professional soldiers are usually recruited from specific native or nonnative groups. However, they may be recruited from outcasts, prisoners of war, and other "displaced persons." Some of the enlistees come well trained; others need further training. The preeminent qualification for service is allegiance to the regime, above any other loyalties. In many cases, standing formations are reduced to the status of militias as a result of adverse changes in loyalties, combat skills, or regime finances.

From the internal perspective, the image of the Arab warrior has been more prominent in legend than in history per se. It was during the fourth generation of Islam that Arabic historiography came into its mature phase. By then, the Umayyad regime had been thoroughly undermined by factional rivalry. Whatever official accounts or records existed were altered or swept away consequent to the rise of the Abbasids. The previous two centuries were, nonetheless, commemorated as a heroic age, with pre-Islamic and Islamic eras.

In the accounts of the pre-Islamic era, the mere resort to arms has value; the justness of the conflict is seemingly irrelevant. Bedouin warriors have the highest positive profile, although town militias have some share in the glory of local wars. Professional troops are sometimes allies and sometimes opponents of a clan's warriors. In the latter case, some accounts downplay the military capability of the professionals. With the rise of Islam, the bedouins take on an adversarial role. They are the enemies of the standing units, militias, and auxiliaries of the Islamic regime. Upon their submission, they become part of the Islamic military establishment, instruments of Islamic power. They and the two other force types lose their distinctness in the image of an entire people (Arabic, *nās*) under arms, serving the cause of Islam. Differentiation of military functions is similarly lost, so that light-armed horsemen are erroneously portrayed as shock troops. This image of the people (Muslim Arabs) under arms remains consistent through the wars of the two Islamic conquest eras. Likewise, the adversaries in the early civil wars are depicted in a nondescript way, the people of one belief or faction (tribal bloc) fighting the people of another belief or faction. As in the pre-Islamic conflicts, the mere resort to arms has value.

During the long Abbasid era (of five centuries), Arab fighting men continued to participate in the warfare between Christendom and Islam, albeit in decreasing numbers. Their exploits at the Anatolian frontier have been commemorated in legend and historical romance, which employ raid motifs of the pre-Islamic era of the herioc age. The men of the frontier militias and garrisons have been depicted both as tribal warriors and as fighters for the faith. During the same period, the composition of the caliphal guard corps and key garrisons of the central Islamic lands was altered such that Arabs were displaced by Iranians, Turks, and others. Despite this change, the literary-historical image of the military professionals remained positive, although it was shallow. Bedouin warriors and clan militias were no doubt involved in rebellions and sectarian wars as either supporters or adversaries of the Abbasid state. However, their identity became blurred in nondescript references to regime or rebel forces.

With the prolongation of the Crusading movement, the theme of fighting for the faith again becomes prominent in Arabic historiography. The Muslim professional troops and their leaders, who were mostly non-Arab, are acclaimed for their martial deeds. As for the Arab militias and bedouin warriors, their participation in campaigns is at least acknowledged. The counter-Crusading effort encompasses most of the Muslim fighting men of Egypt and Greater Syria, but the professionals are distinctly the heroes. With the final eviction of the Crusaders from the Levant, concern with military affairs recedes from the consciousness of Arab society until it becomes ravaged by Tamerlane's army (1400–1401/803). At this point in time, the famous Ibn Khaldūn commemorates the historic role of bedouins in war—albeit in a somewhat misleading way.

From later Mamluk through classical Ottoman times, the arena of conflict in the Near East was primarily restricted to the Western frontiers of Shiite Persia. Arab irregular forces served in campaigns at that front as well as in internal security roles throughout Arabistan. However, their service was hardly notable to a ruling class that was largely Turkish in culture. In late Ottoman times (18th–19th centuries), the allegiance of the Arabs to Istanbul started to waver when the puritanical Wahhabis challenged the legitimacy of Ottoman authority in Arabia. Among the Wahhabi forces, the bedouins seemingly had more visibility than the town and village militias, although the latter were the mainstay of the military establishment. From the Ottoman loyalist perspective, the Wahhabis were heretics and lawless marauders. From the obverse, Wahhabi perspective, the Ottoman forces were the henchmen of a religiously corrupt regime. Moreover, the reputation of the regime and its professional "Turkish" soldiers was further discredited when Western forces broke through the Ottoman shield at the end of the 18th century and continued to intervene in the affairs of Egypt and Syria. The tensions between subjects and rulers eventually devolved to the point that Arab separatists initiated a revolt against the Turks during World War I. With this revolt, which came to be seen as a nationalist conflict, the Arab East passed from the Islamic age into the modern age.

With the advent of modernity, the bedouin population in the Arab East drastically declined. The image of the bedouin warrior became an anachronism. Militias continued to safeguard the interests of clans and communities—often in opposition to the central political authority of their country. Being distrustful of militias, newly independent Arab regimes turned to veterans of the former Ottoman army to form cadres for the new national forces. This development has been ignored by modern Arab historians, deliberately so by nationalist writers, with the consequence that most outside observers are oblivious of the underlying cultural continuum. True, the Arab people were, in general, long excluded from the Ottoman central bureaucracy and military class. However, they were included during the last decades of the empire. The subsequent wide-scale emergence of Arab "free officer" movements (i.e., military intervention in politics) can be traced to immediate, Turkish influences as well as older, Islamic ones.

Turk and Arab ideologues similarly see the military as an agent of societal modernization and progress. However, they differ in their justification of military intervention in politics. With the Turks, the impetus is the danger to a vital interest of the nation-state. With the Arabs, the impetus is the righteousness of one faction. The Arab paradigm is in a certain sense a throwback to earlier Islamic times, as the following considerations suggest. The Umayyad dynasty became established during an era of factional conflict. The House of Umayya held on to power by playing off the main tribal factions against one another. Its power base was undermined when the cohesion of the Syrian army succumbed to factional influences. The Abbasids exploited this military factionalism in their rise to power. They then purged, more than once, the elite units of the Islamic military establishment—the caliphal guard corps and the garrisons of key sites. The need to counter factionalism became one of the tenets of classical Islamic government. Two others were to expand, or at least defend, the Islamic dominion and to maintain the jurisdiction of Islamic law.

The intense factionalism that has undermined the political cohesion of the Arabs through history reflects the following cultural imperative. The extended family (or kin group) is the fundamental unit of political and social action, and kinship usually dictates loyalties. According to this paradigm, a kin group first looks to its own fighting men, not to the state's armed forces, to ensure its survival and protection and promotion of its interests. Subconsciously, the resort to arms for the sake of one's clan is a higher ideal than military service to the state. The obligation of jihad (fighting to expand or defend the Islamic dominion) receives considerable attention in the literary and historiographic heritage of the Arabs. However, the call to jihad has seldom been effective where clan interests were not directly affected.

By taking an essentially ethnocentric approach to this study, I have had to forego some chronological continuity. However, there is virtually no way to pursue a coherent study of warfare or militarism in the Near East without being selective in the treatment of topics. One might trace the historical development of Islamic arms through the successive contributions of Arabs, Iranians, and Turks (to include the manpower of the Caucasus region).[4] Yet each of these nations had pre-Islamic military traditions and practices. Those of the Turks and, to a lesser extent, the Iranians derive from Central Asian culture—a considerable expansion in scope. Moreover, Islamic history per se ends with the onset of World War I—a chronological limitation. Many variant influences converge and interact in the civilization and military culture of Islam. I, for one, believe that, to make sense of the Islamic composite, it is better to separate out the distinct ethnocultural strands. These can be studied in their pre-Islamic, Islamic, and modern-day stages. Having said that, it is necessary to admit that the primary source material will be scarce for the pre-Islamic stage and perhaps spotty for the Islamic one. This is the case regarding research on the military aspects of Arab history.

As mentioned previously, the Arabic literary heritage lacks any genre comparable to military history in the Western world. Moreover, there is very little genuine primary source material for the pre-Islamic and early Islamic eras. The extant record of relevant events is found in the writings of later generations. These include historical romances, chronicles, and other traditional historical works, many of which have been translated or otherwise retransmitted in whole or in part. The works in this corpus selectively draw from earlier sources, which largely belong to the genres of salvation history or tribal epic. The extant sources present two challenges for research on Arab military practice. First, they are anachronistic; that is, their authors interpret and portray earlier events from the perspective of their own time. Second, they generally ignore or distort aspects of warfare because of the authors' motives or use of literary conventions. Distortion notwithstanding, these sources have inspired popular histories in both the Arab world and the West. The full scholarly history of the great Arab (or Islamic) conquests, the civil wars of early Islam, and the incessant Muslim-Byzantine struggle remains to be written.

For the above reasons, Part I of this sourcebook addresses the Arab warfare of ancient and early medieval times in terms of "traditions." The relevant events fall more in the realm of myth or legend than of history. The secondary sources reveal some of the problems of primary-source interpretation and also the disagreement among scholars as to the historicity of events. The number of valuable references is not extensive. Many of the bibliographic citations are works of European Orientalists, and several of these demonstrate philological rather than social science methods.

We come closer to the realm of history with the later Abbasid period. By this time, though, most of the standing formations of Islamic armies consisted of non-Arab soldiery. Still, Arab militias and bedouin warriors fought in the rebellions of the 10th/4th century, the counter-Crusading campaigns, and the Mamluk-Mongol wars in northern Syria. Their role in the counter-Crusades is more in evidence because of the many sources that recount the fighting of that epoch. However, there exists no comprehensive study of "irregular forces" in the conflicts of medieval Islam. Such an effort will require the careful examination of many contemporary or nearly contemporary works whose subjects are other than war. The preponderance of the secondary sources for this period address two main subjects: (1) military technology—armor, weaponry, fortification, and siege techniques and (2) various aspects of the slave-soldier institution and, especially, the famous Mamluk military establishment. For the Crusading era in particular, Western scholars have found it more feasible to undertake comparative studies of warfare. Yet even with this era, genuine historical inquiry is hampered by the legend and romance that surround the careers of Saladin and, to a lesser extent, Baybars and their "defeat of the infidels."

Except for the conquest of Egypt and Arabistan, the achievements of Ottoman arms in the Arab East have been neglected by both contemporary and modern Arab historians. It might be possible to reconstruct the role of Arab irregulars in Ottoman armies. However, this effort would necessitate the meticulous examination of a multitude of potential sources in Ottoman Turkish. Neither modern Arab historians nor Western Ottomanists have been inclined to undertake such a project. Thus, Part II, my discussion of military roles in medieval Islam, ends with the Ottoman conquest of the Arab East.

My survey of relevant topics resumes in Part III with the period of Ottoman decline and Western intervention—the beginnings of the modern Middle East. Potentially useful sources for the period from 1798 to the present are much more abundant than those for earlier periods. We have many personal observations of Westerners who served in various capacities in the Arab East. The growth of journalism has added to the opportunities for direct observation. Moreover, a few Arab officers have been willing to breach the customary secrecy that pervades military activity in the Arab World. The Western student of Arab military affairs has, thus, been freed from dependence on the arcane accounts of court scholars and historians.

Considering the nature of the works cited within, the bibliographies of Part III differ somewhat from those of Parts I and II. The sources as a whole are probably easier to use. There is more firsthand reporting by both Western and native participants in events. There are fewer academic, interpretative works, as indigenous writing styles have gradually taken on modern form. Regarding the more scholarly endeavors among the Western sources, social science methodology displaces philology. There is a high proportion of English-language sources, which reflects the growing dominance of British and then American influence and interest in the Arab East. The one period for which French sources are prevalent is that of Muḥammad ʿAlī's rule in Egypt.

For the past half century, there is a disproportionately large amount of information on the battlefield performance of Arab armies and the role of the military in Arab society. This gain notwithstanding, the researcher must still be attentive to the author's bias in many potential sources. Direct involvement or observation has brought not only more detail but also more emotion and partiality. Moreover, the coalescence of the Arab-Israeli Conflict and the Cold War (between the Soviet- and U.S.-led blocs) has in many cases strengthened adversarial viewpoints. I have consciously excluded the more biased works from the bibliographic listings. These contribute nothing to my aim, which is to suggest correlations between present and past institutions, symbols, thought patterns, and values.

NOTES

1. See, for example: Daniel W. Engels, *Alexander the Great and the Logistics of the Macedonian Army* (Berkeley: University of California Press, 1978); Victor Davis Hanson, *The Western Way of War: Infantry Battle in Classical Greece* (New York: Alfred A. Knopf, 1989); and Yann Le Bohec, *The Imperial Roman Army* (New York: Hippocrene, 1994).

2. Scholarly research in this field once largely resided in collections of articles, for example: V. J. Parry and M. E. Yapp, eds., *War, Technology, and Society in the Middle East* (London: Oxford University Press, 1975); David Ayalon, *Studies on the Mamlūks of Egypt (1250–1517)* (in Chap. 5, Bibliog. 3); and Robert Elgood, ed., *Islamic Arms and Armour* (London: Scholar Press, 1979). For more recent endeavors in Islamic and Arab military history, see John W. Jandora, *The March from Medina* (in Chap. 2, Bibliog. 4); Reuven Amitai Preiss, *Mongols and Mamluks* (in Chap. 5, Bibliog. 4); and S. A. El-Edroos, *The Hashemite Arab Army 1908–1979* (in Chap. 6, Bibliog. 3).

3. See Emmanuel Sivan, *Modern Arab Historiography of the Crusades* (Tel Aviv: Tel Aviv University, 1973).

4. The parameters of such a study are implied in Muhammad Naeem, *Muslim Military History: A Preliminary Bibliography*. 1st ed. (Islamabad, Pakistan: Islamic Research Institute, 1985).

Glossary: Terms and Names with Militaristic Significance

Authors and publishers use varying conventions to render words and names of Arabic origin in English. The entries below appear with full diacritics, although they may appear elsewhere without. Variant forms are listed only when different characters are used to represent the same foreign sound.

Ajnādayn
(var. Ajnādīn). First major victory in the Arab-Islamic conquest of Syria. Muslim Arab forces, led by Khālid ibn al-Walīd and ʿAmr ibn al-ʿĀṣ, engaged and defeated the Byzantines to the southwest of Jerusalem in 634/13. The events of Ajnādayn are often confused with those of the later Yarmūk campaign. As a consequence, the battle of Ajnādayn has virtually no historical profile. See chapter 2.

amīr.
Arabic word meaning *governor*, *ruler*, or *commander*. It is traditionally used to designate the head of a state, tribal group, or military force. One of the caliph's titles was Amīr al-Mu'minīn (Commander of the Faithful).

Amorium.
City in Anatolia, the object of several Muslim-Arab attacks during the 7th–9th/1st–3rd centuries. The raid on Amorium in 838/223 was the last significant Abbasid land offensive against the Byzantines. This event was commemorated in a famous poem by Abū Tammām. See chapters 1 and 3.

ʿAmr ibn al-ʿĀṣ.
One of the most competent leaders of the first generation of Islam. ʿAmr had a key role in the conquest of Palestine and the lead role in the conquest of Egypt. He sided with Muʿāwiya against ʿAlī in the first Islamic civil war, and consequently his deeds have been slighted or maligned in many Arabic historical works. See chapters 2 and 3.

Anṣār.
Arabic word, plural form, literally meaning *helpers* or *supporters*. In traditional sources, al-Anṣār designates the natives of Medina who gave their allegiance to the Prophet Muḥammad and fought for the Islamic cause. They became an important interest group in early Islam. The Anṣār were distinguished from the Muhājirūn, those people of Quraysh who, with the Prophet, emigrated from Mecca to Medina. In modern times, Arab militias and militant groups have used the word Anṣār in their titles.

ʿAyn Jālūt.
Decisive Muslim victory over the Mongols and their allies. In 1260/658, the Mamluk army, under Sultan Quṭuz, marched through Crusader territory to counter the Mongol threat from Syria. The Mamluks intercepted and overwhelmed an advance force of the Mongol army at this site near Nazareth in Palestine. The Mongols made no further advance toward Egypt. See chapter 5.

ʿAyn Shams.
First major victory in the Arab-Islamic conquest of Egypt. Muslim Arab forces, led by ʿAmr ibn al-ʿĀṣ, defeated the provincial troops massed at that site (now part of modern Cairo) in 640/19. From then on, the Byzantines could only fight defensively. The battle at ʿAyn Shams led to the Muslim investment of surviving Byzantine forces at the famous fortress of Babylon. See chapter 2.

Ayyām al-ʿArab.
See ***yawm***.

Badr.
First victory of Muslim arms over pagan Arabia. The Prophet Muḥammad, leading some 300 Muslims, engaged and defeated a larger Meccan force at the wells of Badr (southwest of Medina) in 624/2. The victory was taken to be a sign of divine providence. See chapter 2.

Baṭṭāl.
Arabic word meaning *hero*; honorific name of a famous Muslim Arab war leader. ʿAbdullah al-Baṭṭāl (d. circa. 740/122) had a key role in the frontier warfare against the Byzantines in Anatolia. His exploits have been commemorated in fictionalized form in popular legend and historical romance. See chapter 1.

Baybars I.
Legendary Mamluk war leader and sultan. Baybars had important roles in the victories over the Crusaders at Gaza and over the Mongols at ʿAyn Jālūt. As sultan, he extended the Mamluk realm into Nubia, Libya, and Syria and established a protectorate over the Hijaz, with its two holy cities. Baybars also initiated the series of offensives that brought an end to the Crusader presence in the Levant. See chapter 5.

Bayt al-Muqaddas
(var. Bayt al-Maqdis). Alternate Arabic names for Jerusalem. See **Quds**.

Camel, Battle of the.
Initial battle of the first Islamic civil war. Forces loyal to ʿAlī ibn Abī Ṭālib defeated the forces of his opponents (ʿĀ'isha, Ṭalḥa, and al-Zubayr) near al-Baṣra in 656–57/36. The name of the battle recalls that intense fighting supposedly took place around the camel that bore ʿĀ'isha's litter. See chapter 3.

Dhū Qār
(var. Dhū Ḳār). One of the most famous battles of pre-Islamic Arabia. Arab tribesmen of Shaybān b. Bakr defeated a force of Sassanid cavalry and tribal auxiliaries in A.D. 602 at this site on the lower Euphrates. Arab historians of later times viewed this victory as a testament to the martial superiority of Arabs over Persians. See chapter 1.

fāris.
Arabic word meaning *horseman* or *mounted man at arms*. It correlates to English *knight* but without the connotations of feudal rank and duty. See chapter 4.

Fatḥ
(var. Fatah). Arabic word meaning *opening* and, in an extended sense, *conquest*. The name, as a reverse acronym, designates the Palestinian political-military organization that was established by Yāsir ʿArafāt and Abū Khalīl al-Wazīr during the 1950s. Fatḥ has had a dominant influence within the Palestine Liberation Organization. See chapter 7.

Fedayeen
(Ar. *fidā'iyīn*). Literally, *those who sacrifice themselves (for a cause)*. This term commonly denotes Palestinian militiamen in general. It alludes to their willingness to carry out suicide or high-risk missions against the Israelis. See chapters 7 and 8.

fitna.
Arabic word with primary meaning of *strife*, used to designate civil war in traditional sources. Of the three major civil wars of early Islam, the first involved the Alid-Umayyad struggle for the caliphate. The second involved Umayyad efforts to preserve their dynasty. The third involved internal conflict among the Umayyads and their overthrow by the Abbasids. See chapter 3.

furūsīya.
Arabic technical term denoting horsemanship skills in a collective sense. This term appears in military manuals of the Mamluk era, which address the training of Muslim cavalrymen. Furūsīya includes the handling and care of mounts as well as the handling of weapons by mounted troops. See chapters 4 and 5.

futūḥ
(pl. *futūḥāt*). Arabic word meaning *conquest*. The plural *futūḥāt* refers to the two-phased expansionist movement of Islam. The early conquests, which occurred from 633/11 to 645/24, included Arabia, Syria, Palestine, Egypt, Persia, Mesopotamia, and Armenia. The follow-on, Umayyad conquests, which mostly occurred from

698/79 to 715/96, included North Africa, Spain, Transoxiana, and northern India. The traditional Arabic historical record of these conquests is sometimes referred to as *futūḥ* literature. See chapters 2 and 3.

ghāzī.
Arabic word for *raider*. The term was applied to the Muslim frontier troops who raided into infidel territory in Anatolia and south-central Asia during the 8th–10th/2d–4th centuries. The ghāzī ethos was eventually assimilated in Turkish military tradition. See chapter 1.

ghazw.
Arabic word for *raid*. See ***ghāzī*** and ***maghāzī***.

ghulām.
See ***mamlūk***.

ḥarb.
Arabic word meaning *war* in a generic sense. The term has a neutral connotation, unlike *fitna* (internal strife or civil war) and *jihād* (war against non-Muslims).

Ḥaṭṭīn
(var. Ḥiṭṭīn). Decisive Muslim victory over the Crusaders. The army of Saladin crushed the Crusader forces near Lake Tiberias in Palestine in 1187/583. By this victory, the Muslim forces reversed the tide of the Crusading movement. The Latin states of the Levant survived this disaster, but they never regained their former military superiority. See chapter 5.

Ikhwān.
Arabic word, plural form, meaning *brethren*. In Arabia, Ikhwān denotes the militiamen who constituted the mainstay of the Saudi army in the early 1900s. To create this force, the Saudi regime settled bedouins in colonies throughout central Arabia, where they were trained in religious doctrine, agriculture, and war craft. See chapter 6.

Jalūlā'.
Decisive victory in the Arab-Islamic struggle against Sassanid Persia. In 637/16, Muslim forces, led by Hāshim ibn ʿUtba, drove the Sassanid army from its last foothold in Mesopotamia. The battle was apparently won when the Muslims penetrated the Persians' defensive works. This victory opened the way for the Islamic invasion of upper Mesopotamia and the Iranian plateau. See chapter 2.

jaysh.
Arabic word for *army*. In early Arabic sources, *khamīs* also denotes army, while *jaysh*, used in plural form *juyūsh*, often translates as contingents, troops, or military forces.

jihād.
Arabic word meaning literally *endeavor* and, by extension, *physical or mental endeavor in the cause of Islam*. When denoting a military effort, *jihād* translates as *holy war* (the usual meaning of the English loan word). It is struggle against non-Muslim forces with the aim of extending or defending the Islamic dominion. One

who participates in such warfare is called *mujāhid*, pl. *mujāhidīn* (Eng. vars. mujahideen, mujahedin). See chapter 3.

jundī.
Arabic word for *soldier*, an adjectival derivative of *jund*. In early Islamic times, the word *jund* denoted a military district, particularly in Syria, or the body of troops that was garrisoned within such a district. In modern times, *jundī* designates the rank that corresponds to the English private.

Karāma
(var. Karameh). Town in northern Jordan, once the site of a Palestinian militia base. The base was the objective of a large-scale Israeli reprisal attack in March 1968. Although the Palestinians sustained considerable losses, their propagandists transformed this event into a symbolic victory for Palestinian resistance. See chapter 7.

Karbalā'.
Shiite holy site in southern Iraq, battle of the second Islamic civil war. At the summons of the anti-Umayyad Shī'a of al-Kūfa, Ḥusayn ibn ʿAlī proceeded there to become their caliph. Umayyad forces blocked his entourage, which included only seventy men at arms, at Karbalā'—some twenty-five miles northwest of the city. Ḥusayn and his men fell in battle on 10 Muḥarram 61 (10 October 680). See chapter 3.

katība
(pl. *katā'ib*). Arabic term for a military unit of intermediate size. The word is used ambiguously in traditional sources for early Islam to designate a company or squadron size unit. In modern usage, *katība* correlates with the Western concept of battalion in most Arab armies. The members of the main Maronite militia in Lebanon took the name *katā'ibiyīn* (an adjectival derivative of the plural form), which the Western press normally rendered as the French word *Phalangists*.

Khālid ibn al-Walīd
(vars. Chaled, Waleed). The foremost Muslim Arab military leader of the early Conquest era. Known as the "Sword of Allah," he had a key role in numerous campaigns in Arabia, Iraq, and Syria, including the great victories of Ajnādayn and al-Yarmūk. Aside from his own battlefield accomplishments, Khālid was apparently the mentor of several other successful commanders. See chapter 2.

Khandaq.
Third significant encounter between the early Muslims and pagan Arabs. The word, which means *trench* in Arabic, was aptly chosen to denote this engagement. While allied enemy forces of Meccans, Jews, and bedouins surrounded Medina in 627/5, the Muslims constructed earthworks for their protection. Their enemies failed to penetrate these defenses, and the hostile alliance consequently fell apart. See chapter 2.

liwā'.
Arabic word that originally designated a military banner of some sort. The terminology for the early Islamic period is ambiguous. It seems that *liwā'* denotes a

guidon (that is, a position marker), whereas *rāya* denotes a battle standard. In modern usage, *liwā'* generally correlates with the Western concept of brigade.

maghāzī.
Arabic word, plural form, meaning *military campaigns* or *raiding expeditions*. Early Arabic historiography includes a genre of works that recount the military exploits of the Prophet Muḥammad and his Companions. The authors of these works ostensibly viewed earlier events from the perspective of their own time, when Muslim military activity was generally limited to cross-border raiding. See chapter 1.

Mamlūk
(var. Mameluke). Arabic passive participle meaning *owned* and, by extension, *enslaved*. The term derives from the practice of medieval Islam whereby the manpower of elite military units (and also government bureaus) was recruited from slaves and prisoners of war. Thus, *mamlūk* denotes a soldier who belonged to such a unit. The word *ghulām* is used synonymously. See chapter 4. Mamlūk is also the name of the dynasty that ruled from Cairo over Egypt, Syria, and adjacent lands from 1250/648 to 1517/922. See chapter 5.

maʿrika.
See ***yawm***.

Marj Rāhiṭ.
Umayyad victory of the second Islamic civil war. Troops loyal to Marwān ibn al-Ḥakam defeated troops loyal to Ibn al-Zubayr at this site near Damascus in 684/64. The Syrian army had split according to factional allegiance. Henceforth, military factionalism remained a key factor in Umayyad politics. See chapter 3.

Marwān II.
Last Umayyad caliph (744–750/127–132). Prior to his accession, he was a popular commander of troops at the Caucasus frontier. As caliph, Marwān changed the Muslim battle array from a close-order, linear formation (*ṣaff*) to an open one with base and maneuver echelons (*kurdūs*). Marwān was unable to curtail the military factionalism in Syria, which undermined the Umayyad dynasty and contributed to its overthrow. See chapter 3.

Muʿāwiya.
Famous founder of the Umayyad dynasty (661–750/41–132). Muʿāwiya participated in the Islamic invasion of Syria and eventually became the provincial governor at Damascus. From his strong power base there, he successfully challenged the claims of ʿAlī and his sons (relatives of the Prophet) to the caliphate. Both as governor and caliph, Muʿāwiya directed numerous campaigns against the Byzantines. See chapters 1 and 3.

Muḥammad ʿAlī Pasha
(var. Mehmet Ali). Ottoman-appointed governor (1805–1848), renowned as the founder of modern Egypt. Muḥammad ʿAlī implemented many military and governmental reforms with the aim of strengthening his power base. By means of numerous military campaigns, he subjugated much of the Near East and eventually challenged the authority of the Ottoman sultan. European intervention negated much that he had accomplished. See chapter 6.

Mujahideen
(var. Mujahedin). See ***jihād.***

Mūsā ibn Nuṣayr.
Renowned military governor of North Africa (700–715/81–96). He subjugated the littoral lands from Carthage to the Atlantic. One of his subordinates led the Muslim invasion of Spain. See chapter 3.

Nihāwand.
Called the "victory of victories," decisive engagement in the Arab-Islamic conquest of Iran. Muslim Arab forces from the garrisons of Kūfa and Baṣra advanced into central Iran and engaged the Sassanid army there in 641/20. They feigned a withdrawal to lure the Persian troops from their strong defensive positions and beat them in an open-field battle. See chapter 2.

Qādisīya.
Decisive victory which assured the Arab-Islamic conquest of lower Iraq. Muslim Arab forces, under Saʿd ibn Abī Waqqāṣ, fought a successful defensive action when the Sassanid army attacked across the Euphrates near Lake Najaf in 636/15. Reinforcements from Syria arrived at a decisive moment and counterattacked. As the Sassanid troops fell back across the river, their retreat degenerated into a rout. See chapter 2.

Quds, Bayt al-Muqaddas, Bayt al-Maqdis.
Arabic name for Jerusalem, third holiest city in Islam. The Temple Mount, located there, is believed to be the site from which the Prophet made his night journey to heaven. It is also believed to be the site at which the true believers (Muslims) will be gathered on the day of judgment. The Muslims lost but regained control of Jerusalem during the Crusades. See chapter 5. They lost control of the city during the Arab-Israeli Wars; for the pious, there is a religious obligation to retake it. See chapter 7.

Qutayba ibn Muslim.
Muslim war leader, renowned for the conquest of Transoxiana. In a series of campaigns lasting from 705/86 to 715/96, Qutayba retook or subjugated anew much territory in Central Asia. See chapter 3.

al-Rashīd, Hārūn
(var. Rasheed). Fifth Abbasid caliph (786–809/170–193), made famous worldwide by the romantic tales of the "Thousand and One Nights." Hārūn is also renowned in Arab-Islamic lore for reviving the official pilgrimage to Mecca and for reviving annual raid activity against the Byzantines in Anatolia. See chapters 1 and 3.

ridda.
Derivative of an Arabic word which, by extension, means to *retract (allegiance)* or *renounce (faith)*. In traditional Arabic sources, *ridda* designates the wars of early Islam (632–633/11–12) in which the Muslim regime at Medina suppressed various tribal rebellions against its authority. The implication is that the rebels renounced Islam; therefore, English works refer to the "Wars of Apostasy."

Saʿd ibn Abī Waqqāṣ.
Known as the "Archer of Islam," he was one of the early Companions of the Prophet. Although disabled, he held nominal command of the Arab-Muslim forces at the decisive battle of Qādisīya. Afterward, Saʿd twice served as governor at the garrison town of al-Kūfa. See chapter 2.

Ṣāʿiqa.
Arabic word for *thunderbolt.* Ṣāʿiqa was taken as a name by one of the Palestinian military organizations. Originally established with Syrian support, Ṣāʿiqa withdrew from the Palestine Liberation Organization in 1983 and remained estranged from it. As for the thunderbolt symbol, it is the emblem of various elite units among the armed forces of the Arab world.

Saladin
(Ṣalāḥ al-Dīn Yūsuf ibn Ayyūb). Counter-Crusading hero, renowned for his chivalry in both Islamic and Western lore. Saladin became the effective ruler of Egypt in 1169/564. In his effort to unite the Islamic world, he deposed the Fatimid caliph, conquered the lands adjacent to Egypt, and took many of the Zangid possessions in Syria and Mesopotamia. Saladin eventually turned against the Crusaders and defeated them in the battle of Ḥaṭṭīn. See chapter 5.

Ṣawārī.
Arabic word for *masts*. The expression *Dhāt al-Ṣawārī* denotes the naval battle at which the Muslim Arabs defeated the Byzantines near Phoenix off the Lycian coast of Anatolia in 655/34. See chapter 2.

Ṣiffīn.
Indecisive battle of the first Islamic civil war, which pitted the heroes of the conquest of Syria against the heroes of the conquest of Iraq. In the spring of 657/36, ʿAlī led an army of some 50,000 into Syria to depose Muʿāwiya. His advance was checked by Muʿāwiya's forces on the plain of Ṣiffīn near al-Raqqa. The ensuing confrontation ended with an agreement to settle the issue of governmental legitimacy through arbitration. See chapter 3.

talīʿa
(pl. *talāʾiʿ*). Arabic term designating a body of scouts or out riders. The word, as used in the title of at least one contemporary militant group, has been translated as *vanguard.* Technically, the *talīʿa* is the mounted patrol that moves ahead of the van or advance guard (Ar. *muqaddima*).

Ṭāriq ibn Ziyād.
Muslim war leader renowned for invading Spain. As a subordinate of Mūsā ibn Nuṣayr, Ṭāriq led several thousand troops onto the peninsula in 711/92. He quickly defeated the Visigothic army and captured Toledo and Cordoba. His name has been commemorated in the toponym Gibraltar, the site where he crossed with his army from North Africa. Gibraltar is a liguistic corruption of Jabal Ṭāriq, which means Mount Ṭāriq. See chapter 3.

thughūr.
Arabic word, plural form, designating the frontier fortresses of Anatolia. Control of these forts was contested between the Muslim Arabs and Byzantines in the seesaw struggle that occurred during the 8th–10th/2d–4th centuries. See chapter 1.

waqʿa.
See ***yawm***.

Yarmūk.
(var. Yarmouk). Decisive victory that assured the Arab-Islamic conquest of southern Syria. The campaign evolved as a Byzantine counteroffensive which recovered Homs and Damascus. The Muslim Arabs retreated before the massed enemy army. Assembling all forces within the Syrian theater, they made a stand near Wādī al-Yarmūk in the summer of 636/15. The Muslims lured the Byzantine cavalry into a trap, enveloped and drove it from the field, then routed the Byzantine infantry. Khālid ibn al-Walīd was very likely the field commander, although Abū ʿUbayda ibn al-Jarrāḥ was evidently the nominal commander in chief. See chapter 2.

yawm
(pl. *ayyām*). Arabic word meaning, in general, *day* but, in special usage, *battle day*. In traditional lore, *yawm* is used in construct with the names of sites to designate the battles and skirmishes of the pre-Islamic Arabs. These engagements are collectively known as Ayyām al-ʿArab. See chapter 1. Arabic sources for the Islamic period use the words *waqʿa* and *maʿrika* to denote a battle.

Islamic Dynasties of the Arab East

Abbasid.

Second dynasty of Arab caliphs, which gained power in 750/132. The Abbasids moved the seat of the caliphate from Syria to Iraq, gradually lost control of the more distant provinces, and lost effective authority to commanders of the guard corps and then the Buyid viziers. The Mongols terminated the Baghdad caliphate in 1258/656. The Ayyubids restored the Abbasid caliphate in Egypt, but as a symbolic office only. See tables 1, 2, and 3 and chapters 1, 4, and 5.

Ayyubid.

Family of sultans of Kurdish origin. The line originated with Salāḥ al-Dīn Yūsuf ibn Ayyūb, the famous Saladin, who deposed the Fatimids of Cairo in 1171/567 and then reconstituted their empire. Saladin's sons and brother divided his realm upon his death. See tables 1, 2, and 3 and chapter 5.

Buyid.

Line of viziers of Iranian origin who usurped Abbasid authority at Baghdad and ruled over Iraq and Iran (945–1055/334–447). This dynasty was founded by the three sons of Būyeh (or Buwayh). See table 1 and chapter 4.

Fatimid.

Line of Shiite caliph-imams (909–1171/297–567). The dynasty originated with Saʿīd ibn Ḥusayn, who claimed to be a descendant of ʿAlī and Fāṭima. The Fatimids first rose to power in North Africa, but they expanded eastward and eventually established their capital in Egypt. See tables 2 and 3 and chapters 4 and 5.

Table 1
Dynastic Rule, Iraq

Dynasty/Dates	Capital	Domain
Umayyad control (661–750/41–132)		
Abbasids (750–945/132–334)	Baghdad al-Sāmarrā'	Iraq, Syria, Egypt, Arabia, Armenia, Iran, Transoxiana, N. India, N. Africa, Spain. Sphere of control eventually reduced to areas near Baghdad.
Buyids (945–1055/334–447)	Baghdad	Iraq, Iran
Hamdanids (927–1000/317–391)	Mosul	N. Iraq
Uqaylids (990–1096/380–489)	Mosul	N. Iraq, N. Syria
Seljuk control (1055–1152/447–547)		
Zangids (1127–1250/521–648)	Various	N. Iraq
Abbasids (1152–1258/547–656)	Baghdad	S. Iraq
Ayyubids (1185–1260/581–659)	Various	N. Iraq (Ruled from Cairo under Saladin)
Il-Khanid control (1256–1335/654–735)		
Jalayirid/Timurid control (1336–1410/736–813)		
Turcoman control (1410–1508/813–914)		
Safavid control (1508–1534/914–941)		
Ottoman control (1534–1918/941–1336)		

Note: As used here, the term *Iraq* equates to the older Mesopotamia (the land of the Tigris-Euphrates basins).

Hamdanid.
Line of Shiite Arab amirs who ruled parts of northern Iraq and northern Syria (927–1004/317–394). The eponymous ancestor of this family was Ḥamdān ibn Ḥamdūn of the Taghlib tribe. The Hamdanids engaged in border warfare with Byzantium and eventually fell victim to the great Byzantine counteroffensive that began in 969/358. See tables 1 and 2 and chapter 4.

Table 2
Dynastic Rule, Syria

Dynasty/Dates	Capital	Domain
Umayyads (661–750/41–132)	Damascus	Syria, Egypt, Arabia, Iraq, Armenia, Iran. Later Conquests: Transoxiana, N. India, N. Africa, Spain
Abbasid control (750–877/132–263) (905–937/292–325)		
Tulunid control (877–905/263–292)		
Ikhshidid control (937–969/325–358)		
Hamdanids (945–1004/333–394)	Aleppo	N. Syria, N. Iraq
Fatimid control (969–1078/358–470) (997–1023/387–414)		(S. Syria) (N. Syria)
Petty dynasties (1023–1094/414–487)	Various	N. Syria
Seljuks/Atabegs (1078–1154/470–549)	Various	N. Syria, Inner Syria
Crusader control (1098–1291/491–690)	Various	Coastal Syria
Zangids (1146–1181/541–577)	Aleppo Damascus	Inner Syria
Ayyubids (1183–1260/579–658)	Various	Inner Syria (Ruled from Cairo under Saladin)
Mamluk control (1260–1517/658–922)		
Ottoman control (1517–1918/922–1336)		

Note: As used here, the term *Syria* includes Palestine.

Ikhshidid.
Line of autonomous rulers of Egypt (935–969/323–358). The dynasty was founded by Muḥammad ibn Ṭughj, a Turk, who held the title *ikhshīd*. Shortly after becoming the governor of Egypt, al-Ikhshīd took control of Syria and the Hijaz. See tables 2 and 3 and chapter 4.

Mamluk
(Baḥrī, Burjī). Two continuous lines of sultans who were former slave-soldiers or descendants of slave-soldiers (1250–1517/648–922). The dynasty originated with Sharaj al-Durr and her husband Aybeg, an exslave (*mamlūk)*, who brought an end to the Ayyubid rule in Egypt. The Mamluks drove the Crusaders from the Lev-

Table 3
Dynastic Rule, Egypt

Dynasty/Dates	Capital	Domain
Umayyad control (661–750/41–132)		
Abbasid control (750–868/132–254) (905–935/292–323)		
Tulunids (868–905/254–292)	al-Fusṭāṭ	Egypt, Syria
Ikhshidids (935–969/323–358)	al-Fusṭāṭ	Egypt, Syria, W. Arabia
Fatamids (969–1171/358–567)	al-Qāhira (Cairo)	(a) Egypt, Syria, W. Arabia, N.E. Sudan (b) N. Africa, Sicily (until later 11th/5th century)
Ayyubids (1171–1260/567–648)	Cairo	(a) Egypt, W. Arabia (b) Syria, N. Africa (under Saladin)
Mamluks (1250–1517/648–922)	Cairo	(a) Egypt, Syria, W. Arabia (b) Libya, Nubia (under Baybars)
Ottoman control (1517–1805/922–1220)		
Muḥammad 'Alī Family (1805–1952)	Cairo	(a) Egypt, Sudan (b) W. Arabia, Crete, Syria (briefly under Muḥammad ʿAlī)

antine Coast and checked the Mongol advance in Syria. See tables 2 and 3 and chapter 5.

Muḥammad ʿAlī family
(Khedive). The last line of hereditary rulers of Egypt (1805–1952). Muḥammad ʿAlī, as governor of Egypt (1805–1848), achieved autonomy from the Ottoman regime and the right of hereditary succession to his office. Among his descendants, Ismāʿīl attained the distinctive title of *khedive*. See table 3 and chapter 6.

Rashidi.
Line of amirs who ruled north-central Arabia (1832–1923). The dynasty originated with ʿAbdallah ibn Rashīd. The Rashidis were successively allies, overlords, and then rivals of the Saudi family. See chapter 6.

Rāshidūn.
The first four "rightly guided" caliphs of Islam. Abū Bakr and ʿUmar held the caliphate during the early conquest movement. ʿUthmān and ʿAlī, both victims of violence, had to cope with the internal dissent that followed the rapid expansion of the Islamic dominion. See chapters 2 and 3.

Saudi (or Wahhabi).
Family of Arab nobles who rose to power in east-central Arabia as champions

(and imams) of the Wahhābī religious reform movement. Their political fortunes vacillated for a century and a half (1746–1887/1159–1305), as they sought to expand their domain in areas of direct or indirect Ottoman rule. ʿAbd al-ʿAzīz, known as ibn Suʿūd, established the present-day kingdom in 1927. See chapter 6.

Seljuk (and Atabegs).
Various families of sultans (1038–1194/429–590) who were descendants of the Ghuzz Turk leader Seljuk. The rise of the Seljuks led to the restoration of Sunni rule in Iran, Iraq, and most of Syria. However, the practice of dividing dominions among a deceased ruler's sons led to the emergence of numerous rival and unstable states. Seljuk rulers customarily entrusted the upbringing of their sons to senior officers, called *atabegs*, who sometimes usurped the authority of their nominal masters. See tables 1 and 2 and chapters 4 and 5.

Sharifian.
Various noble families who governed the Hijaz. They held the title of sharif as descendants of the Prophet Muḥammad and ruled at Mecca from the mid-10th/4th century. The sharifs were usually subject to one of the regional powers. They were subject to Ottoman authority when Ḥusayn ibn ʿAlī of Hashemite lineage launched the so-called Arab Revolt during World War I. Ḥusayn lost the Hijaz to the Saudis, but his sons became the titular rulers of Transjordan and Iraq. See chapter 6.

Tulunid.
Line of autonomous rulers of Egypt and Syria (868–905/254–292). The dynasty originated with Aḥmad ibn Ṭūlūn, the son of a Turkish slave who had been in the service of Caliph al-Ma'mūn. See tables 2 and 3 and chapter 4.

Umayyad.
First dynasty of Arab caliphs (661–750/41–132). The Umayyads prevailed over the followers of ʿAlī and also those of Ibn al-Zubayr in the early civil wars of Islam. They directed the second phase of the Arab-Islamic conquests (698–715/79–96). Their hold on power was gradually undermined by factionalism within the army. After the Abbasid takeover, a scion of the House of Umayya established a new dynasty in Spain. See tables 1, 2, and 3 and chapters 3 and 4.

Zangid.
Family of nobles of Turkish origin, who ruled parts of northern Iraq and inner Syria (1127–1250/521–648). The dynasty was founded by the *atabeg* ʿImād al-Dīn Zangī, one of the great counter-Crusading heroes of Islam. At Zangī's death, his dominion was divided among his sons. See tables 1 and 2 and chapter 5.

Zaydi.
(Qasimid). Line of imams of the Zaydī sect, who governed northern Yemen (1592–1962/1000–1382). The Zaydīya were Shiite followers of Zayd ibn ʿAlī, grandson of al-Ḥusayn, grandson of the Prophet. The Qasimids, who had overthrown Ottoman authority, were again subjected to it from 1849–1911. The Zaydi imamate was abolished consequent to a "republican" coup. See chapter 8.

Part I

Warfare in Arab Traditions

1

The Mystique of the Raid

The mystique of the raid is one of the key elements of Arab militarism. It derives from the Arab-Byzantine conflict in Anatolia which endured as a virtual stalemate for over two hundred years (8th–10th/2d–4th centuries). The relevant imagery has two distinct motifs. One is the glory of the camel raid conducted by one bedouin tribe against another. The other is the glory of the border raid conducted by Muslim warriors against infidels.

In less than a century, Muslim Arab forces conquered most of the lands of Classical antiquity. Nonetheless, the momentum of these conquests had stalled by the mid-8th/2d century. On several fronts the Arab advance stopped at geographic, rather than military, barriers. In Anatolia, Arab troops continued to battle the forces of the Byzantine Empire; however, the nature of war changed. Where campaigning once had many facets (i.e., sieges, pitched battles, raids, and security operations), cross-border raiding became the prevalent military activity. Consistent deep penetration of Byzantine territory ceased after the unsuccessful second siege of Constantinople (716–717/98–99).

This change in warfare came about as the Byzantines perfected their defensive strategy. In its developed form, their border disposition consisted of an outer belt of depopulated tracts of land and an inner belt of isolated strong points and fortresses. The fortified sites served as garrisons for the small standing formations, marshaling points for the territorial militiamen, and safe havens for the noncombatants. Upon commencement of a Muslim incursion, the defensive reaction was to avoid combat initially, maintain surveillance, assemble forces, and eventually intercept in force. With this defensive scheme in place, Arab forces could no longer effect permanent gains. Nonetheless, there were still opportunities for military heroism. There evolved a new rationale for military service at the frontier. Whereas Arab troops had once gained merit through the capture of territory, they now gained it through the conduct of raids.

From pre-Islamic to pre-modern times, raiding was an important facet of the tribal society of Arabia. Since the possession of camels amounted to wealth—especially among the bedouins, camel raiding was an opportunity for one tribal group to gain an economic advantage at the expense of another. This practice was apparently carried on with minimal violence in most cases. However, sometimes a raid became the flash point for a tribal war which brought about considerably more bloodshed. In either situation, the conduct of a raid afforded a test of courage and martial skill for the tribesmen involved. Arab tribes originally commemorated their most significant raids through oral traditions and poems. This lore was eventually recorded in historical works, commentaries on poetry, and historical romances. It is debatable as to when the traditions and poems were first committed to written form. However, there is little doubt that the underlying tribal "epics" were composed during the Umayyad Era (661–750/41–132). Other purposes notwithstanding, they would have served to motivate Arab troops at the Anatolian frontier.

The tribal epics, which projected the bedouin raid motif, easily lent themselves to the culture of the border warriors. Key terms were the same. The border raid was called *ghazw* (variants *ghazwa*, *ghazya*, and derivative *maghzā*), as was the camel raid. (The word *ghazya* eventually became the English loan word *razzia*.) Similarly, the border raider was called *ghāzī*, as was the camel raider. In time, the word *ghāzī* was applied to all frontier forces, irrespective of their military activity.

Two of the famous early *ghāzīs* were ʿAbdullah al-Baṭṭāl and ʿAbd al-Wahhāb ibn Bukht. Although the historical evidence is scant, it does indicate that both men participated in military operations against the Byzantines in the early 8th/2d century. ʿAbd al-Wahhāb was killed during an expedition in 731–32/113. Al-Baṭṭāl was killed in battle some years later; 740/122 is the most commonly cited date for his death. The exploits of both men were celebrated long after their own days. They were fictionalized, transposed in time, and forged into popular legends and an Arabic historical romance entitled *Sīrat Dhāt al-Himma wa al-Baṭṭāl*.[1] Segments of the romance have survived as folklore in parts of the modern Arab world.[2] The deeds of later Arab ghāzīs, such as Zufar ibn ʿĀṣim al-Hilālī and Maʿyūf ibn Yaḥyā al-Kindī, were recorded in annals, but they seemingly were not commemorated in legend.

As the border forces of the Islamic state came to include a larger percentage of Turks, the *ghāzī* tradition was eventually assimilated into Turkish military culture. The personage of al-Baṭṭāl was transformed into the ancestor of the Turkish *ghāzīs*. The legends of his exploits were merged with other elements in the Turkish historical romance *Sayyid Battal* (Lord Battal). As the Seljuk Turks took the lead in the Muslim struggle against Byzantium in the 12th/6th century, the *ghāzī* tradition broke from its Arab origin.[3] Consequently, modern Arabic historiography remembers the Seljuks and especially the Ottomans as the *ghāzīs* par excellence. It does not elaborate on the deeds of the Arab border warriors. Al-Baṭṭāl and ʿAbd al-Wahhāb have in a sense lost their place in history. They remain obscure for two likely reasons. No scholarly attempt has been made to sort fact from fiction in the Dhāt al-Himma romance. Arabic historical writing portrays other heroes as raiders.

Arabic historiography seemingly reached maturity during the mid-8th/2d century, and it reflects the political-military circumstances of that time, including the stalemate in Anatolia and the Abbasid overthrow of the Umayyad Caliphate. Consequent to the fall of the Umayyad regime, the Byzantines seized some of the Muslim frontier posts in Anatolia. In retaking these positions, the Abbasid army gained momentum toward the offensive. That momentum, however, quickly dissipated. The Abbasids found the Byzantine defensive scheme as formidable as had their predecessors. They reverted to the raiding routine of Umayyad days.

Except during times of internal crisis, the Abbasids launched at least one expedition into Anatolia each summer. They conducted a few long-range operations; however, these were seemingly not on the scale of early Umayyad campaigns. Al-Muʿtaṣim's march to Amorium (ʿAmmūriya) in 838/223 was perhaps the most renowned expedition undertaken by the Abbasids. It was, in any case, their last serious offensive. Although the Abbasids did not overcome the Byzantine defensive effort, they did succeed in establishing settlements in the no-man's-land of the Umayyad era.

Abbasid society apparently adjusted to the military stalemate in Anatolia without loss of morale. Muslim scholars endowed the border raid with new prestige. In their written works, they acclaimed raiding as both a religious duty and a long-established tradition. Al-Balādhurī thus recorded the perspective of his society:

> When Abū Jaʿfar al-Manṣūr ruled, he inspected the forts and towns of the coast, populated and fortified them, and built in them what needed to be built. He did likewise with the frontier towns. When al-Mahdī became caliph, he completed what remained to be done in the towns and forts and added to their garrisons. Muʿāwiya ibn ʿAmr states, "What we have seen was really great regarding the effort of the Commander of the Believers Hārūn in conducting raids and his acute discernment in

Map 1.1
The Arab-Byzantine Frontier in Anatolia, 8th–10th/2d–4th Centuries

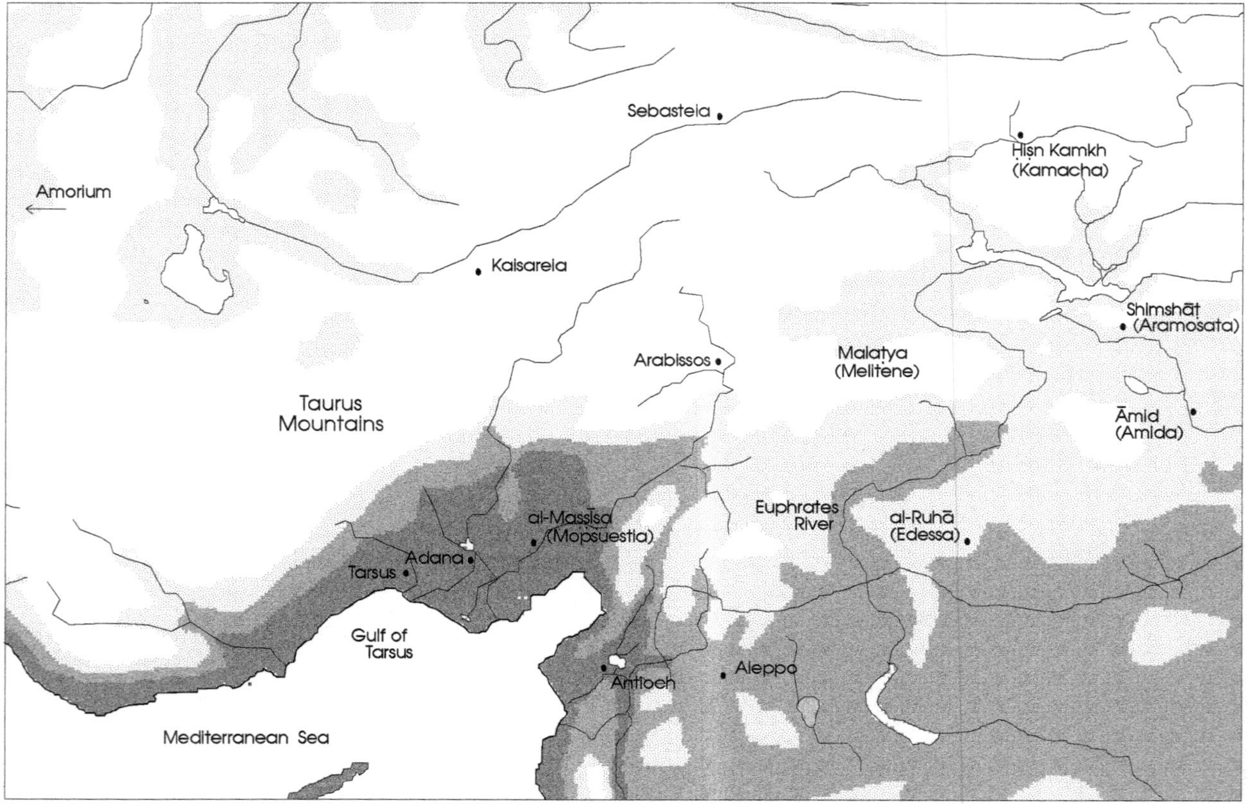

> waging holy war. He undertook what had not been undertaken before. He distributed wealth in the frontier and coastal areas. He brought distress on the Romans and subdued them." . . .
>
> I was informed by certain shaykhs of Antioch and by others that in the days of ʿUmar and ʿUthmān, and after their time, the frontier cities of Syria were Antioch and other towns which al-Rashīd called al-ʿAwāṣim. The Muslims used to conduct raids beyond these towns as they now raid what is beyond Tarsus.
>
> . . . I found in the book *Maghāzī Muʿāwiya* that in the year 31 he conducted a raid, setting out from near al-Maṣṣīṣa (Mopsuestia), and reached Darūlīya (Dorylaeum). When he went out, he did not leave standing any fortress between himself and Antioch. (*Futūḥ al-Buldān*, edited by de Goeje, pp. 163–65)

The above-cited source *Maghāzī Muʿāwiya* is not extant. We can only conjecture as to its full content and purpose. The title suggests that it belongs to a genre that is exemplified by al-Wāqidī's *Kitāb al-Maghāzī*—the book of Muḥammad's campaigns.[4] This work and other related ones that survive as fragments portray the Prophet and his Companions as war leaders or at least as veteran campaigners. Indeed, this theme carries through in the Muslim historiography of the present day. Paraphrasing the old sources, S. A. Salik recounts the deeds of the future caliphs. Abū Bakr

> took part in the battle of Hunayn and in the siege of Tayif and the expedition against Tabuk. Though no fighting took place in the last of these expeditions, it was a difficult campaign as it was undertaken at the time of scarcity and in the hottest part of the year.[5]

ʿAlī, in 9 A.H.,

> was sent out with a detachment of 200 horse to destroy a temple belonging to the Beni Tay. He thoroughly accomplished the task assigned to him and returned with a good many prisoners and plunder. . . . When setting out for the expedition against Tabuk in 9 A.H., the Prophet left Hadzrat Aly at Medina to look after his household affairs. Some of the disaffected persons maliciously told Hadzrat Aly that he was left behind as an unnecessary burden. On account of the taunt he armed himself, and proceeded to the holy Prophet.[6]

The Arabic word *maghāzī* may be translated as either campaigns or raiding expeditions, depending on the context. It is significant that the

Kitāb al-Maghāzī mentions over fifty raids, in addition to the few famous battles and sieges of Muḥammad's time. Beyond the literary aim though, the high count of raids should not be taken uncritically. The pertinent accounts consist largely of dates, place names, personal names, and individual deeds and quotes. They are so devoid of operational details that it is difficult to discern exactly what military activity took place. In many cases, the absence of fighting suggests that the events commemorated were actually security (or counterraid), reconnaissance, and show-of-force operations. It is likewise difficult to discern the purpose or objective of some of the raids. Among the possibilities are punitive strikes, intimidation tactics, or booty hunts. Beyond the challenge of interpretation, such considerations call into question the prevailing notion of the ethos of nascent Islam. Was it really to fight the unbelievers until they accepted Islam? Or was it to force the nomadic and seminomadic tribesmen to submit to the temporal authority of Medina? This issue suggests itself as a worthwhile topic for further study.

As the descriptions of the campaigns of the Prophet are lacking in operational information so too are the descriptions of the caliphs' campaigns in Anatolia. Even those writers who were near contemporaries of events forego transmitting militarily significant reports. It would seem that the Muslim scholarly class was concerned with the who, when, and where of a raid or expedition, but not with how it was conducted. E. W. Brooks ("The Arabs in Asia Minor," 1898) has compiled a comprehensive index of relevant accounts, in translation. The following excerpts from the histories of al-Ṭabarī and al-Yaʿqūbī (Ibn Wāḍiḥ) are representative of this corpus.

> Among the events of that year (92 A.H.) was the raid of Maslama bin ʿAbd al-Malik and ʿUmar bin al-Walīd into the land of the Romans. Three fortresses were taken by Maslama. The people of Susana moved into the interior of the Romans' country. (*Ta'rīkh al-Rusul wa al-Mulūk*)
>
> During his government, in the year 106, Muʿāwiya bin Hishām made a raid with the men. He sent al-Waḍḍāḥ, the leader of the Waḍḍāḥīya, to burn the crops and the villages because the Romans had burnt the pasture lands. Saʿīd bin ʿAbd al-Malik made a summer raid in the north. (*Ta'rīkh al-Yaʿqūbī*)

With source information being so limited, it is not possible to recover the life of the border warriors. David Nicolle and Angus McBride, working from Byzantine church artifacts, have at least been able to reconstitute an image of their attire and armament.[7] Regarding their propensity to fight, it would seem that frontier forces were motivated by pay, booty, and self-protection. The majority of their service time was probably spent in local, raid/counterraid and security activity. Haldon and Kennedy ("The Arab-Byzantine Frontier," 1980) conjecture that most of the minor raids were no more than stock-rustling ventures. Moreover, the inevitable competition for grazing land would have created tensions inside as well as across borders. The romance of Dhāt al-Himma clearly indicates that the Arab frontier militias engaged in internecine conflict. Western scholars have already established a macro-level view of settlement and building patterns along the frontier.[8] It may be feasible to refine that view through further archeological research.

Assuming that considerable assimilation occurred in the frontier zones, ethnicity was probably not a factor in the recruitment of border forces until the Seljuk period. The sources indicate that, over time, the frontier forces included Arabs, Aramaean natives of northern Syria and Mesopotamia, Persians, Slavs, Armenians, and Turks—proportions unknown. We cannot know what each group contributed to the culture of the borderlands. However, it was seemingly the Arabs who endowed Muslim frontier society with the mystique of the raid.

Apart from historic border warfare, the raid as a feature of bedouin life has been and continues to be an important theme in Arab culture. It is an element of what Raphael Patai (*The Arab Mind*, 1983) calls the "bedouin substratum" of the value system of Arab society. To the settled Arab, the bedouin tribesman is the exemplar of the free man. He has the wherewithal to forego employment as a laborer or tradesman, to relocate his household and possessions with relative ease, and to resist governmental control. This image is now more fiction than fact due to the changes brought about by modernization in the Arab world. Nonetheless, it remains an ideal. Within that same ethos, participation in a camel raid is a dramatic test of courage, skill, and selfless dedication to the goals of the tribal group.

The first literary glorification of raiding activity drew on the legends of tribal conflict in pre-Islamic Arabia. Before the conquests and the emigration from Arabia, tribal groups probably transmitted vague memories of ancestral deeds through oral traditions. After the tribes became part of the Islamic political-military establishment, their learned men recast the traditional lore in stylized poetry and narrative accounts, in some cases creating epics. In similar fashion they commemorated the tribes' exploits in the early conquests.

Hishām ibn Muḥammad al-Kalbī and Abū ʿUbayda Maʿmar ibn al-Muthannā, who were early authorities on the lore of the so-called Southern and Northern Tribes, included many narrative accounts in various works on the pre-Islamic Arabs. Although the most relevant of their works are not extant, segments were preserved by later authors writing on history, geography, genealogy, poetry, and other subjects. In works about the early conquests, Abū Mikhnaf and Sayf ibn ʿUmar recounted respectively the exploits of Azd and their allies and of Tamīm and theirs. These works too have been lost; only segments are preserved in the famous histories of al-Balādhurī and al-Ṭabarī.

Such literary efforts probably served to buttress the claims of some groups to higher nobility or merit vis-à-vis other groups. It is known that through the early Umayyad period, the pay and pension system of the Islamic state was based on lineage and military service to Islam, among other factors. Moreover, Umayyad society was beset by political power struggles between rival tribal blocs. Early Arabic "histories" may well have served as propaganda tracts. It is also plausible that Arabic historical writing evolved in part from efforts to justify rank status on the state payroll—an issue deserving further research.

Whatever their purpose, these works created a heroic image of the Arabs' ancestral age. Pre-Islamic tribal conflicts were commemorated in terms of battle days (Arabic sing., *yawm*; pl., *ayyām*). The encounters at Buʿāth and al-Habā'a were called, for example, Yawm Buʿāth and Yawm al-Habā'a. The number of pre-Islamic *ayyām* has been placed as high as 132. However, the subject struggles were of varying magnitude. Among other scholars, E. Mittwoch ("Ayyām al-ʿArab," 1960) has observed that many of them commemorate "insignificant skirmishes, or frays, in which instead of the whole tribes, only a few families or individuals opposed one another." Some of these incidents were recounted in full detail. In contrast, there appear to have been some major conflicts, but the relevant battle accounts are rather uninformative.

These accounts identified winners and losers, but without discrediting the losers. The resort to combat seemingly bestowed honor on both sides. In a few traditions, the prowess of one side received special acclaim. Such was the case of the Day of Dhū Qār. In that famous engagement, tribesmen of Shaybān b. Bakr defeated a force of Sassanid cavalry and tribal auxiliaries. The account of the victory of Bakr was interpreted by later generations as a testament to the martial superiority of Arabs over Persians. However, the author of the Dhū Qār tradition more likely intended to extol the victory of free tribesmen over hired soldiers. It is relevant that Bakr defeated armored cavalry (*aṣāwira*). Those troops may well have been Persian, but there is no indication of ethnicity. Moreover, the same theme was used in at least one other case. In verse commemorating al-Qurnatayn, men of ʿĀmir boasted that they had captured the half-brother of the Lakhmid king and had mutilated the troops of the kings (called *ṣanā'iʿ*). According to these sources, tribal warriors sometimes did engage and defeat professional soldiers. However, the circumstances were not recorded with clarity or detail. The tribesmen may have had the advantage of numbers, position, surprise, or some other factor.

In the raid motifs of Arab culture, the bedouin warrior is an exemplar of martial prowess. Ibn Khaldūn presents what is perhaps the classic statement on the superiority of the bedouins:

> Superiority comes to nations through boldness and courage. Whichever (tribal) group is more firmly rooted in bedouin life and more savage is more likely to be superior when there is approximate equality in number and group solidarity.
>
> In this connection, compare the (tribe of) Muḍar with the earlier Ḥimyar and Kahlān . . . and also Rabīʿa. . . . The Muḍar retained their bedouin ways; the others moved before them toward a life of abundance and opulence. How bedouin life sharpened their edge in attaining superiority! They laid hold of what they (the others) had and wrested it from them. (*al-Muqaddima*, chap. ii, sec. 15)

This image has been taken for granted, yet it should be reassessed here. The ability to rustle a camel or two or to conduct a larger raid in retaliation does not equate to military battle drill.

Despite the cultural significance of the raid motif, the actual technique of raiding has not been a subject of interest to Arab scholars or literateurs. Most of our knowledge comes from the observations of Westerners who traveled in Arabia before the onset of modernization.[9] Their accounts reveal that raid activity, although it varied greatly as to numbers involved and distance traveled, followed certain norms: travel light, move quickly, avoid detection, strive to achieve surprise, avoid (or minimize) bloodshed, take camels only—no captives, no loot. They also provide limited insight into motivation, preparation, decision making, leadership, organization, and the requisite skills of scouting, tracking, and navigating desert terrain, with the degree of difficulty left largely to conjecture. Camel raiding sometimes led to tribal war. However, such conflicts were not known to be great blood-letting events. The objective was not to force submission but to restore the balance of honor or the balance of livestock. It was usually when states or kingdoms sought to impose control over the desert tribes that warfare became intense.

From experience in raiding, bedouins would be well suited to perform the classic light cavalry functions of scouting, screening, raiding, foraging, harassing, and pursuing defeated foes. They would not be suited to serve as troops of the line (i.e., shock troops). The historical-literary record indicates that bedouin tribesmen, when involved in the defense system of states, served as auxiliary troops or as frontier security or police forces. True, Arab tribesmen did serve in the standing formations of the Roman Empire, the early Islamic state, and the Saudi Kingdom. However, those who had been bedouins became good soldiers not because of their origin but because of better diet, systematic training, and other conditioning.

In pre-modern Arabia, camels were both a cause and a means of war. Contrary to popular notions, the Arabs did not ride camels into battle. In longer range operations, they used camels to move to the objective area, then dismounted to fight on foot or horseback. If horses were used by the attacking force, they were led, not ridden, during the march to the objective. Likewise contrary to popular notions, the camel, although it has represented wealth, does not have any other symbolic meaning among the Arabs.

Camel rustling was not the only raid activity undertaken by the bedouins. They also preyed on the caravans that conveyed trade goods and, after Islam, religious pilgrims through Arabia. Unlike the camel raids, the caravan raids were not idealized in Arab urban culture and literature. In these undertakings the bedouins could be ruthless since their victims were of a different social order. Because they were not fellow nomads, they were not encompassed in the laws and protocols of nomadic life.

Caravan raiding was a threat to the economic well-being and the Islamic legitimacy of states bordering the desert. To counter that threat, the rich merchants and rulers recruited available manpower to serve as caravan guards and bedouin police. These troopers, like their antagonists, would have needed skills in navigating desert terrain, scouting, tracking, and camel handling. The repulse, interception, or successful pursuit of a raiding party no doubt afforded opportunity for heroism. Even so, these security forces would not be the heroes of Arabic literature and folklore. Their historic role in state formation in Arabia has largely passed into oblivion. There is some indirect evidence that the military élan of early Islam developed from the experience of desert security operations, although the extant sources portray a different theme. At least, we can reconstruct the rigors of that work from comparative evidence. George Green ("The Organization and Employment of Camel Corps," 1885) has recorded particularly good perspectives on the operations of a desert security force.

It is again the writing of Westerners that affords us some insight on the difficulty of negotiating desert terrain by traditional means (i.e., without motor vehicles and roads). The following observations are relevant. The camel provides the capability to travel long distances at a sustained rate. Both with and without camels, the Arabs move relatively quickly over open terrain. Still, they have to follow landmarks during daylight and navigate by the stars at night. They also have to compensate for obstacles (shifting sand dunes, lava fields, precipitous terrain) that cause diversion from the correct route. The all-important consideration is to stay within reach of water sources. As a result of this imperative, Arab tribesmen do not move freely across the desert. The routes of a raiding party, a retaliatory force, or a caravan are all to a large extent predictable to one who knows the local topography.

Through the course of history, conflict in Arabia was conditioned by the harsh environment. In general, the land did not sustain large populations, and so the scale of human undertakings, including warfare, was relatively small. Within that world of experience, raiding may well have been the epitome of warlike behavior. Despite the experience of the Islamic conquests, the Arabs seemingly retained that notion, both consciously and subconsciously. Raiding was an act of man and redounded to his glory. Conquest, in contrast, was an act of God (Allah) and redounded to his much greater glory.

NOTES

1. This romance portrays al-Baṭṭāl's mother as a main character and heroine. Her name, Dhāt al-Himma (meaning she of noble purpose), is also rendered as Dalhamma or Delhemma.

2. See Edward William Lane, *An Account of the Manners and Customs of the Modern Egyptians* (London: East-West Publications, 1978), vol. 2, chap. 10. In the Dhāt al-Himma romance, al-Baṭṭāl is first and foremost a champion of the Kilāb Tribe. He is implicitly a champion of Islam in those episodes where he prevails against Byzantine foes.

3. At the eastern frontier of Islam, a Turkish *ghāzī* ethos had already emerged by the turn of the 10th/4th century.

4. See chapter 2 for a further discussion and bibliography.

5. Saiyed Abdus Salik, *The Early Heroes of Islam* (in Chap. 2, Bibliog. 3), p. 202.

6. Ibid., pp. 436–37.

7. See *The Armies of Islam 7th–11th Centuries* (in Chap. 4, Bibliog. 1), illus. H2 and annotation, p. 39.

8. See Bibliog. 1, works by H. Ahrweiler, Marius Canard (1957), John Haldon and Hugh Kennedy, and A. A. Vasiliev et al.

9. See Bibliog. 4, works of H.R.P. Dickson, Johann Jakob Hess, Alois Musil, and Wilfred Thesinger.

BIBLIOGRAPHY

1. The Arab-Byzantine Frontier

Ahrweiler, H. "L'Asie Mineure et les Invasions Arabes." *Revue Historique* 227 (1962): 1–32.

Bonner, Michael. "The Emergence of the Thughūr: The Arab-Byzantine Frontier in the Early Abbasid Age." Ph.D. diss., Princeton University, 1987.

Bosworth, C. E., trans. *The History of al-Tabari*. Vol. 33, *Storm and Stress along the Northern Frontiers of the ʿAbbasid Caliphate*. Albany: State University of New York Press, 1991.

Brooks, E. W. "The Arabs in Asia Minor (641–750), from Arabic Sources." *Journal of Hellenic Studies* 18 (1898): 182–208.

———. "Byzantines and Arabs in the Time of the Early Abbasids." *English Historical Review* 15 (1900): 728–747; 16 (1901): 84–92.

Bury, J. B. "Mutasim's March through Cappadocia in A.D. 838." *Journal of Hellenic Studies* 29 (1909): 120–29.

Canard, Marius. "ʿAmmūriya." *EI* 1 (new ed.): 449.

———. "Quelques Observations sur l'Introduction Géographique de la Bughyat at'T'alab de Kamal ad-Din d'Alep." *Annales de l'Institut des Études Orientales* 15 (1957).

Cheira, M. A. *La Lutte entre Arabes et Byzantines: La Conquête et l'Organization des Frontières aux VIIe et VIIIe Siècles*. Alexandria, Egypt: Société de Publications Égyptiennes, 1947.

Haldon, John, and Hugh Kennedy. "The Arab-Byzantine Frontier in the Eighth and Ninth Centuries: Military Organization and Society in the Borderlands." *Zbornik Radova Vizantoloski Institut* 19 (1980): 78–116.

Lilie, Ralph-Johannes. *Die Byzantinische Reaktion auf die Ausbreitung der Araber*. Miscellanea Byzantine Monacensia 22. Munich: Institut für Byzantinistik und Neugriechische Philologie der Universität, 1976.

Petrusi, A. "Tra Storia e Leggenda: Akritai e Ghazi sulla Frontiera Orientale di Bisanzio." In *Rapports de XIVe Congrès International des Études Byzantines II*, 27–72. Bucharest: Editions de l'Academie de la Republique Socialiste de Roumanie, 1971.

Ramsay, W. M. "The Attempt of the Arabs to Conquer Asia Minor (641–964 A.D.) and the Causes of Its Failure." *Academie Roumaine Bulletin de la Section Historique* 2 (1924): 1–8.

Rosser, J. "The Role of Fortifications in the Defense of Asia Minor against the Arabs from the Eighth to the Tenth Century." *Greek Orthodox Theological Review* 27 (1982): 135–43.

Vasiliev, A. A. et al. *Byzance et les Arabes*. Brussels: Institut de Philologie et d'Histoire Orientales, 1935–1950. See vol. 2, pp. 98 ff. on border warfare.

Wellhausen, Julius. "Die Kämpfe der Araber mit den Romäern in der Zeit der Umaijiden." *Nachrichten von den Königl Gesellschaft der Wissenschaften* (Göttingen: Universität serial) 8 (1901): 414–47.

Williams, John A., trans. *Al-Tabari, the Early ʿAbbasi Empire*. 2 vols. Cambridge, England: Cambridge University Press, 1989.

2. Raid Motifs in Arab Culture

Bravmann, M. M. "Heroic Motifs in Early Arabic Literature." *Islam* 33 (1958): 256–79; 35 (1960): 1–25; 36 (1960): 4–36.

Canard, Marius. "al-Baṭṭāl." *EI* 1 (new ed.): 1102–03.

———. "Delhemma, Épopée Arabe des Guerres Arabo-Byzantine." *Byzantion* 10 (1935): 283–300.

———. "Dhu 'l-Himma." *EI* 2 (new ed.): 233–39.

———. "Les Expéditions des Arabes contre Constantinople dans l'Histoire et la Légende." *Journal Asiatique* 208 (1926): 61–121. See pp. 116 ff.

———. "Les Principaux Personnages du Roman de Chevalerie Arabe Ḏāt al-Himma wa-l-Baṭṭāl." *Arabica* 8 (1961): 158–73.

Della Vida, Giorgio Levi. "Pre-Islamic Arabia." In *The Arab Heritage*, edited by Nabih Amin Faris. Princeton, N.J.: Princeton University Press, 1944. See references to tribal lore, pp. 43 and 47–48.

Meeker, Michael E. *Literature and Violence in North Arabia.* Cambridge, England: Cambridge University Press, 1979. See especially pts. 2 and 3.

Mélikoff, Irène. "Ghāzī." *EI* 2 (new ed.): 1043–45.

Newbury, Gordon D. "Ibn Khaldun and Frederick Jackson Turner: Islam and the Frontier Experience." In *Ibn Khaldun and Islamic Ideology*, edited by Bruce B. Lawrence. International Studies in Sociology and Anthropology, Vol. 40. Leiden, Netherlands: E. J. Brill, 1984.

Paret, Rudi. *Die Legendäre Maghāzī-Literatur: Arabische Dichtungen über die Muslimischen Kriegzüge zu Mohammeds Zeit.* Tübingen, Germany: J.C.B. Mohr, 1930.

Patai, Raphael. *The Arab Mind.* Rev. ed. New York: Charles Scribner's Sons, 1983. See pp. 78–81 and 209–15.

Renard, John. *Islam and the Heroic Image.* Columbia: University of South Carolina Press, 1993. See pp. 43–53, 237–43, and 258–59.

3. Pre-Islamic Tribal Wars

Beeston, A.F.L. *Warfare in Ancient South Arabia (2d–3rd Centuries A.D.).* (Qahtan: Studies in Old South Arabian Epigraphy, no. 3). London: Luzac and Co., 1976.

Caskel, Werner. "Aijam al-ʿArab. Studien zur Altarabischen Epik." *Islamica* 3 (1930), facicule 5 (Ergänzungsheft): 1–99.

Fück, J. W. "Fidjār." *EI* 2 (new ed.): 883–84.

Jandora, John W. "The Rise of Mecca: Geopolitical Factors." *Muslim World* 85 (1995), 333–44.

Mittwoch, E. "Ayyām al-ʿArab." *EI* 1 (1960 and new ed.): 793–94.

Olinder, Gunnar. *The Kings of Kinda of the Family of Ākil al-Murār.* Lund, Sweden: C.W.K. Gleerup, 1927.

Veccia-Vaglieri, Laura. "Dhū Ḳār." *EI* 2 (1965): 241.

4. Bedouin Prowess, Raiding versus Soldiering

Asad, Talal. "The Bedouin as a Military Force: Notes on Some Aspects of Power Relations between Nomads and Sedentaries in Historical Perspective." In *The Desert and the Sown—Nomads in the Wider Society*, edited by Cynthia Nelson. Berkeley, Calif.: Institute of International Studies, 1973.

Burckhardt, Johann Ludwig. *Notes on the Bedouins and Wahabys.* Reading, England: Garnet Publishing, 1992. See vol. 1, pp. 133–48 and 291–312.

Dempsey, Thomas A. "Desert Guerrillas: Psychological, Social, and Economic Characteristics of the Bedouin Which Lend Themselves to Irregular Warfare." Fort Leavenworth, Kans.: U.S. Army Staff and General Command College, 1989.

Dickson, H.R.P. *The Arab of the Desert: A Glimpse into Badawin Life in Kuwait and Sau'di Arabia.* London: George Allen and Unwin, 1949. See chap. 26.

Gellner, Ernest. "Tribalism and the State in the Middle East." In *Tribes and State Formation in the Middle East*, edited by Philip Khoury and Joseph Kostiner. Berkeley: University of California Press, 1990.

Hess, Johann Jakob. *Von den Beduinen des Innern Arabiens.* Zurich: M. Niehan, 1938.

Johnstone, T. M. "Ghazw." *EI* 2 (1965): 1055–56.

Kay, Shirley. *The Bedouin*. This Changing World Series. New York: Crane, Russak & Company, 1978. See chap. 7.

Kostiner, Joseph. "Transforming Dualities: Tribe and State Formation in Saudi Arabia." In *Tribes and State Formation in the Middle East*, edited by Philip Khoury and Joseph Kostiner. Berkeley: University of California Press, 1990.

Musil, Alois. *The Manners and Customs of the Rwala Bedouins*. New York: American Geographical Society, 1928. See pp. 506–40 and other references to raiders and raids in the index.

Oppenheim, Max. *Die Beduinen*. Leipzig, Germany: Otto Harrassowitz, 1939.

Sweet, Louise E. "Camel Raiding of North Arabian Bedouin: A Mechanism of Cultural Adaptation." *American Anthropologist* 67 (1965): 1132–50.

Thesinger, Wilfred. *Arabian Sands*. New York: E. P. Dutton, 1959. See discussion of tracking skills (pp. 51–52) and raid/counterraid strategy (pp. 57–59).

5. War in the (Premodern) Desert Environment

Several monographic studies are listed below. For excellent incidental comments on this topic, see Chapter 6: Bibliog. 1, works by Bankes, Sabini, Sadleir, and Weygand; Bibliog. 2, works by Glubb, Habib, Philby (1926 and 1928), and Winder; Bibliog. 3, works by Falls, Lawrence (1927 and 1935), and Parker.

Armstrong, Godfrey. "Camels at War." *Fighting Forces* 22 (April 1945): 44–47.

Davies, Reginald. *The Camel's Back: Service in the Rural Sudan*. London: J. Murray, 1957. Chap. 5 discusses recruitment of scouts; chap. 7 discusses the hazards of using camels as mounts.

Gardavsky, J. "Military Operations in the Desert." *Military Review* 23 (April 1943): 70–72. This article addresses North Africa but has good applicability to desert operations in general.

Gimond, Andre. "Desert Warfare." *Military Review* 28 (August 1948): 73–83. This article provides insights on environmental factors, which have been constant through history.

Green, George W. "The Organization and Employment of Camel Corps in Warfare." *RUSI Journal* 29 (1885): 521–37. This article discusses the Sudan but remains an excellent source on desert security and counterraid operations.

2

The Archetypal Victories of Islam

The so-called Arab (or Islamic) conquest movement has long presented one of the great anomalies of world history. In 622 A.D., the Prophet Muḥammad and a few hundred followers migrated from Mecca to Medina and established a new community there. By 645/24, this community evolved into a state which controlled Arabia, Syria, Palestine, Egypt, Persia, Mesopotamia, and Armenia. In 661/41 the Umayyad regime of Damascus replaced the Medinan regime as the seat of Islamic power. By 715/96 (the end of al-Walīd's reign), the Umayyads extended the Islamic dominion to North Africa, Spain, Transoxiana, and northern India. Modern historians have seen these conquests as unparalleled in their rapidity and extent. Yet, their attempts at interpretation have largely foundered owing to the dearth of primary source material (i.e., contemporary or near-contemporary references to events) and the canonical or partisan character of the oldest extant accounts.

The Arabic historical writing of the second Islamic century included fragmentary information that seemingly derives from firsthand sources. It is not clear how that information was acquired or transmitted. There is no evidence that Arab scholars of Umayyad times were interested in military aspects of recent wars, although the caliphs undoubtedly sought information on the military practices of hostile nations. As mentioned in chapter 1, there once existed a book on the campaigns of Muʿāwiya, the founder of the Umayyad dynasty. This work may have been a literary record, perhaps the only contemporary one, of the conquest of geographic Syria. If so, its uniqueness can in part be explained by the fact that, of the first five caliphs, Muʿāwiya was the only one to "take the field" against the Byzantines. As conjecture, it is also possible that this work was the prototype of the *maghāzī* genre, which recounted the political-military activity of the Prophet and his Companions. Whatever the case, early Arabic historiography apparently produced no integral literary record of the achievements of Muslim arms.

Ibn Isḥāq's work on *maghāzī*, as redacted in Ibn Hishām's *al-Sīra al-Nabawīya* (Life of the Prophet), eventually became the substance of the Islamic "myth of origin." It is largely the content of this work that created the perception of nascent Islam as a militant movement. The *Sīra* is sometimes referred to as a biography of the Prophet. However, that description is not really accurate because the work focuses on the formation of a community-state—an achievement brought about by forceful means. The *Sīra* is not a story of religious conviction, preaching, or conversion as a personal experience. It is, rather, a story of countering and overcoming political-military opposition.

Although the *Sīra* is a story of struggle, it merely takes for granted the existence of a Muslim military establishment. There are a few fleeting references to a close-order battle array, a squadron of fully armored troops, and other aspects of Muslim war making. However, details of recruitment, training, armament, organization, and deployment are for the most part lacking. The focus is on what was accomplished, not how. This inattention to military matters creates the impression that the whole Muslim society is engaged, not just the men at arms.

Similarly, the opposing forces are largely nondescript. They consist of pagan Meccans, settled Jewish tribes, and nomadic or seminomadic pagan tribes. Key actors are rarely identified. This vagueness may be intentional, showing sensitivity to the fact that many persons and groups who initially opposed Islam eventually became its adherents. In a few exceptional cases, the *Sīra* does vilify individuals. For example, Abū Jahl takes the brunt of antipathy for all the Meccan foes of the Prophet. It seems that he cannot be redeemed by the deeds of his son ʿIkrima, who distinguished himself and died in the service of Islam.

The composition reveals what appear to be literary conventions of the time. Among the more interesting cases, the theme of struggle is implicitly developed as a play on the number three. As noted above, there are three groups of enemies. The preeminent Jewish enemies are the three tribes of Qaynuqā', Naḍīr, and Qurayẓa. There are three major battles involving the pagan Meccans—First Badr, Uḥud, and al-Khandaq. In each of these, the Muslims are outnumbered by about three to one. Moreover, the size of the opposing forces progressively increases by an approximate factor of three: 300/1,000, 1,000/3,000, 3,000/10,000.

Map 2.1
Campaigns of the Prophet Muḥammad, 624–630/2–9

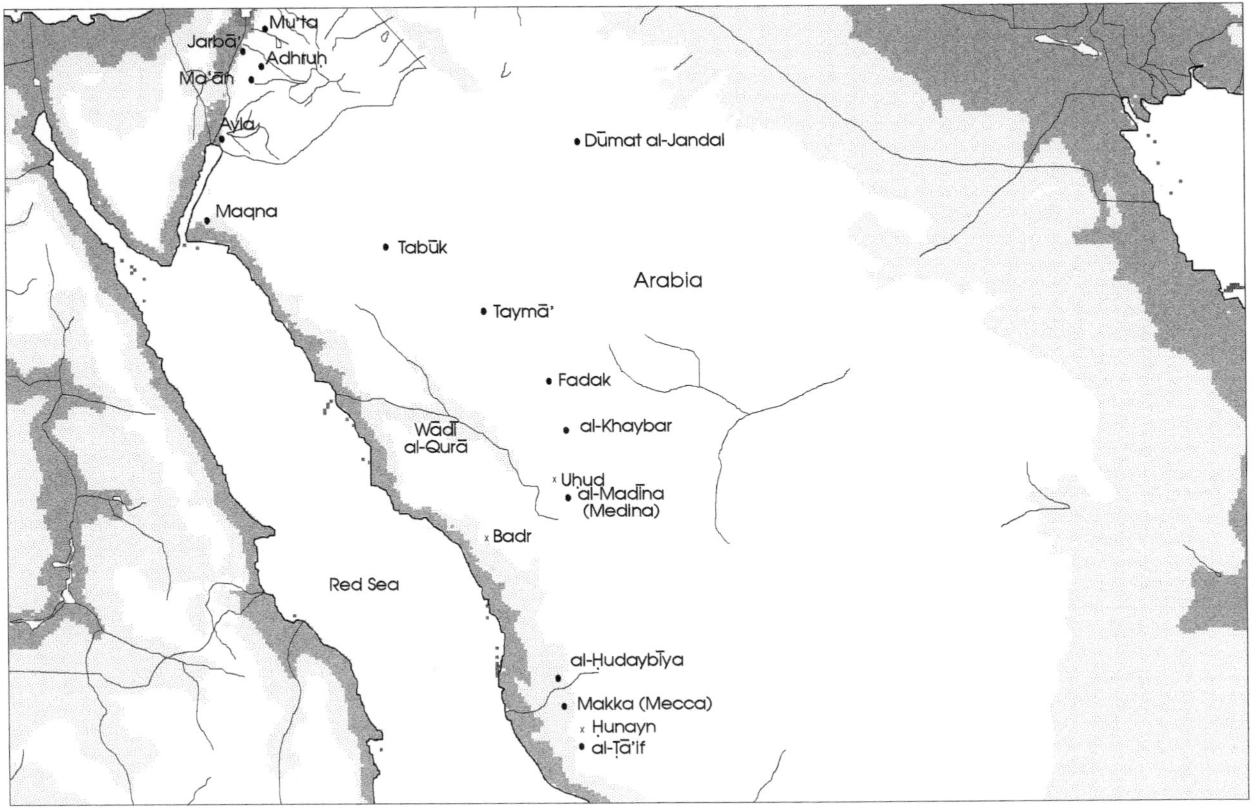

Among the major engagements, First Badr is the archetypal Muslim victory over pagan Arabia. It is the turning point in the venture of Islam. It marks the decision of the Muslims first to fight against their Meccan kinsmen and second to fight at a numeric disadvantage. In the outcome, God sends angels to support the Muslims, and they are victorious. The message to the believers is to trust in God, and you shall prevail, even against great odds. The *Sīra*'s coverage of Badr is better than its coverage of other engagements.[1] Moreover, a full listing of those who fought on the Muslim side is appended to the account. This contrasts with the treatment of other battles for which only the Muslim fatalities are listed.

The listing of names is a departure from the tenor of the battle accounts in which the combatants are, for the most part, anonymous. The citation of fatalities obviously promotes the theme of martyrdom for the cause of Islam. This edification, however, stops short of describing the circumstances of death in the majority of cases. As for the full listing of the veterans of Badr, it has a different purpose. It attests to the ennoblement of the Arab Muslim elite—descent from a veteran of Badr came to be an entitlement to high status, pension, and privilege.

According to the traditionally accepted view, the encounter at Badr occurred more by chance than by design. At the outset, Muḥammad was leading a force of over 300 men; their aim was to raid a large Meccan caravan returning from Syria. The caravan leader, Abū Sufyān ibn Ḥarb, received word of the Muslim moves and sent to Mecca for help. The Quraysh reacted quickly and sent a force to protect their property. Meanwhile, Abū Sufyān eluded the Muslims by diverting the caravan to the coastal route. The Muslims continued moving toward the wells of Badr, where they had hoped to conduct the raid. The Meccan relief force headed for the same location. Although the caravan was safe, Abū Jahl convinced the majority of the Meccans to bivouac at Badr to uphold their prestige among the surrounding tribes. With their enemies in sight, both sides opted to fight. The opposing forces formed ranks, and a few champions from each side went forward to engage in individual combat. Afterward, the two formations closed on each other. The Muslims stood firm as the Meccans probed their line. Muḥammad eventually ordered his men to attack. They broke the Meccan line, routed their foes, and won the day.

The pathos of the event is that the Muslims were compelled by circumstances to shed the blood of kinsmen. Nonetheless, the mystique of Badr justifies the resort to battle in the defense and expansion of the Islamic regime. The *Sīra*'s portrayal of other incidents seemingly condones other means—assassination (the fate of Abū ʿAfak, Kaʿb ibn al-Ashraf, and others), deportation (the fate of the Banū Qaynuqā'), and mass execution (the fate of the Banū Qurayẓa). Such measures are consistent with the practice of the times. Yet, their portrayal in the *Sīra* confirms the impression that Islam is spread by force.

The Islamic conquest of the Medina region, as depicted in the *Sīra*, may be summarized as follows. After Badr, Muḥammad moved against the Jewish tribe of Qaynuqā' at Medina (then known as Yathrib) and some neighboring bedouin tribes. His forces then incurred a setback at Uḥud, where the Meccans avenged their earlier defeat. The Muslim loss was interpreted as a test and as a punishment from God for disobedience to the Prophet. The Muslims recovered quickly and drove the Jewish Banū al-Naḍīr from Medina. They then had to confront an alliance of the three enemy groups. Meccans, Jews, and bedouins combined forces and besieged Medina in an event known as the Battle of the Trench (*al-khandaq*) because of the Muslims' reliance on defensive works. The defenses held, the alliance fractured, and the enemy forces withdrew. The Muslims then punished the Jewish Banū Qurayẓa for their supposed treachery during the siege and thus completed their quest for local dominance.

Following the action at Medina, the Muslims adopted an offense-oriented policy. The Prophet sent expeditions on show-of-force missions in bedouin territory, imposed the Treaty of al-Ḥudaybiya on Mecca, and moved against the settlements north of Medina. His forces subjugated al-Khaybar, Fadak, Wādī al-Qurā, and Taymā'. He even sent a raiding force into Byzantine territory, although it was repulsed by troops guarding the desert routes east of the Dead Sea. Within a few months of that event, Muḥammad provoked a final confrontation with his Meccan adversaries. He accused them of violating the Treaty of al-Ḥudaybiya, sent his army against Mecca, and seized control of the town. After taking Mecca, the Muslim army defeated the massed warriors of Hawāzin and its allies at Wādī Ḥunayn and went on to besiege the town of al-Ṭā'if. When he faced a stalemate there, Muḥammad again redeployed his forces northward. He exacted tribute from Tabūk, Ayla, Dūmat al-Jandal, and other towns.

Upon his return to Medina, Muḥammad accepted the submission of the people of al-Ṭā'if. Meanwhile, his agents and envoys had already extended Muslim authority, or at least influence, southward into Yemen and the Sarāt Lands (the high country between Mecca and Najrān) and eastward into the territory of al-Baḥrayn (the island now known as Bahrain and the adjacent mainland) and al-ʿUmān (a region approximating the present state of Oman). Delegations from these and other areas under Islamic influence converged on Medina seeking audiences with the Prophet. Muḥammad died soon after the meetings concluded. The *Sīra* thus leaves the impression that almost all of Arabia was subject to Islamic rule.

Although the *Sīra* ends with the death of the Prophet, Ibn Isḥāq continues the history of the early Islamic community in his *Kitāb al-Futūḥ* (Book of Conquests). This book is a prototype of later works by al-Wāqidī and Ibn Saʿd. These can be classified as salvation history. They represent one of two historiographic genres included in the broad category of Arab (or Islamic) conquest literature. The other genre is represented by the works of Abū Mikhnaf, Sayf ibn ʿUmar, al-Walīd Ibn Muslim, Abū Hudhayfa (Isḥāq ibn Bishr), and al-Madā'inī. These can be classified as epic history. They are based on selective collection and integration of tribal traditions regarding the conquests. None of the above-mentioned works of either genre are extant. However, segments of them are included in al-Ṭabarī's annalistic history, al-Balādhurī's monograph on the conquests, and many other, less renowned works.

The corpus of early conquest literature reflects many inconsistencies. About the only point of consensus is that, because of certain battles, certain regions and cities fell to the Muslim Arabs. Information on dates, personalities, and circumstances is often contradictory or lacking. Like the *Sīra*, the salvation histories depict war as an anonymous undertaking, but probably for a different reason. Their aim is to show that God ensures victory and that the Muslims collectively carry out His design. Hence, no particular individuals or contingents deserve glory. In contrast, the tribal epic histories are attentive to force composition and leadership. They provide relatively more detail overall. However, their veracity is suspect because they seemingly aim to aggrandize the role of a certain tribe or tribal bloc. Partial listing of fatalities is also attested in the conquest literature, and this practice affords some insights on the composition of the Arab armies, apart from the histrionics of the tribal traditions.

Of the many battles that constituted the conquest movement, two have been preeminent in Arab-Islamic historical awareness: al-Yarmūk and al-Qādisīya. The first was a victory over the Romans (more precisely, Byzantines), which ensured the Muslim conquest of Syria. The second was a victory over the Sassanid Persians, which led to the Muslim conquest of lower Mesopotamia, called al-ʿIrāq by the Arabs. These battles were both major engagements, but they were not the only ones within their respective theaters of war. Two years before the battle of al-Yarmūk, Muslim Arab forces won a large-scale battle, known as Ajnādayn, against the Byzantines in Palestine. Some five years after al-Qādisīya, Muslim arms achieved the "victory of victories" over the Sassanids at Nihāwand in Persia.[2]

The apparent reason for the preeminence of al-Yarmūk and al-Qādisīya was that they became part of the historical tradition, respectively, of the great Arab cities of Damascus (Dimashq) and al-Kūfa. In the course of the conquests, the Islamic regime established troop concentrations in garrison camps at al-Jābiya near Damascus, al-Kūfa (in Iraq), and other sites. The military settlement at al-Jābiya was eventually abandoned in favor of Damascus itself, which had a large Arab population even before the conquest of Syria. In contrast, the garrison town of al-Kūfa grew through a constant influx of settlers into a large city. Both Damascus and al-Kūfa were centers of Arab-Islamic culture.

The battle of Ajnādayn took place approximately twelve miles southwest of Jerusalem, yet the memory of that event has been all but lost. Commemoration of a major Byzantine defeat was an unlikely topic for the tradition of a city which for some time retained a large Christian population. Because of several coincidences, the events of Ajnādayn became confused and combined with those of al-Yarmūk in the broader works of Muslim historiography. The battle called Ajnādayn by the Arabs involved Byzantine forces encamped at three sites, one of which was Jermūchā (phonetic /Yarmūchā/). As de Goeje notes (*Mémoire sur la Conquête de la Syrie*, 1900), the similarity of Aramaic /Yarmūchā/ and Arabic /Yarmūk/ undoubtedly led to much of the confusion. Apart from this factor, Khālid ibn al-Walīd played a key role in both of the Muslim victories. Among other prominent Arab commanders, ʿAmr ibn al-ʿĀṣ and Shuraḥbīl ibn Ḥasana were present at both battles. Among the Arab rank and file, many of the veterans of Ajnādayn were also veterans of al-Yarmūk. The literati of a later generation probably found it difficult to sort out the stories of old soldiers.

In the extant histories, the accounts of Ajnādayn have virtually no substance. Al-Balādhurī mentions only that

> about 100,000 Romans took part, most of whom Heraclius (the Byzantine emperor) sent in contingents, the rest having assembled from places nearby. On that day, Heraclius was staying in Ḥimṣ. The Muslims fought an intense battle against them, and Khālid ibn al-Walīd distinguished himself. Thereupon, Allah routed His enemies and broke them apart, a great many being killed. (*Futūḥ al-Buldān*, edited de Goeje, p. 113)

Al-Ṭabarī's account is similarly succinct and nondescript. It describes the battle as a major encounter between Muslim forces under ʿAmr ibn al-ʿĀṣ and Roman forces under an unnamed tribune.

The received version notwithstanding, there are a number of factors that allow us to distinguish between Ajnādayn and al-Yarmūk. An important clue is the list of fatalities appended to al-Balādhurī's account. It includes four prominent men of Makhzūm: ʿIkrima ibn Abī Jahl, Habbār ibn Sufyān ibn ʿAbd al-Asad, Salama ibn Hishām ibn al-Mughīra, and al-Ḥārith ibn Hishām ibn al-Mughīra. Al-Ṭabarī further informs us that, prior to Ajnādayn, ʿIkrima led forces north from Yemen, and his column included a Himyarite contingent. Various other sources indicate that the clan of Makhzūm had long-standing ties to South Arabia. The relevance of this link is that South Arabians were not indisposed to fight at night, as were the North Arabian tribesmen. Although he misplaced the event, al-Ṭabarī recounts that Khālid found his slain cousin ʿIkrima in the Roman camp at dawn, following the night battle. An early, independent source, the Latin Chronicle of Fredegarius, mentions that a decisive blow befell the

Byzantines during the night hours.[3] This evidence indicates that at Ajnādayn the Muslims attacked at least one Byzantine camp during the night. This tactic should not be confused with references to panic in the Byzantine camp at al-Yarmūk. That situation occurred because the Muslims cut the line of retreat to the north, not because they directly attacked the camp.

Despite the evidence for two distinct scenarios, most Western scholars have insisted on combining the events of both in their reconstructions of al-Yarmūk. The resulting panorama is a battle that lasted several days and involved a constant change of front—as if the opposing armies had the mobility of modern mechanized forces! The contrary view is that the Muslims had very little tactical mobility and finished the fight in one day.[4] They lured the Byzantine heavy cavalry into a trap, forced it to retreat away from its infantry support, threatened the infantry's line of retreat, and watched their ranks collapse in panic.

There is no such confusion or controversy in regard to the equally famous battle of al-Qādisīya. The sources describe the terrain in some detail, which is exceptional, and attest that the Muslim Arabs occupied a strong defensive position. The campaign unfolds as a Sassanid effort to effect a river crossing and dislodge the Arabs. There is some allusion to cavalry skirmishing and individual heroics in the tribal traditions. However, the key to the Muslims' victory lies in their infantry's holding its ground until cavalry reinforcements arrive from Syria. The Persians' use of elephant teams turns into a debacle. The Syrian veterans react quickly to exploit the situation, charge, and break the enemy's battle line.

Most of the details we have regarding the great Islamic victories derive from tribal epic sources. The salvation history genre presents terse accounts and attributes the victories to divine intervention. Thus, Ibn Isḥāq's account, as redacted and combined with other sources in al-Ṭabarī, mentions that the fighting was heavy at al-Yarmūk and that the Muslims' camp was penetrated.

> Then, Allah the Blessed and Exalted granted victory. The Romans and the contingents marshalled by Heraclius were defeated. Seventy thousand of the Romans, Armenians and Christian Arabs, were killed. Allah killed the Sacelarius and Bahan (another Roman commander). (*Ta'rīkh al-Rusul wa al-Mulūk*, edited by de Goeje, 1. 2349)

Quite similarly, an account of al-Qādisīya from the same source relates that God defeated the armies of Persia and killed Rustam (the Persian commander).

The early Arabic historiography of the conquest of other regions is similarly lacking in militarily relevant details. This is understandable, especially given the case of Egypt. Al-Fusṭāṭ (now ruins in the south of Cairo) was established as a garrison on the same model as al-Jābiya-Damascus and al-Kūfa. However, its population apparently grew more through native resettlement than through an influx of Arabs. Its literary activity did not reach the level of Damascus and al-Kūfa. Al-Fusṭāṭ was only a provincial capital, while the other two were respectively the capital and second city of the Umayyad caliphate. Perhaps these reasons, as well as the place's subsequent destruction by fire, account for the paucity of literary-historical traditions regarding the Muslim victories in Egypt.

In the course of time, the original works on the conquests disappeared, although segments of them were cited in various later works dealing with general history, geography, local or regional history, topical history, and genealogy. The received notion of the conquest movement thus reflected a disjointed experience. The theme of divine intervention was perhaps the only part of the historiographic heritage that gave that experience some meaning, beyond being the circumstances of change in governmental authority. The Muslim Arabs made no apparent attempt to write the "lessons of the conquests" into tactical treatises or other militarily relevant works.

Muslim society did not relook the conquest experience until the later part of the Crusading era (or early Mamluk period, that is, the second half of the 13th/7th century). By then, the people of Greater Syria (including Palestine) and Egypt had endured decades of incessant warfare—and the consequent population displacement, economic disruption, and threat or reality of infidel rule. However, the ascendancy of the Mamluk regime in Cairo finally brought an end to the Crusader occupation of the Levantine coast. The scholarly class of Syria and Egypt recorded these events in histories and chronicles, but they did not specifically correlate the contemporary Muslim victories with those of the early conquest era. Instead, some writers developed a new form of conquest literature by combining portions of earlier works with local folklore and legend and observations on the current conflict involving the Crusaders. They apparently sought to impart some credibility by attributing the authorship to the famous early historian al-Wāqidī. Nonetheless, the resulting compositions were largely fantastic descriptions of Muslim military prowess and bravery.

Without precise dating for this pseudo-*futūḥ* literature, as it is called, the reasons for its emergence remain subject to conjecture. The relevant works are ostensibly not intended to instruct the military class in a technical way. However, they may aim at encouraging the new political-military leadership to continue the fight. They clearly suggest that Muslim arms can defeat the enemies of Islam, however strong, through persistence and trust in God. Conversely, they may derive from a groundswell of popular euphoria over Muslim military achievements. It is conceivable that the same themes motivated both authors and storytellers, who entertained the illiterate populace of the towns and cities. In any case, the pseudo-

Plate 1. Facsimile of artwork in *al-Ḥaras al-Waṭanī (Journal of the Saudi Arabian National Guard)* 3, No. 12 (Rabīʿ II 1403/Jan. 1983). In the popular history of both the Arab and Western cultures, early Islamic warfare is generally conceived to have consisted of intense cavalry skirmishing.

futūḥ works seem to present in fictional form the warrior heritage of the Mamluk regime.

Despite the appearance of pseudo-Wāqidī works, later Muslim scholars maintained some objectivity in regard to the early conquest period. In the 14th/8th century, the renowned Ibn Khaldūn, remarking on historical differences in Arab methods of war, wrote,

> Every battle at the beginning of Islam was fought in closed formation. The Arabs had known only the attack and withdrawal technique. However, two things induced them to fight the other way at the beginning of Islam. First, their enemies used to fight in closed formation, so they were compelled to fight them that way. Second, they sought to die in holy war because they wished to persevere and were firm in their faith. The advance in close order is more appropriate for seeking death. (*al-Muqaddima*, chap. iii, sec. 35)

The last sentence indicates, though, that the battles of the early conquest period were still topics of salvation history. They apparently did not become topics of Arabic military writing until modern times.

In both the Western and Islamic Worlds, recent efforts to reconstruct the Arab conquests have been hindered by the unrealistic and uninformative nature of the available sources. Egyptian video and cinema reinstill the traditionally accepted view of light horsemen charging the enemy in

Plate 2. Exterior of the famous "Iron Gate" of the Roman fortress, Old Cairo. According to tradition, the Muslim Arab besiegers directed their main effort against this part of the fortress. The shoring has recently been added to offset stress caused by earthquakes. (Author's photograph)

reckless abandon (of formation and caution). This image has also influenced modern Arab military thought, perhaps in some cases subconsciously. We find it portrayed in military magazines (see Plate 1). Still, the same journals reflect some sense that the early Muslim military leadership adhered to time-tested precepts for battlefield success; for example, to devise stratagems to achieve surprise, to resort to maneuver or negotiation to avoid fighting at a disadvantage, and to strike toward the flanks and rear rather than the solid front of the enemy force.

Modern-day writing in Arab and Islamic countries also reflects an interest in the deeds of the early Muslim Arab war leaders. The traditional sources contain considerable information about Khālid ibn al-Walīd, as he led forces in numerous campaigns. They recall that Saʿd ibn Abī Waqqāṣ, the commander at al-Qādisīya, was renowned as the "Archer of Islam." Perhaps it is more than a coincidence that Arab archery had an important role in the outcome of the battle. Otherwise, the traditional works slight several contemporaries of Khālid, who were very militarily competent:

ʿAmr ibn al-ʿĀṣ, ʿIyāḍ ibn Ghanm, Hāshim ibn ʿUtba, Abū Mūsā al-Ashʿarī, and others. Thus, there is source material for articles, but only in the case of Khālid ibn al-Walīd, the "Sword of Allah," is there sufficient material for whole books.[5]

Regardless of historiographic efforts, the people of the contemporary Arab world are generally aware of the location of early Islamic battle sites. Some have been covered by urban sprawl. Others have been covered only by nature. However, the recurrence of war in the Middle East and heightened security awareness have inhibited their exploration. Nor do the respective Arab governments seem interested in encouraging pertinent archeological and cultural projects. The only significant relic of the Arab conquest era is Old Cairo's Roman fortress, which Muslim forces, under ʿAmr ibn al-ʿĀṣ, captured in 641/20. Even there, much of the older structure has been reworked. Outside access to the towers, wall, and gate of ʿAmr's time is blocked by a cemetery and some dwellings. It would seem that the human aspect of the conquest movement is still far from attaining full recognition in Arab culture.

NOTES

1. As a further measure of Badr's importance, it is noteworthy that al-Wāqidī devotes about one-third of his *Kitāb al-Maghāzī* to that battle.

2. Other major battles of the early conquest era were those of Jalūlā' (Iraq), ʿAyn Shams (Egypt), and Dhāt al-Ṣawārī (naval engagement near Phoenix on the Lycian coast of Anatolia).

3. Cited in Walter E. Kaegi, *Byzantium and the Early Arab Conquests* (Bibliog. 4), p. 125.

4. Compare the view of John W. Jandora ("The Battle of the Yarmūk" [Bibliog. 2] and *The March from Medina* [Bibliog. 4], pp. 61–65) with those of Kaegi (*Byzantium and the Early Arab Conquests* [Bibliog. 4], pp. 112–46); John Bagot Glubb (*The Great Arab Conquests* [Bibliog. 3], pp. 139–46 and 173–85); and Jim Bloom, "Sword of Allah," *Command Magazine* 44 (January–February 1993); pp. 57–61. Kaegi's neglect of Ajnādayn further poses the anomaly that the Byzantines took nearly thirty months to respond in force to the Arab invasion of Syria-Palestine. Bloom's article reflects an extreme degree of misinterpretation in its undocumented, noncritical approach.

5. Muṣṭafā Ṭalās' work is unique in that he expands on the traditional sources' rather nondescript references to raids, making them full-blown military operations. One example is his treatment of the Anbār campaign. See *Sayf Allāh, Khālid ibn al-Walīd* (Damascus: n.p., 1978), pp. 256–62.

BIBLIOGRAPHY

1. Campaigns of the Prophet

Ahmad, Gulzar. *Battles of the Prophet of Allah.* 2 vols. Chicago: Kazi Publications, 1986.

Bosworth, C. E. "Armies of the Prophet." In *Islam and the Arabs*, edited by Bernard Lewis. London: McClelland and Stewart, 1976.

Gabrieli, Francesco. *Muhammad and the Conquests of Islam*. Translated from the Italian by Virginia Luling and Rosamund Linell. New York: McGraw-Hill, 1968.

Gauba, K. L. *The Prophet of the Desert*. Lahore, Pakistan: Lion Press, 1962. See chaps. 5 and 6.

Hamidullah, Muhammad. "The Battlefields of the Prophet Muhammad." *Islamic Review* (June 1953): 12–15; (July 1953): 11–14; (September 1953): 12–14; (October 1953): 13–17. Reprinted as *The Battlefields of the Prophet Muhammad*. Karachi, Pakistan: Huzaifah Publications, 1979.

Ibn Hishām. *The Life of Muhammad*. A translation of *Sirat Rasūl Allāh* with introduction and notes by Alfred Guillaume. London: Oxford University Press, 1955.

Lecker, M. "The Ḥudaybiyya-Treaty and the Expedition against Khaybar." *JSAI* 5 (1984): 1–11.

Malik, S. K. *The Quranic Concept of War*. Lahore, Pakistan: Wajidalis, 1979.

McDonald, V. M., trans. *The History of al-Tabari*. Vol. 7, *The Foundation of the Community*. Albany: State University of New York Press, 1987.

Poonawala, Ismail K., trans. *The History of al-Tabari*. Vol. 9, *The Last Years of the Prophet*. Albany: State University of New York Press, 1990.

Watt, W. Montgomery. "Badr." *EI* 1 (new ed.): 867–68.

———. "Khandaḳ." *EI* 4 (new ed.): p. 1020.

———. *Muhammad at Medina*. Oxford, England: Clarendon Press, 1956.

2. Decisive Battles

Friedmann, Yohanan, trans. *The History of al-Tabari*. Vol. 12, The Battle of al-Qadisiyyah and the Conquest of Syria and Palestine. Albany: State University of New York Press, 1992.

Jandora, John W. "The Battle of the Yarmūk: A Reconstruction." *Journal of Asian History* 19 (1985): 8–21.

———. "Developments in Islamic Warfare: The Early Conquests." *Studia Islamica* 64 (1986): 101–13.

Lo Jacondo, C. "La Battaglia di Ağnādain Secondo il *Kitāb al-Futūḥ* di Ibn Aʿṯam al-Kūfī." In *Studi in Onore di Francesco Gabrieli nel suo Ottantesimo Compleanno*. A cura di R. Traini. Rome: Università di Roma "La Sapienza," Dipartimento di Studi Orientali, 1984.

Nicolle, David. *Yarmūk 636: The Muslim Conquest of Syria*. Campaign Series, no. 31. London: Osprey Publishing, 1994.

Yusuf, Sayyid Muhammad. "The Battle of al-Qādisiyya." *Islamic Culture* 19 (1945): 1–28.

3. Early Conquests, Traditional Accounts (Translation/ Paraphrase)

Akram, A. I. *The Muslim Conquest of Egypt and North Africa*. Lahore, Pakistan: Ferozsons, 1977.

———. *The Muslim Conquest of Persia.* Rawalpindi, Pakistan: Army Education Press, n.d.

———. *The Sword of Allah.* Karachi, Pakistan: National Publishing House, 1970.

al-Balādhurī. *Origins of the Islamic State.* Vol. I, translated with annotations by Philip K. Hitti; vol. 2, translated with annotations by Francis Clark Murgotten. New York: AMS Press, 1968.

Blankinship, Khalid Yahya, trans. *The History of al-Tabari.* Vol. 11, *The Challenge to the Empires.* Albany: State University of New York Press, 1993.

Donner, Fred M., trans. *The History of al-Tabari.* Vol. 10, *The Conquest of Arabia.* Albany: State University of New York Press, 1993.

Ghevond (Lewond), Erēts[c]. *Histoire des Guerres et des Conquêtes des Arabes.* Translated by Zaven Arzoumanian. Wynnewood, Pa.: St. Sahag and St. Mesrob Armenian Church, 1982.

Glubb, John Bagot. *The Great Arab Conquests.* Englewood Cliffs, N.J.: Prentice-Hall, 1967.

Humphreys, R. Stephen, trans. *The History of al-Tabari.* Vol. 15, *The Crisis of the Early Caliphate.* Albany: State University of New York Press, 1990.

Juynboll, Gautier H. A., trans. *The History of al-Tabari.* Vol. 13, *The Conquest of Iraq, Southwestern Persia, and Egypt.* Albany: State University of New York Press, 1989.

Muir, William. *Annals of the Early Caliphate.* Amsterdam: Oriental Press, 1968.

Raisuddin, Abu Nayeem Md. "ʿAmr b. al-ʿĀṣ and His Conquest of Egypt." *Islamic Culture* 55 (1981): 277–90.

Salik, Saiyed Abdus. *The Early Heroes of Islam.* Lahore, Pakistan: Book House, 1976.

Smith, G. Rex, trans. *The History of al-Tabari.* Vol. 14, *The Conquest of Iran.* Albany: State University of New York Press, 1994.

4. Early Conquests, Critical Interpretation

Amelineau, Emile. "La Conquête de l'Égypte par les Arabes." *Revue Historique* 119 (1915): 273–310; 120 (1915); 1–25.

Beckmann, L.H.H. "Die Muslimischen Heere der Eroberungszeit, 622–651." Ph.D. diss., University of Hamburg, 1953.

Butler, Alfred J. *The Arab Conquest of Egypt and the Last Thirty Years of the Roman Dominion.* Oxford, England: Clarendon Press, 1902.

Caetani, Leone. *Annali dell'Islam.* 10 vols. Milan and Rome: U. Hoepli, 1905–1926.

Canard, Marius. "L'Expansion Arabe: Le Problème Militaire." *L'Occidente e l'Islam nell'Alto Medioevo* 1 (1965): 37–63.

De Goeje, Michael Jan. *Mémoire sur la Conquête de la Syrie.* 2d ed. (Mémoires d'Histoire et de Géographie Orientales, 2.) Leiden, Netherlands: E. J. Brill, 1900.

Donner, Fred McGraw. "The Arab Tribes in the Muslim Conquest of Iraq." Ph.D. diss., Princeton University, 1975.

———. *The Early Islamic Conquests.* Princeton, N.J.: Princeton University Press, 1981.

Guillou, André. "Prise de Gaza par les Arabes au VIIe Siècle." *Bulletin de Correspondance Hellénique* 81 (1957): 396–404.

Hill, Donald Routledge. "The Role of the Camel and the Horse in the Early Arab Conquests." In *WTS.*

———. *The Termination of Hostilities in the Early Arab Conquests, A.D. 634–656.* London: Luzac and Company, 1971.

Hinds, Martin. "The First Arab Conquests in Fars." *Iran* 22 (1984): 39–53.

Jandora, John W. *The March from Medina: A Revisionist Study of the Arab Conquests.* Clifton, N.J.: Kingston Press, Inc., 1990.

Kaegi, Walter E. *Byzantium and the Early Arab Conquests.* Cambridge, England: Cambridge University Press, 1992.

———. "The First Arab Expedition against Amorium." *Byzantine and Modern Greek Studies* 3 (1977): 19–22.

Manandian, H. A. "Les Invasions Arabes en Arménie." *Byzantion* 18 (1948): 163–92.

Mayerson, Philip. "The First Muslim Attacks on Southern Palestine (A.D. 633–634)." *Transactions and Proceedings of the American Philological Association* 95 (1964): 155–99.

Nicolle, David, and Angus McBride. *Armies of the Muslim Conquest.* Men-at-Arms Series, no. 255. London: Osprey Publishing, 1993.

Posner, Nadine F. "The Muslim Conquest of Northern Mesopotamia: An Introductory Essay into Its Historical Background and Historiography." Ph.D. diss., New York University, 1985.

———. "Whence the Muslim Conquest of Northern Mesopotamia?" In *A Way Prepared: Essays in Honor of Richard Bayly Winder*, edited by Farhad Kazemi and R. D. McChesney. New York: New York University Press, 1988.

Shoufani, Elias. *Al-Riddah and the Muslim Conquest of Arabia.* Toronto, Ontario: University of Toronto Press; and Beirut: Arab Institute for Research and Publishing, 1973.

5. Source Critique

Bashear, S. "Apocalyptic and other Materials on Early Muslim-Byzantine Wars: A Review of Arabic Sources." *JRAS* ser. 3, 1 (1991): 173–207.

Conrad, Lawrence I. "Al-Azdi's History of the Arab Conquests in Bilad al-Sham: Some Historiographic Observations." In *Proceedings of the Second Symposium on the History of Bilād al-Shām during the Early Islamic Period up to 40 A.H./640 A.D.*, edited by Muhammad Adnan Bakhit. Amman: University of Jordan, 1987.

———. "The Conquest of Arwād: A Source-Critical Study in the Historiography of the Early Medieval Near East." In *The Byzantine and Early Islamic Near East: Papers of the First Workshop on Late Antiquity and Early Islam*, edited by Avril Cameron and Lawrence I. Conrad. Princeton, N.J.: Darwin Press, 1992.

Hinds, Martin. "Al-Maghāzī." *EI* 5 (new ed.): 1161–64.

Jones, J.M.B. "The Chronology of the Maghāzī—A Textual Survey." *BSOAS* 19 (1957): 245–80.

———. "Ibn Isḥāq and al-Wāqidī: The Dream of ʿĀtika and the Raid to Nakhla in Relation to the Charge of Plagiarism." *BSOAS* 22 (1959): 41–51.

Kister, Meir J. "The Expedition to Bi'r Maʿūna." In *Arabic and Islamic Studies in Honor of Hamilton A. R. Gibb*, edited by George Makdisi. Leiden, Netherlands: E. J. Brill, 1965.

———. "Notes on the Papyrus Text about Muḥammad's Campaign Against the Banū al-Naḍīr," *Archiv Orientální* 32 (1964), pp. 233–236.

Noth, Albrecht, and Lawrence I. Conrad. *The Early Arabic Historical Tradition: A Source-Critical Study*. Translated by Michael Bonner. Princeton, N.J.: Darwin Press, 1994.

Paret, Rudi. ''Die Legendäre Futuh-Literatur, ein Arabisches Volksepos?'' In *La Poesia Epica e la sur Formazione*. Rome: Accademia dei Lincei, 1970.

Schacht, J. ''On Mūsā b. ʿUqba's Kitāb al-Maghāzī.'' *Acta Orientalia* 21 (1953): 288–300.

3

The Struggle Within and Without the Islamic Domain (Fitna and Jihad)

Thc rapidity of the early Arab-Islamic conquests was due in large part to the cohesion of the Muslim political-military leadership. However, some twenty-two years after the Muslim invasion of Syria, that cohesion was seriously shattered, and it would never be fully restored. In the winter of 656–657/36, two Muslim Arab armies fought the so-called Battle of the Camel, in the vicinity of al-Baṣra. One force was led by the Prophet's cousin and son-in-law ʿAlī, who had recently attained the caliphate. The other force was led by ʿĀ'isha, who was one of the Prophet's widows, and al-Zubayr and Ṭalḥa, who were two of the Prophet's preeminent Companions. These three had taken to arms to avenge the murder of the caliph ʿUthmān and to challenge ʿAlī's succession. The battle ended in victory for ʿAlī. As for his opponents, Ṭalḥa was fatally wounded, al-Zubayr was killed outright, and ʿĀ'isha retired to Medina and henceforth kept out of governmental affairs.

According to the received history, the prelude to the Battle of the Camel (i.e., ʿĀ'isha's camel) was the climax of growing popular resentment toward the ruling elite's abuse of power. Certain inhabitants of the garrison towns of al-Fusṭāṭ, al-Kūfa, and al-Baṣra conspired among themselves to march on Medina and demand governmental changes and reform. When faced with their animosity, the aged caliph ʿUthmān vacillated. The dissidents from al-Fusṭāṭ became distrustful of his intentions. They pressed their demands with renewed vehemence, beleaguered the

Map 3.1
The Islamic Dominion at ʿUthmān's Accession, 644/23

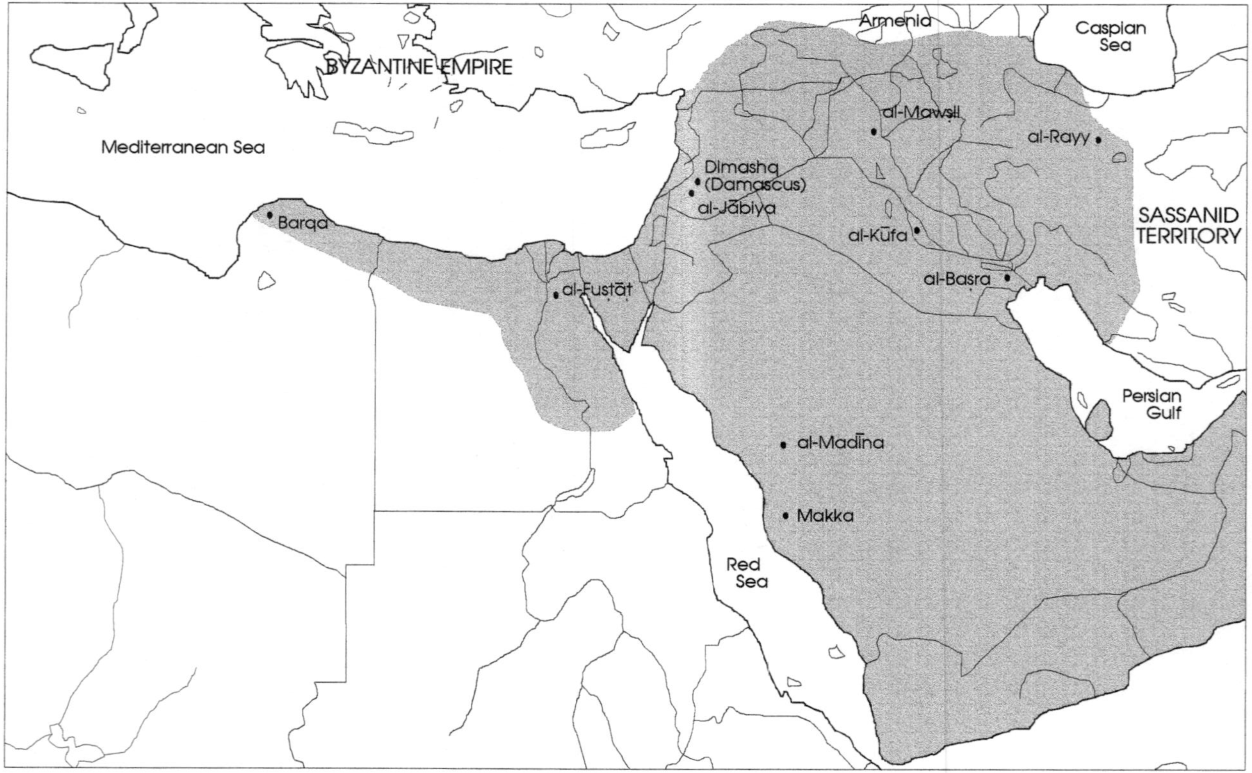

caliph in his palace, and eventually killed him. They prevailed on the citizens of Medina to choose a new caliph and then confirmed the selection of ʿAlī. Certain accounts of these events hint at ʿAlī's complicity in the coup, since he refrained from actively defending ʿUthmān. Moreover, his following came to include many of those who had attacked the old caliph.

ʿAlī's victory near al-Baṣra eliminated an immediate challenge but did not compel the allegiance of all Islam. Many of ʿUthmān's kinsmen (of the Umayyad clan of Quraysh) and allies were well established in Syria, where the governor Muʿāwiya was the champion of their cause. Having that secure base, they refused to acknowledge ʿAlī as caliph until he avenged ʿUthmān's murder by punishing the regicides. Since ʿAlī could ill afford to alienate his current supporters, he had to confront the Umayyad opposition and depose Muʿāwiya.

During the month following the Battle of the Camel, ʿAlī moved his seat of government to al-Kūfa as a result of the support he received from that city. There, he assembled forces to strike at his opponents. In the spring of 657/36, he led his army of some 50,000 into Syria. The main force crossed the Euphrates in the vicinity of al-Raqqa and came in contact with Muʿāwiya's army south of the town on the plain of Ṣiffīn. That encounter involved skirmishing over a period of weeks, followed by an armistice, fruitless negotiations, more skirmishing, and then resort to all-out battle. After a few days of combat, the opposing sides agreed to settle the issue of governmental legitimacy by binding arbitration. When the arbiters finally met several months later, their decision went against ʿAlī's claim to the caliphate.

Even before this judgment was passed, ʿAlī had lost the allegiance of many vehement opponents of the Islamic aristocracy, who wanted to finish the fight against Muʿāwiya. Several thousand fighting men separated themselves from ʿAlī's army on the return march from Ṣiffīn. They encamped at the village of Ḥarūrā' near al-Kūfa, where they were joined by others of like mind. These separatists denounced the conventional notion of an elect group within Islam and the concomitant belief that the caliph must be of the lineage of Quraysh. They and their successors developed a new creed, which emphasized the equality of all Muslims and refuted the moral doctrine of justification by faith (vice deeds). Their secessionist movement, which came to be called Kharijite (Arabic *Khārijīya*), created the first major rift within the Islamic domain.

The Kharijites held to a militant, fanatically self-righteous stance. They raided and killed in any vulnerable Muslim community that would not accept their beliefs. Because of the Kharijite insurrection, ʿAlī was preempted from taking further action against Muʿāwiya. He did deploy forces for another campaign in Syria, but he was compelled to countermand their march orders. Reacting to reports of Kharijite atrocities in Iraq, ʿAlī moved against their new camp by the Nahrawān Canal (in the vicinity of modern Baghdad). Most of the 4,000 insurgents dispersed, but some 1,800 zealots offered resistance against overwhelming odds, only to be slaughtered. Those who avoided the carnage continued to proselytize and spread dissent. As a consequence, ʿAlī had to cope with several Kharijite uprisings in the final two years of his reign. His own demise came at the hands of an assassin who sought to avenge some of the Kharijites killed at the Battle of Nahrawān. ʿAlī's oldest son Ḥasan was acclaimed the new caliph. However, Muʿāwiya persuaded him to abdicate and proceeded to take control of the eastern lands of Islam.

The received account of the above events derives from an era when anti-Umayyad feelings were prevalent. Nonetheless, mainline Arabic historiography is not altogether partial to ʿAlī. The events of this first civil war (or *fitna*, in Arabic) are generally described in a matter-of-fact manner, without the invective and ascription of right and wrong that are found in various sectarian tracts. The accounts of the fighting seem to have the same model as those of the pre-Islamic tribal conflicts, or *Ayyām al-ʿArab*.[1] The champions of the opposing forces boast of their martial prowess and incite their comrades to fight. The battle is obscure since there is little or no mention of tactical formations or maneuvers. Sometimes valor prevails, sometimes stratagem. Both sides gain honor from the test of arms. The early historians point out that the major tribal groups were divided in their allegiance. However, this observation only confirms that local, clan interests were then, as they are today, more fundamental determinants of loyalty than eponymous identity with a larger group.

In this story of strife, ʿAlī is portrayed as an ill-fated hero. He is the paragon of manly virtue—eloquent in speech, wise in counsel, loyal in friendship, patient in adversity, valiant in war, and magnanimous in victory. Despite his virtues, his efforts are undermined by vacillating supporters and nondiscerning counsellors. The sources convey this overall favorable impression, yet they also hint at ʿAlī's shortcomings in statecraft. Indeed, it seems that, prior to becoming caliph, ʿAlī had had little experience in fighting wars or making peace.

In comparison, Muʿāwiya did much more to further the cause of Islam. Relying on his loyal Syrian forces, he ensured internal stability for nearly twenty years. Meanwhile, he improved the government and extended the frontiers of the Islamic dominion. The termination of the first civil war allowed the resumption of the struggle against Byzantium. Muslim forces pressed the Byzantines on two fronts. In the north, they raided deep into Anatolia on a regular basis, temporarily occupied Crete and Rhodes, and twice besieged Constantinople. In the west, they conquered a large part of the North African littoral. Muslim forces also campaigned on the eastern frontiers of Islam, where they completed the conquest of Khurasan and raided beyond the Oxus River.

While he still lived, Muʿāwiya arranged for his son Yazīd to succeed to the caliphate. Despite this precaution, Yazīd's accession led to another civil war. The first resistance came from Medina, where some members of the Muslim elite refused to acknowledge him as caliph. When Yazīd pressed for their oath of allegiance through the local governor, ʿAbdullah son of al-Zubayr and Ḥusayn son of ʿAlī sought refuge at Mecca. Of the two, Ḥusayn was first to challenge Yazīd. In response to multiple summons from al-Kūfa, pledging loyalty and support, he decided to reclaim his father's place there. Ḥusayn set out from Mecca with his entire household, a number of kinsmen, and an escort—an entourage which, according to tradition, included only seventy fighting men. When Umayyad forces blocked the roads into al-Kūfa, the group encamped in the plain of Karbalā', about twenty-five miles northwest of the city. The inevitable negotiations foundered, and the Umayyad troops eventually attacked, killing Ḥusayn and all the men with him. This "martyrdom" of Ḥusayn on 10 Muḥarram 61 (10 October 680) was the impetus for the second major schism within Islam. Henceforth, the supporters of the House of ʿAlī (now called Shiites, by derivation from Arabic *shīʿat ʿAlī*) denounced mainstream Islam and, like the Kharijites, formulated their own religio-political doctrine.

The events at Karbalā' did not end the challenge to the Umayyads but rather sparked a second period of civil war. With Ḥusayn eliminated as a rival, ʿAbdullah ibn al-Zubayr assumed the leadership of the anti-Umayyad movement. His support initially came from the people of Mecca and Medina, the latter having revoked their allegiance to Yazīd, and from Kharijite groups in other parts of Arabia and al-Baṣra. Yazīd sent a punitive expedition against the two rebellious cities in the Hijaz (al-Ḥijāz, Western Arabia). The Umayyad troops defeated the defense force of Medina in the Battle of the Ḥarra (i.e., the nearby lava field) and subsequently occupied and pillaged the town. They then marched on Mecca and laid siege to it. The siege operations were suspended though, when news of Yazīd's death induced the Umayyad force to withdraw. The succession issue became a crisis for the Umayyads. Meanwhile, Ibn al-Zubayr was acknowledged as caliph throughout much of the Islamic domain. His supporters in Syria, led by al-Ḍaḥḥāk ibn Qays al-Fihrī, almost carried that province as well. However, Marwān ibn al-Ḥakam, the former secretary of Caliph ʿUthmān, was able to retrieve the Umayyad position there. He assembled an army, which defeated al-Ḍaḥḥāk's forces at Marj Rāhiṭ near Damascus in 684/64.

Ibn al-Zubayr was unable to press the Umayyads in Syria, as he had to contend with threats to his own rule in Iran and Arabia. Various Kharijite groups renounced him and resumed their violent activity. Meanwhile, the Shīʿa rose up under the leadership of Mukhtār ibn Abī ʿUbayd. Mukhtār, who is depicted as an adventurer in the sources, gained control over al-Kūfa and its dependent territories in the troubled years following the death of Ḥusayn ibn ʿAlī. In 685/66 he claimed the caliphate for Muḥammad, son of ʿAlī by a woman of Ḥanīfa (i.e., he was not a descendant of the Prophet). He also claimed for himself the status of regent to legitimize his hold on power.[2] In the summer of 686/67, Mukhtār's army checked the Umayyad forces that had been sent to depose him and defeated them at the Khazir River near Mosul. Mukhtār's victory, however, was short lived. The following year, his movement was crushed—not by the Umayyads but by the Zubayrid governor of al-Baṣra.

From the time of the Battle of the Ḥarra, it was nine years before the Umayyads could again move against Ibn al-Zubayr at Mecca. Marwān's son ʿAbd al-Malik, who had since succeeded him as caliph in 685/65, completed the restoration of Umayyad rule. With Iraq in turmoil, he was able to defeat the Zubayrid forces in that province. He then sent an army under the famous al-Ḥajjāj to subjugate the Hijaz. The Umayyad forces prevailed in the ensuing second siege of Mecca, and Ibn al-Zubayr fell in the final fighting. ʿAbd al-Malik and his successors preserved the unity of the Islamic dominion for more than five decades. Their dynasty was overthrown in 750/132, consequent to yet another period of civil strife.

In the received Arabic history of early Islam, the events of the civil wars lead up to the emergence of the righteous, Abbasid dynasty. The historians of the Abbasid era somewhat begrudgingly credit the Umayyads with preserving the unity of the Islamic dominion. They establish the cause of the Alid-Umayyad conflict. However, they generally withhold comment on the other disruptive developments which beset Muslim Arab society of the Umayyad era.

The analytic work of several Western scholars has defined the trends that adversely affected the political cohesion of the early caliphate, that is, other than the struggle for preeminence within the aristocracy, the antiaristocratic stance of the egalitarian Kharijites, the rivalry between tribal political-military blocs, and the self-assertion of non-Arab Muslims. Despite this ground-breaking analysis, there have yet to be follow-on studies of pattern variances in time and location. Regarding the factor of Arab factionalism, for example, the accepted notion of rivalry between two major blocs (Muḍar versus Yemen, Tamīm versus Azd, and so on) seems to be an oversimplification, given the number of exceptions to the normative alignment. We are similarly lacking a systematic study of how the stability of the caliphate was affected by the manning and administration of the Muslim armies.

Since the Arabic sources generally distinguish groups on the basis of tribal/clan or sectarian affiliation, they overlook the military aspect of events. In the case of ʿUthmān's demise, for example, they depict as extremist dissidents the people who initially protested against and then killed the caliph. In actuality, they were mutinous soldiers. Their attack on ʿUthmān was the first of several instances in which Arab soldiers revolted against the reigning caliph. The behavior of the soldiers, though, may have been moderated by some cultural constraints in this early period of Islam. It is significant that, except for the Kharijites, there is no evidence of mutineers arrogating to themselves alone the right to name a new ruler.

A number of Western scholars have conjectured that the traditional bedouin disdain for governmental control may have been a contributing factor in the recurrent mutinies. Similarly, the raiding activity of the Kharijites may have been a reversion to the predatory habits of bedouins, although the code that constrained violence in the desert was no longer upheld. Sectarian differences seemingly changed group dynamics and justified bloodletting on a wider scale. Although such hypotheses have yet to be fully tested, governmental problems were ostensibly more severe in Iraq and the conquered lands to the east, where Arab migration was heaviest. To check the unruly tendencies there, the Umayyads took various measures, including deploying Syrian troops, manipulating the local tribal rivalries, and maintaining "private armies."

Until later Umayyad times, Syria did not experience the factiousness prevalent in the Islamic East. This situation probably resulted from the Umayyads' policies regarding immigration and manpower. Except for the movement of the Qays ʿAylān into Northern Syria, they apparently barred Arab migration into Syria-Palestine. Despite this restriction, the Umayyads sustained a large military establishment within their home province. The Syrian army included the caliphal guard, regional garrisons, frontier defenses, and expeditionary forces. As usual, the Arabic histories offer few hints as to how this army's manning was sustained. It is known that the respective tribal/communal contingents that constituted the original armies of invasion were attrited by war and plague. Nevertheless, units with the same tribal lineage remained in active service for decades. It would seem then that they were sustained through enrollment of offspring, clients (*mawālī*), and slaves. Apart from the induction of Syrians as clients, there is evidence that non-Arab native converts formed their own units and that native Christians served in the army as well. By inference, the army of Syria had a large proportion of natives in its ranks and, eventually, a large number of enlistees who were offspring of marriages between conquerors and natives.[3]

There is no indication that the Syrians had any special military qualities per se; however, the sources do attest to their discipline and loyalty and, hence, their reliability. The inference is that the Umayyad government was successful because the regime had reliable troops to deploy to critical areas. This advantage lasted into the reign of Hishām (724–743/105–125), when Umayyad princes began to develop personal ties to certain units. As a consequence, the Syrian army split along factional lines in the succession struggle that followed the death of Hishām. The rivalry between the tribal blocs of Kalb and Qays ʿAylān also undermined the stability of Syria, but this case may be overstated in the sources.

It is clear that the Umayyads had to contend with factionalism as a consequence of assimilating the manpower of Arabia (including the Syrian Desert) into their military establishment.[4] It is not clear, however, how they did it. Depending on circumstances, they abetted, suppressed, or exploited the factionalism in the garrison towns. Given the high potential for instability, the regime sought to attain some security at the higher levels of government through the formation of guard units (Arabic: *shurṭa, shuraṭ).*[5]

The significance of the *shurṭa* as an institution has gone largely unnoticed. The early Arab authors, who vaguely noted the existence of guard units, somewhat confused the historical record by using the terms *shurṭa* and *ḥaras* interchangeably. Western scholars have seemingly been misled by the terminology, as *shurṭa* has come to mean military police, while *ḥaras* means guard in a generic sense. By inference, the *shurṭa* of the caliph consisted of an elite corps of highly loyal troops who accompanied him, his heir, or his deputy during war and perhaps guarded them during peacetime functions.[6] The *shurṭa* of the governor similarly consisted of highly loyal troops who served as his private army. This force was probably just large enough to influence the local, factional balance of power, when necessary, without being able to suppress major revolts by itself. In critical situations, the Umayyads deployed units of the Syrian army to pacify the provinces.

Over the decades, the evolution of this institution took an unfavorable turn. Two Umayyad princes, who eventually became rivals, developed personal ties with certain military units as a consequence of campaigning with them against the Byzantines. Sulaymān ibn Hishām went as far as maintaining his own army.[7] This development contributed to the severity of the succession struggle that followed the death of the caliph Hishām. Despite Marwān II's victory, enmities within the military establishment lingered on and undermined the dynasty, which soon was overthrown.

The second civil war (Ibn al-Zubayr versus the Umayyads) and the recurrent uprisings in the provinces temporarily interrupted the surge of Arab-Islamic conquest. However, ʿAbd al-Malik's effective consolidation of power in the central provinces eventually allowed for the resumption of offensive action at the frontiers. In the west, Mūsā ibn Nuṣayr advanced with forces from Qayrawān to the Atlantic shore of North Africa. He and his freedman Ṭāriq ibn Ziyād then undertook the conquest of Spain. In the east, the Muslims subjugated Kabul and its dependent territories and then continued their advance on two fronts. Troops from Iraq, reinforced by Syrians, conquered northern India. Another Iraqi force, under the famous Qutayba ibn Muslim, retook or conquered anew the lands in the Oxus-Jaxartes region of Central Asia (ancient Bactria and Sogdiana) and

Map 3.2
Umayyad Conquests, West, 661–715/41–96

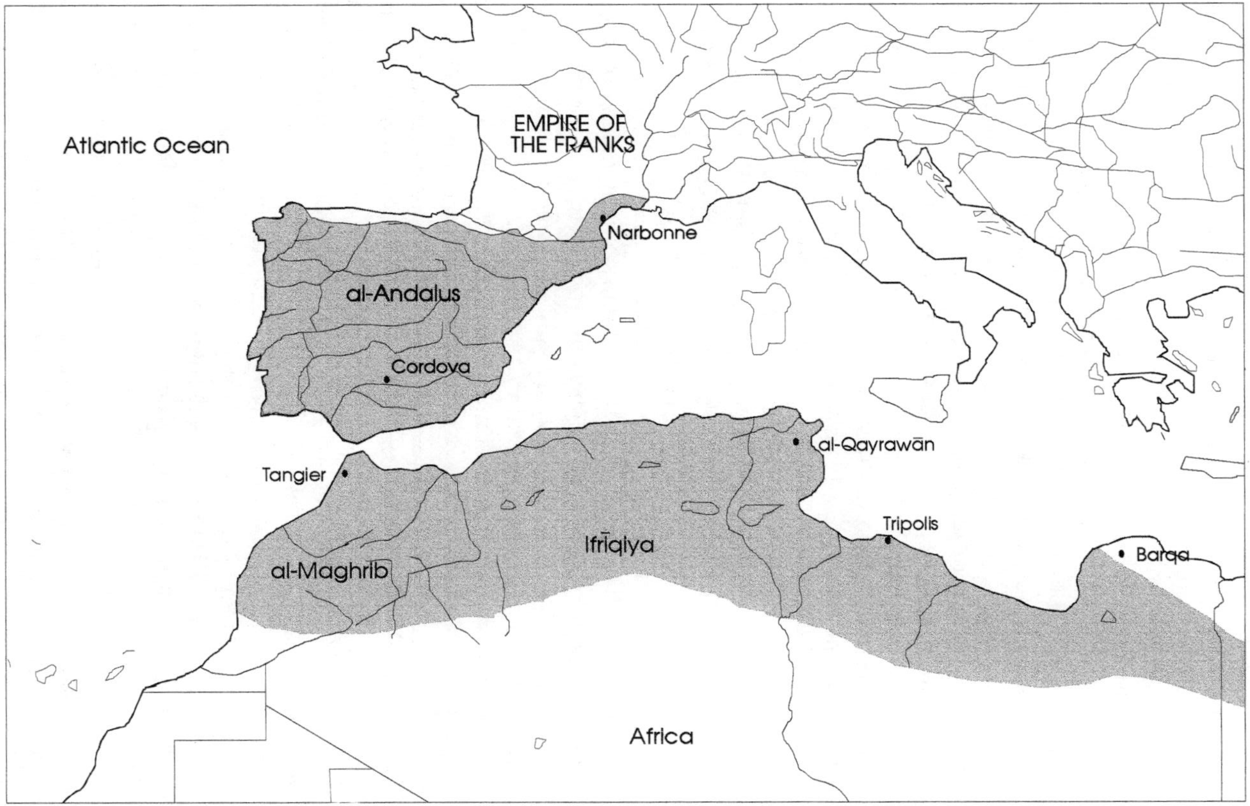

Map 3.3
Umayyad Conquests, East, 661–715/41–96

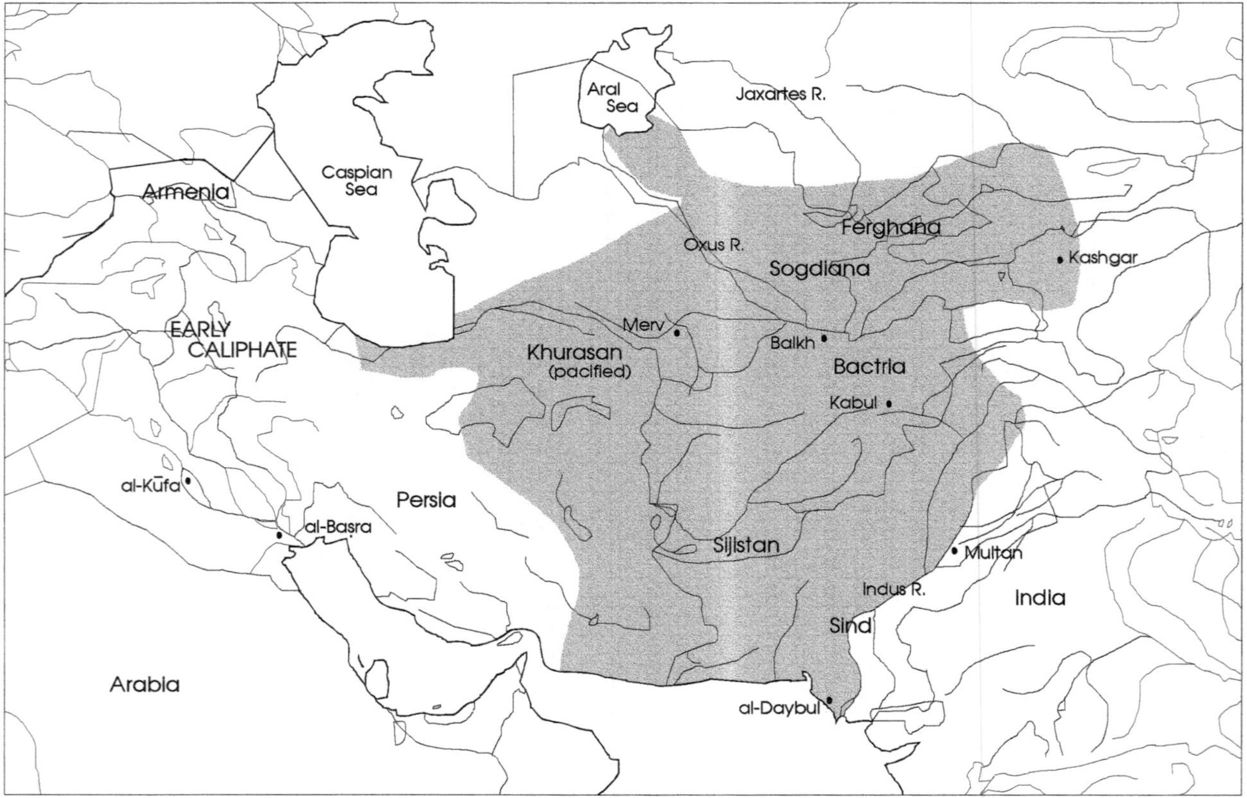

established a foothold beyond the Jaxartes in Ferghana. In the north, Muslim forces recovered the Armenian lands that had thrown off Islamic rule.

While their provincial governors (or viceroys) extended the far frontiers of Islam, the Umayyads themselves launched yet another expedition against Constantinople. Maslama, one of the many sons of ʿAbd al-Malik, led the Muslim forces in a year-long siege of the Byzantine capital (late summer 716/97–98 to late summer 717/98–99). The Muslims were thwarted by various counter moves and finally lifted the siege upon the death of their caliph Sulaymān. As events transpired, that would be the last effort made by Arab troops to take the great city on the Golden Horn.

As with the initial conquests, early Arabic historiography provides few militarily relevant details regarding the campaigns of the Umayyad era. This is especially the case for those events that took place at a great distance from the culture of the caliphal and viceregal courts and main areas of Arab settlement. Nonetheless, modern Arabic historiography proudly recalls, albeit with some vagueness, the military achievements of the Umayyad dynasty and the subsequent development of centers of Islamic culture in Spain, northern India, and Central Asia. In contrast, early modern Western historians tend to focus on the culmination of the Muslim Arab threat to Europe. The two key events are the break-off of the siege of Constantinople and the defeat at Tours (or Poitiers) in 732/114, which checked the Muslim incursion through Spain into southern France. One overarching relevant issue which has yet to be adequately studied is the Umayyads' reliance on non-Arab manpower to sustain so many military endeavors.

The Islamic dominion was at its greatest expanse during the caliphate of Hishām, that is, approximately one hundred years from the onset of the Arab conquest movement. Within that relatively short period of time, the Muslim Arabs created the largest empire the world had yet seen. Even after the tide of conquest had ebbed, successive Islamic dynasties continued to threaten southern and eastern Europe for centuries—the Ottomans were the vanguard of Islam in premodern and early modern times. More recently, various Muslim governments and extremist groups have called for a jihad (either outright war or militant activity) in reaction to the foreign policy moves of America and its allies. With this historical perspective, Western scholars and other intellectuals have raised the issue of the inherent militancy of Islam. Social science generalists usually affirm the hypothesis. However, specialists in Islamic studies are better able to look beyond the external evidence of events. Their analysis focuses on the Muslim attitude to war, as it has been affected by temporal circumstances, foreign influences, and native traditions.[8] Comparative evidence indicates that Muslim society, as a historical continuum, has been no more militant than others.

At its inception, Islam appears as a militant movement in that the

Prophet sanctioned the use of force to convert the pagans of Arabia. This injunction is conveyed both explicitly and implicitly in a number of places in the Qur'ān. Nonetheless, the Muslim scripture as a whole does not concern itself much with the subject of war—certainly no more than the Old Testament. Despite the claims of *ḥadīth* (study of the Prophet's non-revelatory words and deeds), it remains a matter of conjecture as to whether Muḥammad would have fully engaged the Byzantines and Sassanid Persians, as his successors did.

The early caliphal regime was indeed militaristic in that it sustained itself largely by war. However, it did not implement any general policy of forced conversion. On the contrary, the Muslim leadership at Medina and then Damascus did not encourage mass conversion and, in some cases, even discouraged it. This record suggests that the motive force of conquest was not religious. During the early Islamic era, being Muslim was tantamount to being a member of the ruling class—a group largely consisting of soldiers. It would seem then that the obligation to fight was a corollary of the system of governing, not a precept for personal salvation.

The scholars of the Ummayad era and later times endeavored to define the Islamic concept of war, as reflected in the Qur'ān, the related corpus of Prophetic traditions, and the practice of the early caliphate. Their analysis differentiated three situations: war against non-Muslims for the advancement or defense of Islam (*jihād*), war between Muslims (*fitna*), and war as a condition of the human experience in general (*ḥarb*). Of the two cases concerning Muslims, jihad was permissible, if not obligatory, but *fitna* was objectionable. Despite the legalistic proscription of *fitna*, the Muslim Arabs often engaged in sectarian conflict. Even then, the legitimacy of the resort to arms could be upheld if one side declared its opponents to be apostates from true Islam. The Shiites and Kharijites often resorted to this expedient.

Emerging Islamic doctrine sanctioned the use of force to achieve the righteous society—one with peace, Muslim government, and fair distribution of wealth. This legitimation of force to attain righteousness created a fundamental tension within Muslim Arab society. The early caliphs were often able to direct that tension outward through wars of conquest. However, with the onset of military stalemate at the frontiers, that tension was released inward as insurrection and civil war. The Kharijites and radical Shiites (Ismailis) were particularly prone to violence against other Muslims.

Regarding jihad as a duty, there were obligations on both the caliph and the generality of Muslims. The caliph was expected to expand or at least defend the frontiers of Islam. Indeed, fulfillment of this role was an important aspect of the early Abbasids' self-image, even though they did not effect any significant territorial gains. The Muslims as a people were expected to support the caliph's call to war. The response, however, usually varied according to the proximity of the conflict. Involvement was seemingly greater where local or personal interests were affected.[9] From Abbasid times on, the call to jihad in Arab society has generally not been an effective means of mobilizing manpower and resources on a large scale. Nonetheless, the contemporary Arabs have been reluctant to let go of this ritual in their war making.

NOTES

1. See discussion in chapter 1.

2. It is relevant to note here that the Alids were not active challengers to the established regime. Mukhtār fulfilled the role of king maker for Muḥammad ibn al-Ḥanafīya, as al-Ashtar ibn al-Ḥārith al-Nakhaʿī did for ʿAlī.

3. Some Arabists and Orientalists may object to this distinction between "native Syrians" and conquering Arabs. Of course, the preconquest population of Syria consisted of Arabs as well as Aramaeans and people of mixed stock. However, the basis of distinction here is cultural rather than ethnic. The people of Syria, to include the seminomadic Arabs of the desert frontier, were accustomed to imperial rule; the people of Arabia proper were not.

4. Actually, discontent among the soldiery had presented problems for Islamic regimes since the latter part of ʿUthmān's caliphate.

5. The sources mention that ʿAlī too had a unit of guardsmen. Muʿāwiya's guard corps distinguished itself at the Battle of Ṣiffīn. See John W. Jandora, *The March from Medina* (in Chap. 2, Bibliog. 4), p. 96, nn. 37 and 38.

6. It is not clear whether the Umayyad caliphs all had distinct units of household, or palace, guards and companion guards.

7. See references to al-Dhakwānīya in Gerald R. Hawting (Bibliog. 1), pp. 97, 100, and 102.

8. See Bibliog. 4, particularly the works of Marius Canard (1936), Fred McGraw Donner, E. J. Jurji, and Albrecht Noth (1966).

9. The Islamic historiography of the Crusading era attests to numerous instances of limited response to an appeal for jihad. For further information, see the works cited in chapter 6, Bibliog. 1.

BIBLIOGRAPHY

1. Civil Wars in Early Islam

Blankinship, Khalid Yahya. *The End of the Jihad State: The Reign of Hisham ibn ʿAbd al-Malik and the Collapse of the Umayyads.* Albany: State University of New York Press, 1994.

Brünnow, R. E. *Die Charidschiten unter der Ersten Omayyaden.* Leiden, Netherlands: E. J. Brill, 1884.

Buhl, Frants. "Ṣiffīn." *EI* (1st ed.; reprint): 406–8.

Dixon, A. A. *The Umayyad Caliphate 65–86/684–705.* London: Luzac, 1971.

Gibb, H. A. R. "ʿAbd Allāh b. al-Zubayr." *EI* 1 (new ed.): 54–55.

Haji Yahaya, Mahayudin. *The Origins of the Khawarij*. Subang Jaya, Selangor, Malaysia: Penerbitan Sarjana (M) Sdn. Bhd., 1984.

Hasan, S. M. Waris. "Some of the Aspects of the Event of Karbala." *Alserāt* 2, iv (1976): 14–20.

Hawting, Gerald R. *The First Dynasty of Islam: The Umayyad Caliphate A.D. 661–750*. Carbondale: Southern Illinois University Press, 1986.

Hinds, Martin. "The Banners and Battle Cries of the Arabs at Ṣiffīn," *Al-Abḥāth* 24 (1971): 3–42.

Howard, I.K.A. "Events and Circumstances Surrounding the Martyrdom of al-Husain b. Ali." *Alserāt* 1, ii (1975): 3–14.

———. "Hujr b. Adi's Rising against Muʿāwiya." *Alserāt* 3, ii–iii (1977), 19–31.

Husayn, S. E. "The Historical Background to the Battle of Karbala." *Alserāt* 8, iii–iv (1982): 3–7.

Kister, Meir J. "The Battle of the Ḥarra." In *Studies in Memory of Gaston Wiet*, edited by M. Rosen-Ayalon. Jerusalem: Hebrew University, 1977.

Moin, Mumtaz. "The Battle of the Camel." *Journal of the Pakistan Historical Society* 27 (1979): 17–31.

Namazi, M. M. "Karbala." *Alserāt* 2, iv (1976): 2–11; 7, iii–iv (1981): 4–15.

———. "Karbala." In *Alserāt: Selected Articles 1975–83*, 77–86. London: Muhammadi Trust, 1983.

Petersen, Erling Ladewig. "ʿAlî and Muʿâwiyah: The Rise of the Umayyad Caliphate, 656–661." *Acta Orientalia* 23 (1959): 157–96.

———. *ʿAlī and Muʿāwiya in Early Arabic Tradition*. Copenhagen, Denmark: Munksgaard, 1964.

Rotter, Gernot. *Die Umayyaden und der Zweite Bürgerkrieg (680–692)*. Wiesbaden, Germany: Deutsche Morgenländische Gesellschaft, 1982.

Rubinacci, R. "Il Califfo ʿAbd al-Malik b. Marwān e gli Ibāḍiti." *AIUON* n.s. 5 (1953): 99–121.

Sellheim, Rudolf. *Der Zweite Bürgerkrieg in Islam*. Wiesbaden, Germany: F. Steiner, 1970.

Sharon, Moshe. *Revolt: The Social and Military Aspects of the 'Abbasid Revolution*. Jerusalem: Hebrew University, 1990.

Thomson, William. "Kharijitism and the Kharijites." In *The MacDonald Presentation Volume*. Princeton, N.J.: Princeton University Press, 1933.

Van Ess, J. "Les Qadarites et la Ġuilānīya de Yazīd III." *Studia Islamica* 41 (1970): 269–86.

Veccia-Vaglieri, Laura. "(Al-)Ḥusayn b. ʿAlī b. Abī Ṭālib." *EI* 3 (new ed.): 607–15.

———. "Il Conflitto ʿAlī-Muʿāwiya et la Secessione Khārigita Riesaminati alla Luce di Fonti Ibāḍite." *AIUON* n.s. 4 (1952): 1–94.

———. "Kharidjites." Part 2. *EI* 4 (new ed.): 1075–76.

———. "Traduzione di Passi Riguardanti il Conflitto ʿAlī- Muʿāwiya et la Secessione Khārigita." *AIUON* n.s. 5 (1953): 1–98.

Veselý, R. "Die Anṣâr im ersten Bürgerkriege (36–40 d.H.)." *Archiv Orientální* 26 (1958): 36–58.

Wellhausen, Julius. *The Arab Kingdom and Its Fall*. Beirut, Lebanon: Khayat, 1964.

2. Expansion of the Umayyad State, Sources

al-Balādhurī. *Origins of the Islamic State*. Vol. 1, translated with annotations by Philip K. Hitti; vol. 2, translated with annotations by Francis Clark Murgotten. New York: AMS Press, 1968.

Blankinship, Khalid Yahya, trans. *The History of al-Tabari*. Vol. 25, *The End of Expansion*. Albany: State University of New York Press, 1989.

Brunschvig, Robert. ''Ibn 'Abdal-Hakam et la Conquête de l'Afrique du Nord par les Arabes.'' *Annales de l'Institut des Études Orientales* 6 (1942–1947): 108–55.

Fishbein, Michael, trans. *The History of al-Tabari*. Vol. 21, *The Victory of the Marwanids*. Albany: State University of New York Press, 1990.

Gateau, Albert, ed. and trans. ''Ibn 'Abd al-Hakam. La Conquête de l'Afrique du Nord et de l'Espagne.'' *Revue Tunisienne* (1931): 233–60; (1932): 71–78; (1935): 247–70; (1936): 57–83; (1937): 63–88. Reprinted as *La Conquête de l'Afrique du Nord et de l'Espagne*. Algiers: Editions Carbonel, 1942.

———. ''Ibn 'Abd al-Hakam et les Sources Arabes Relatives à la Conquête de l'Afrique du Nord et de l'Espagne.'' *Revue Tunisienne* (1938): 37–54; (1939): 203–19.

Hinds, Martin, trans. *The History of al-Tabari*. Vol. 23, *The Zenith of the Marwanid House*. Albany: State University of New York Press, 1990.

Ibn al-Qūṭīya. *Historia de la Conquista de España*. Translated by Julián Ribera. Madrid: Tip. de la ''Revista de Archivos,'' 1926.

———. ''Histoire de la Conquête de l'Andalousie.'' Translated by M. O. Houdas. In *Recueil de Texts et de Traductions*. Paris: L'École des Langes Orientales Vivantes, 1889.

Rowson, Everett K., trans. *The History of al-Tabari*. Vol. 22, *The Marwanid Restoration*. Albany: State University of New York Press, 1989.

3. Expansion of the Umayyad State, Studies

Akram, A. I. *The Muslim Conquest of Spain*. Rawalpindi, Pakistan: Army Education Press, 1980.

Bosworth, C. E. ''Ubaidallāh b. Abī Bakra and the 'Army of Destruction' in Zābulistān.'' *Islam* 50 (1973): 268–83.

Brooks, E. W. ''The Arab Occupation of Crete.'' *English Historical Review* 28 (1913): 431–43.

———. ''The Campaign of 716–718 from Arabic Sources.'' *Journal of Hellenic Studies* 19 (1989): 19–33.

Canard, Marius. ''Les Expéditions des Arabes contre Constantinople dans l'Histoire et la Légende.'' *Journal Asiatique* 208 (1926): 61–121.

Collins, Roger. *The Arab Conquest of Spain 710–797*. Oxford, England: B. Blackwell, 1989.

Fatimi, S. Q. ''First Muslim Invasion of N.W. Frontier of the Indo-Pakistan Sub-Continent, 44 A.H., 664–5 A.D.,'' *Journal of the Asiatic Society of Pakistan* 8, i (1963): 37–45.

Fries, Nicolaus. *Das Heereswesen der Araber zur Zeite der Omayyaden nach Tabari*. Tübingen, Germany: G. Schnurlen, 1921.

Fuller, J.F.C. *A Military History of the Western World*. Vol. 1: *From the Earliest Times to the Battle of Lepanto*. New York: Minerva Press, 1967. See chap. 12.

Gabrieli, Francesco. ''Muḥammad b. Qāsim al-Thaqafī and the Arab Conquest of Sind.'' *East and West* 15 (1964–1965): 281–95.

Gibb, H.A.R. *The Arab Conquests in Central Asia*. London: Royal Asiatic Society, 1923.

Guilland, Rudolphe. ''L'Expédition de Maslama contre Constantinople (717–718).'' In *Études Byzantines*. Paris: Presses Universitaires de France, 1959.

Habib, Muhammad. ''The Arab Conquest of Sind.'' *Islamic Culture* 3 (1929): 77–95; 592–611.

Hashmi, Yusuf Abbas. ''The First Muslim Siege of Constantinople.'' *University Studies* (Karachi) 2, i (1965): 97–114.

Kaegi, Walter E. ''Observations on Warfare between Byzantium and Umayyad Syria.'' In *1987 Bilad al-Sham Proceedings* 2. Amman: University of Jordan and Yarmouk University, 1989.

Lot, Ferdinand. ''Études sur la Bataille de Poitiers de 732.'' In *Recueil des Travaux Historiques de Ferdinand Lot*. Vol. 2. Geneva: Librairie Droz, 1970.

Majumar, R. C. ''Arab Invasions of India.'' In *Sixth All India Oriental Conference*, 1930–1931.

Mercier, Ernest. ''La Bataille de Poitiers.'' *Revue Historique* (May–August 1878): 1–13.

Rashid, K. A. ''The First Muslim Invasion of the North West Frontier of the Indo-Pakistan Subcontinent, 44 A.H./664–5 A.D.'' *Journal of the Asiatic Society of Pakistan* 8, ii (1963): 25–32.

Reinaud, Joseph Toussaint. *Invasions des Sarrazins en France*. Reprint of 1836 edition. Paris: Librairie Orient, 1964.

Ṭāhā, ʿAbdulwāḥid Dhanūn. *The Muslim Conquest and Settlement of North Africa and Spain*. London: Routledge, 1989.

4. The Concept of Jihad

Abedi, Mehdi, and Gary Legenhausen, eds. *Jihad and Shahadat: Struggle and Martyrdom in Islam*. Houston, Texas: Institute for Research and Islamic Studies, 1986. See introduction.

Aho, James A. *Religious Mythology and the Art of War: Comparative Symbolism of Military Violence*. Contributions to the Study of Religion, no. 3. Westport, Conn.: Greenwood Press, 1981.

Ayoub, Mahmoud. ''*Jihād*: A Source of Power and Framework of Authority in Islam.'' *Bulletin of the Institute of Middle Eastern Studies, International University of Japan* 6 (1992): 205–32.

Canard, Marius. *Byzance et les Musulmans du Proche Orient*. London: Variorum Reprints, 1973. See chap. 8.

———. ''La Guerre Sainte dans le Monde Islamique et le Monde Chrétien.'' *Revue Africaine* 69 (1936): 605–23.

Donner, Fred McGraw. ''The Sources of Islamic Conceptions of War.'' In *Just War and Jihad: Historical and Theoretical Perspectives on War and Peace in Western and Islamic Tradition*, edited by John Kelsay and James T. Johnson. New York: Greenwood Press, 1991.

Hamidullah, Muhammad. *The Muslim Conduct of State*. 5th ed.; rev. ed. Lahore, Pakistan: Sh. Muhammad Ashraf, 1968.

Jurji, E. J. ''The Islamic Theory of War.'' *Muslim World* 30 (1940): 332–42.

Khadduri, Majid. *The Law of War and Peace in Islam.* London: Luzac, 1940.

Martin, Richard C. "The Religious Foundations of War, Peace, and Statecraft in Islam." In *Just War and Jihad: Historical and Theoretical Perspectives on War and Peace in Western and Islamic Tradition*, edited by John Kelsay and James T. Johnson. New York: Greenwood Press, 1991.

Noth, Albrecht. "Heiliger Kampf (Gihad) gegen die 'Franken': Zur Position der Kreuzzüge im Rahmen der Islamgeschichte." *Saeculum* 37 (1986): 240–59.

———. *Heiliger Krieg und Heiliger Kampf in Islam und Christentum: Beitrage zur Vorgeschichte und Geschichte der Kreuzzüge.* Bonner Historische Forschungen, no. 28. Bonn, Germany: Röhrscheid, 1966.

Peters, Rudolph. *Jihad in Medieval and Modern Islam.* Leiden, Netherlands: E. J. Brill, 1977.

Sachedina, Abdulaziz A. "The Development of Jihad in Islamic Revelation and History." In *Cross, Crescent, and Sword*, edited by James T. Johnson and John Kelsay. Westport, Conn.: Greenwood Press, 1990.

Sivan, Emmanuel. *L'Islam et la Croisade: Idéologie et Propagande dans les Réactions Musulmanes aux Croisades.* Paris: Librairie d'Amérique et d'Orient, 1968.

Tyan, E. "Djihād." *EI* 2 (new ed.): 538–40.

Part II

Military Roles in Medieval Islam

4

The Muslim Warriors of Medieval Times: Alien Troops and Arab Militias

Marwān II was overthrown in 750/132 by an anti-Umayyad movement that originated in Khurasan (in eastern Iran) and spread rapidly from there. The revolt, which drew its strength from disaffected Khurasani *mawālīs*, affiliates of the Azdi/Yemeni tribal bloc, and Shiites, upheld the claim of the Abbasid House (descendants of the uncle of both the Prophet and ʿAlī) to the caliphate. Since Marwān's own ascendancy to the caliphate and his subsequent policy making had alienated many units within the Syrian army, he had few military resources at hand to counter the threat from the east. His cause was irrevocably lost in a single engagement near the Greater Zab River. Those Syrians who had welcomed the advance of the Abbasid forces would soon regret their stance. With the advent of a new regime, the center of gravity of the Islamic dominion shifted away from Syria to Iraq. Abū al-ʿAbbās, the first caliph of the new dynasty, established his seat of government at al-Kūfa. His successor built and occupied a new court complex at Baghdad, on the Tigris River, which was the Abbasid capital for most of the dynasty's existence.

The early Abbasids were ruthless in consolidating their hold on power. Abū al-ʿAbbās dispatched his henchmen to kill the male members of the Umayyad House and desecrate the tombs of their caliph ancestors. The severity of his rule was reflected in the sobriquet he chose for himself—al-Saffāḥ, the blood shedder. His successor and brother, Abū Jaʿfar al-Manṣūr, ordered the murder of both his uncle ʿAbdullah ibn ʿAlī and Abū

Muslim, whose military victories had initially brought the Abbasids to power. Al-Manṣūr's men brutally crushed a Shiite uprising led by Ibrāhīm and his brother Muḥammad, the great grandsons of al-Ḥasan ibn ʿAlī. They killed and gibbeted Muḥammad in Medina and two months later decapitated Ibrāhīm near al-Kūfa.

Not only did the early Abbasids execute their potential rivals, they also purged the political-military establishment they had taken over. The ethnic makeup of the governmental hierarchy changed when they appointed many Iranians and, particularly, Khurasanians to positions of trust. They chose mainly Khurasani troops for their elite guard corps. Such changes initiated a trend whereby the presence of ethnic Arabs in the standing military formations declined significantly over the course of some eight decades. In a somewhat ironic way, this trend coincided with the increasing Arabization of civil society in the core provinces (Iraq, Greater Syria, and Egypt) of the Islamic state.

The selection of alien troops for the caliphal guard force was actually consistent with older practice. Various sources attest that kings of pre-Islamic Arabia recruited for their "household troops" men without local kinship ties or other conflicting loyalties. South Arabian inscriptions that mention the forces of the Himyarite kingdom distinguished between the "Arabs of the King" and various tribal contingents.[1] An Arabic tradition regarding the legendary Sayf ibn Dhī Yazan, who was apparently the last Himyarite noble to claim the royal title, relates that he was killed by his Abyssinian bodyguards. Commentaries on Arab tribal lore suggest that the professional soldiers (*al-ṣanā'iʿ*) employed by the kings of Kinda were outcasts from their own tribes.[2]

After the mid-9th/3rd century, Arab troops continued to serve at the Muslim-Byzantine frontier in Anatolia. However, it was not until modern times that ethnic Arabs again had a prominent role in the military affairs of Greater Syria, Iraq, and Egypt. Their role in government took a similar course. Arab blood remained a prerequisite for the caliphate. However, that institution was considerably weakened over the course of its long existence. Having attained the caliphate, the Abbasids soon found that they could not preserve the political unity of the Islamic dominion. The first loss came at the hands of ʿAbd al-Raḥmān ibn Muʿāwiya, one of the few Umayyad princes to escape the massacre of his clan. He made his way to Spain, defeated the Abbasid governor, and founded a new Umayyad dynasty there in 756/138. The Umayyads of Spain did not reclaim the title of caliph until several generations had passed. Meanwhile, they retained the simpler title of *amīr* (commander, ruler).

Within fifty years of the turnabout in Spain, the Abbasids lost control of several other provinces. In 785/169, Idrīs ibn ʿAbdullah, yet another great grandson of al-Ḥasan ibn ʿAlī, came as a refugee to the Maghrib (western North Africa). With the support of the recalcitrant Berbers, he eventually established a Shiite dynasty at Fās (Fez), which ruled that region for almost two centuries. Kharijites established another independent regime (Rustamid) on the eastern flank of this Idrisid state. The province of Ifrīqiya (modern Tunisia and Tripolitania) was also lost to the Abbasids when Ibrāhīm ibn al-Aghlab severed ties with the caliph's court soon after he was appointed governor. He and his descendants ruled as independent sovereigns from 800/184 to 909/297. While the Aghlabids ruled at al-Qayrawān, other independent dynasties (Tahirid, Saffarid, and Samanid) similarly emerged in the eastern lands of Islam. The Abbasids even lost their hold on Egypt and Syria. Governors of Turkish origin established two short-lived dynasties (Tulunid and Ikhshidid) at al-Fusṭāṭ in the period from 868/254 to 969/358. Neither was consistently independent of Abbasid authority. However, Egypt's link to Baghdad was completely severed when the Fatimids ousted the Ikhshidids.

As the territorial integrity of the Islamic dominion vanished, so too did the titular integrity of the caliphate. The Kharijites, who struggled for centuries against the Umayyad and Abbasid regimes, acknowledged their own caliphs, or imams. However, their doctrine did not accommodate hereditary rule. (The only notable exception occured in distant ʿUmān.) The myth of the single caliphate was first seriously shaken when adherents of the radical Shiite, Ismaili movement overthrew the Aghlabids at al-Qayrawān in 909/297. They acknowledged as caliph (more precisely, as imam) Saʿīd ibn Ḥusayn, who claimed to be a descendant of the Prophet's daughter Fāṭima. This Fatimid caliphate subsequently extended its control over all of north Africa and the central Mediterranean, eventually taking Egypt and southern Syria in 969/358. Meanwhile, the Umayyad amir of Spain, ʿAbd al-Raḥmān III, had also assumed the title of caliph in 929/317.

Despite the proliferation of dynasties and the erosion of Abbasid prestige, Baghdad became the paramount cultural center of the Islamic world. The development of Arabic historiography, and Arabic literary culture in general, peaked about the time that the Abbasid dynasty approached its first one hundred years of existence. As a consequence, our knowledge of military developments in the Abbasid era (650–1258/132–749), unlike the Umayyad and earlier periods, has benefited from contemporary and near contemporary source information. The documentary and literary record, complemented by archeological evidence, has afforded solid insights into military armament, administration, and, to a lesser degree, tactics. The writers' perspective, though, was the court view, which focused on the expeditionary forces and elite guard units, not on the local security forces and militias.

Fatimid Egypt also experienced a cultural surge inasmuch as the previous regimes had laid the groundwork for greater prosperity there. By withholding tax remittances to Baghdad, the Tulunid and Ikhshidid rulers

Plate 3. Gateway and walls of Fatimid Cairo. This construction marks the emergence of Cairo as the capital of successive Islamic empires. (Author's photograph)

kept more wealth within the country. This "surplus" abetted the economic and cultural growth of al-Fusṭāṭ. After they seized Egypt, the Fatimids added a new quarter (al-Qāhira; the name has evolved through linguistic transfer into Cairo) to the capital city and subsequently established their court there. In time, Cairo replaced Baghdad as the literary and cultural center of Islam.

The standing forces of both the Abbasid and Fatimid regimes were multiethnic. The makeup of the Abbasid armies varied from one time period to another and, within time periods, from one region to another. Force composition was largely determined by local requirements for manpower and regime efforts to counterbalance the strength of the various ethnic contingents within the armed forces—especially the caliphal guard corps. The Abbasid military establishment was successively dominated by Khurasanians, Turkish "slave-soldiers," and Daylami highlanders (from the region south of the Caspian Sea). Despite the loss of their dominant influence, the two displaced groups continued to resource the armies of medieval Islam. Moreover, the forces directly controlled by the Abbasid court also included contingents of Arabs, Armenians, Kurds, and, to a lesser extent, Berbers.

The Fatimids, following the practice of their predecessors in Egypt, recruited local manpower, brought in alien troops, and purchased slaves to serve in the army. The indigenous (African) units consisted of Arabs, Berbers, Nubians, and Sudanese. The alien troops included Armenians, Iranians, and a few Europeans. The units of slave origin included mainly Negros and Turks as well as some Slavs and others. Considering the reliance on nonnative manpower, the role of the Armenians has been largely overlooked. Their service in Egypt continued a long tradition of military employment outside their homeland. Armenians had served in the armies of the Roman-Byzantine, Palmyrene, Parthian, and Sassanian empires. As for the Iranians, they may have come for higher pay. The warriors of Daylam in particular had an excellent reputation as soldiers during the later 10th/4th century. The influence of the East was also manifested in the employment of slave-soldiers (sing. *ghulām, mamlūk*)—a topic of considerable interest among Western scholars.

Various empires of the ancient world had made use of slaves and freedmen in land and maritime warfare. From the onset of Islam, the Muslim Arabs too made soldiers of male captives taken during war or raid activity. These slaves were enrolled in the same units as their masters. Many were given their freedom, and some rose to high rank. Slaves were also employed in civil society. The demand for them probably grew proportionally as the wealth of the Muslim Arab communities increased. The taking of captives at the frontiers in itself may not have satisfied that demand. However, the supply of slaves increased as the Islamic dominion expanded toward areas where slave raiding was endemic. To the east, among the Turkish and Iranian peoples in Central Asia, the more warlike groups were preying on the weaker ones. To the west, in Saharan Africa, the Berbers were preying on Negroid peoples. The systematic slave raiding of the Ghaznavid dynasty (ruling Khurasan, Afghanistan, and northern India, 977–1186/366–582) also enlarged the slave market of the Islamic world.

The fourth generation of Abbasid caliphs were apparently the first Islamic rulers to form units exclusively of former captives. The model for this innovation may have been the practice of the Central Asian Turks. Whatever its source, the Abbasid practice was motivated by the need to ensure the loyalty of the army. In the aftermath of the civil war of 811–813/196–198, al-Ma'mūn found that he was overly dependent on the Khurasani troops who ensured his succession to the caliphate. These were not resident troops; they had come to Iraq as part of an invading force from eastern Iran. Unlike the established Khurasanians, they generally gave first loyalty to the potentates of their homeland, who did not want a strong regime in Baghdad. To secure his hold on power, al-Ma'mūn began to import Turkish slaves for employment in the army and bureacracy.

Of further relevance here is that the demographics of the Khurasani army had changed considerably since the beginning of the Abbasid caliphate. The army that marched with ʿAbdullah ibn ʿAlī and Abū Muslim in 750/132 included large numbers of Arab garrison troops. The army that marched with al-Ma'mūn's general, Ṭāhir, consisted mostly of native Khurasanians, other eastern Iranians, and Transoxianan Turks. A number of modern scholars have drawn attention to this difference.[3]

After changing the composition of the caliphal guard, al-Ma'mūn proceeded to disband the units of Arab tribal affiliation (*muqātila*) whose lineage dated to the early conquest era. By the beginning of the third Islamic century, most of these had become marginal or ineffective for the purposes of active campaigning. Even so, for many Arab and other old Muslim families, they afforded income or entitlement to pension. Their disbandment, therefore, had more of a social than military impact.

Following al-Ma'mūn's efforts, his successor and brother, al-Muʿtaṣim, undertook the large-scale importation of Central Asian Turkish slaves for service in the army. This practice initially involved the purchase of mature male captives who were fit for military service. However, it gradually expanded into the purchase of child slaves, who were brought into the households of the Muslim elite and systematically educated and trained in the military arts. This "military slavery" became a self-sustaining and expansive institution. Former slaves who distinguished themselves in the service of the caliphs rose to positions of high rank, influence, and income. Many of them in turn established their own corps of slave-soldiers, as did some of their descendants and other men of means.

In time, slaves and freedmen came to hold important military posts, such as commander of the caliph's guard. Descendants of slaves were entrusted with key positions within the governmental establishment. Those officials with numerous slave troops of their own had independent power bases. As a consequence, they were able to challenge or ignore the caliph's authority when it was advantageous to do so. Among the manifestations of this trend were the careers of Ṭahir ibn al-Ḥusayn and Aḥmad ibn Ṭūlūn. Descendants of slaves, they entrenched themselves as governors and founded independent dynasties in Khurasan and Egypt, respectively. The erosion of caliphal power continued until the mere tenure of office itself became a prerogative of the mostly Turkish, former slave officers of the caliph's guard corps. They assassinated the caliph al-Mutawakkil in 861/247 and deposed and killed or blinded several of his successors. This trend continued until 945/334, when the Buyid warlords, leading predominately Daylami forces, came to power at Baghdad. The evolution of the Islamic slave-soldier institution resumed in a later era in another capital. It led to the phenomenon whereby ex-slaves became sovereigns.

The slave-soldier institution can be seen as a necessary measure to counter factionalism in the military and indirectly in the wider society. Indeed, it seems to have been a relatively successful measure, except for its effect in the governmental arena, which went quite beyond the original intent. The unexpected outcome of ex-slaves (*mamlūks*) ruling free men has been harshly judged in modern historiography. From the perspective of Arab nationalism, Arab historians have lamented the debasement of the caliphate. From the perspective of liberal political philosophy, Western historians have lamented the debasement of the ideal of freedom, even suggesting that the slave-soldier institution was some kind of aberration. As for the contemporary reality, it probably evoked a different verdict. The Arab historians of medieval Islam recorded with pride the achievements of mamluk regimes. Despite the disestablishment of the *muqātila*, the free Arab populace in many parts of the Islamic dominion still included men at arms.

As mentioned in chapter 1, Arabs were settled as border militia at the Anatolian frontier. Others came there as volunteer fighters (*mutaṭawwiʿa* or *muṭṭawiʿa*) with the major expeditions. They served without pay but with expectation of booty. Tribal auxiliaries similarly reinforced the caliphs' armies in other areas of conflict. In contrary circumstances, Arab warriors who made up the standing forces and militiamen of Kharijite communities were foes of the caliphs' troops. Their uprisings have been recorded. However, the details of their military methods have passed into oblivion, since the court historians tended to view them as anonymous insurgents. Their own societies lacked the scholars and litterateurs who might have commemorated their way of life.

Among other Arab contingents scarcely mentioned in history were local security forces—bedouin police and urban militias (called *al-aḥdāth* in Syria). The *aḥdāth* have received some attention from modern scholars[4]; however, Claude Cahen apparently has been unable to pursue the monographic study of them he once suggested. Modern scholars in both the Arab world and the West have yet to study the correlation between the medieval militia institutions and aspects of militarism in contemporary Arab society.

The Arabs have commemorated the Abbasid era as being primarily one of cultural achievement. Some glimpses of the Arab military life of that time have been preserved in the Dhāt al-Himma romance.[5] However, that collage of tales from different epochs has yet to be systematically analyzed for its full historical value. Material for comparative study has not been lacking. Abbasid military artifacts have found their way into museums in Istanbul, Cairo, and other Middle Eastern cities. Descriptions of military reviews and technical works on horsemanship, archery, and siege craft have survived the ravages of time. This material has become the substance of translations and monographic studies made by specialists. Nonetheless, the complete picture of the end use of weapons and techniques has yet to be reconstructed.

The Abbasid courtiers evidently did not see fit to record the details of how the caliphs' armies assembled for campaign, encamped, moved to contact, deployed in battle array, and engaged their enemy. They did, however, outline the responsibilities of the caliph and his senior officers regarding military administration—pay, provisions, inspections, and such matters. The dichotomy of interests that is thus apparent in the sources may well have existed at the Abbasid court. Due to the political fragmentation of the 9th/3d century, the Abbasids were gradually isolated from the struggles against the infidels. Unlike the Umayyads, they did not wage war on several far frontiers. The famous expedition to Amorium in 838/223 was their last significant military undertaking against the Byzantines. During the period of slave-soldier dominance, the caliph's troops were primarily committed to the internal security and defense of the Abbasid domain, which consisted roughly of Iraq, western Iran, Armenia, the Transcaucasus, and upper Mesopotamia (al-Jazīra). Their major campaigns entailed suppression of the Zanj (black slave) Rebellion in lower Iraq in 870–883/256–270 and the Qarmatian insurrections in Arabia and the Syrian Desert during the 10th/4th century.

The offensive against Christian Byzantium was sustained by the independent Islamic regimes in North Africa and Egypt. For them, the arena of conflict was the Mediterranean and its coasts, and so the environment of war was in most cases maritime. Under the Aghlabids of Qayrawān, the Muslims conducted seaborne raids throughout the central Mediterranean and also drove the Byzantines from Sicily. The conquest of that island began when Aghlabid troops landed at Mazara in 827/212–213. They advanced on Palermo and incurred a setback there, but with reinforcements from Spain, they eventually took that city. Follow-on expeditions gradually reduced the other Byzantine strongholds; the last was taken in 902/289. Meanwhile, Aghlabid forces captured Malta in 869/255. From bases in Sicily, the Muslims struck at the Italian mainland. They temporarily captured the main towns of Calabria, the "heel" of the peninsula, and attacked various cities to the north, including Rome. Apart from the campaigns in Italy, Aghlabid naval forces also raided the coasts of southern France, Corsica, and Sardinia.

The Byzantines recovered Calabria during the second-to-last decade of the 9th century, but they could not fully reverse the Muslim momentum. When the Fatimids came to power in North Africa, they sustained the Muslim naval offensive in the Mediterranean. Their forces raided the coasts of France and Italy and even captured and temporarily held Genoa. After taking Egypt, the Fatimids added to the existing naval assets there. They relied on sea power to control an empire which, at its height (975–996/365–386), included the entire North African littoral, Sicily, Egypt, southern Syria, and all of western Arabia (both the Hijaz and Yemen).

This era of Muslim maritime greatness has a relatively low profile in Arab history. This historiographic neglect can be attributed to several factors. The deeds of the sea raiders, unlike those of the border warriors of Anatolia, never became legends. The historians of the Fatimid capital apparently lived too far from the maritime frontier to have detailed knowledge of the events occuring there. The Fatimids' Shiite profession has made them somewhat unlikely heroes for mainstream Arabic historiography. Both the scholars and the larger society of the modern Arab world have shown little interest in maritime matters. Consequently, the Fatimid navy is seldom studied outside of Mediterranean history, in which it usually appears as the opponent of the Byzantines.

While the Fatimids were securing the maritime frontiers of Islam, the Hamdanids held the land frontier in Anatolia. The Hamdanid dynasty descended from a prominent family of the Arab tribe of Taghlib, which inhabited upper Mesopotamia. They took advantage of the weakness of the Abbasid regime to establish themselves as independent rulers in the Mosul region in 929/317. The Hamdanid amirs eventually extended their rule into northern Syria and, in 945/333, wrested Aleppo (Ḥalab) and Homs (Ḥimṣ) from the Ikhshidids of Egypt. Shortly thereafter, they took up active campaigning against the Byzantines. Although eulogized in Arabic verse, their war effort turned into a disaster for the Muslims of the borderlands. The Byzantines, under the leadership of Nicephoras Phocas, John Tzimisces, and Basil II, carried out a series of major offensives. They attacked and devastated the Hamdanid capital Aleppo. Furthermore, they recovered a considerable amount of territory that had been under Muslim rule for three centuries—Cyprus, Antioch and its surrounding areas, and southeastern Anatolia as far as the Euphrates. The Byzantine advance southward was checked by the Fatimids, who agreed to a peace treaty and a border from just north of Tripoli to the bend in the Euphrates.

The Byzantines subsequently annexed Armenia, but their hold on Anatolia became precarious in 1049/441. At that time, a new force from the Islamic East, the Seljuk (Saljuq) Turks, swept across the Armenian frontier. This movement had started long before, in about 956/345, when Seljuk-led Ghuzz Turks settled in the vicinity of Bukhara and converted to Islam. They gradually moved westward, seizing territory from the Ghaznavid and Buyid states and adding to their military resources. In a southward thrust, the Seljuks reached Baghdad in 1055/447, at which time they drove the Buyid governor from the city. They acknowledged the nominal authority of the Abbasid caliphs and henceforth acted as their protectors. Meanwhile, Turcoman bands, encouraged by the Seljuks, had pressed on into Anatolia where they took on the role of border raiders (*ghāzīs*). The Seljuks, advancing with their regular forces, undertook yet further conquests. They captured the capital of Christian Armenia in 1065/457 and temporarily wrested most of Syria from the Fatimids in 1070/462–463.

While the Seljuks were campaigning in Syria, the Byzantines struck at their strongholds in Armenia. The Seljuks reacted quickly and consolidated their forces in Azerbaijan. They subsequently engaged and defeated the Byzantine army in the famous, decisive battle of Manzikert in 1071/463. The subsequent collapse of the Byzantine defensive system led to a

Map 4.1
The Near East, Late 10th/4th Century

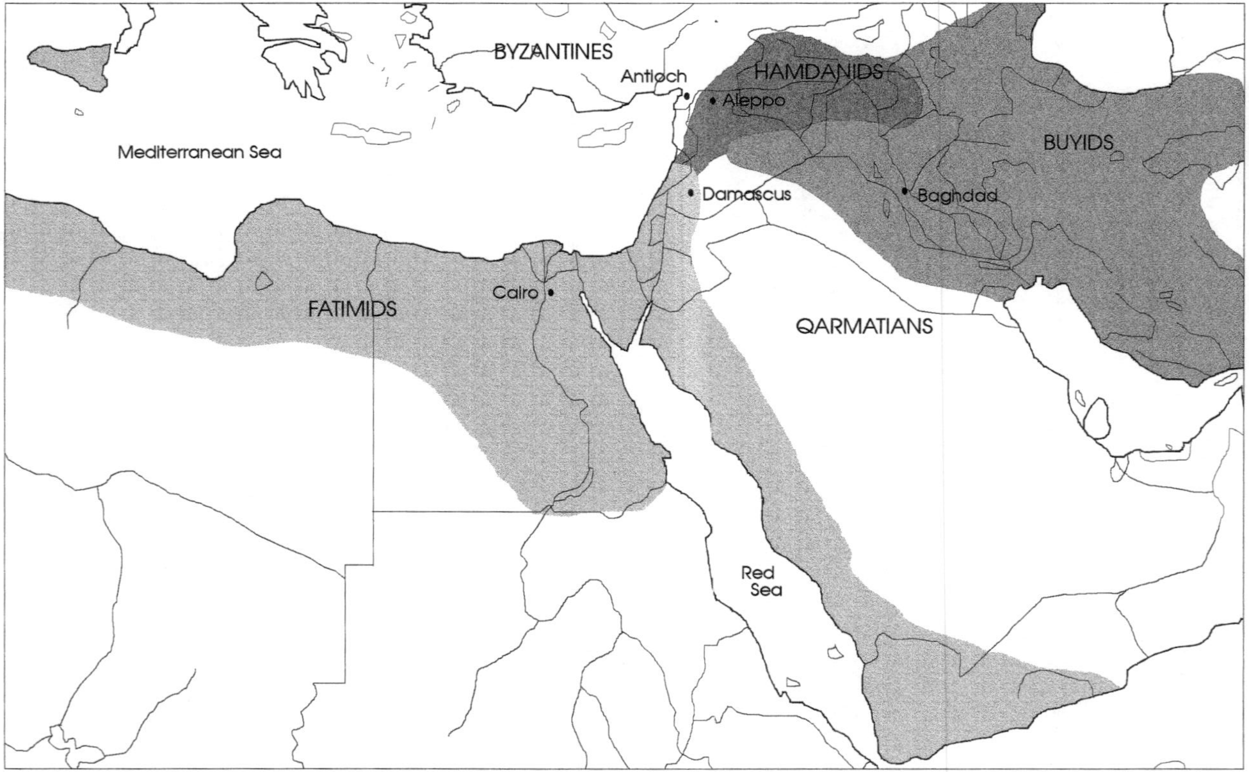

large-scale incursion of Turcoman tribes into the Anatolian heartland. The Seljuk prince Süleymān, who was banished there after a family power struggle, secured the loyalty of some of these tribes. He captured Nicaea (Iznik) in 1075/467 and made it the capital of a new Seljuk state. The Turcoman migration also affected northern Syria. There, Seljuk amirs and *atabegs*, Turcoman warlords, and Arab amirs all contended against one another for control of the main towns and dependent lands. Farther south, the Seljuks continued to contend with the Fatimids for regional dominance.

Meanwhile, the Byzantines were hard pressed to stop the depredation of the Turcomans in Anatolia. Emperors Michael VII and Alexius Comnenus appealed to the rulers of Catholic Europe, through the papacy, to send troops to Constantinople. The papacy, which had its own aim regarding Jerusalem, exploited both the Byzantine appeals and the concurrent stories of mistreatment of Christians in the Holy Land. Pope Urban II was eventually able to mobilize forces to march against the Muslims in the Levant. Thus commenced the great Crusading movement, which lasted for more than three centuries and came to represent the archetypal Christian-Muslim struggle of Western history.

The Crusades have had a somewhat different profile in Arabic historiography. Although they devastated Syria and, to a lesser extent, Egypt, they were not considered to be a major disaster for the Islamic world as a whole. In contemporary and near contemporary sources, the Crusaders are seen to be the allies of Byzantium, and the Crusades are regarded as the continuation of the age-old struggle at the Muslim-Byzantine frontier. The Crusades set the scene for a resurgence of Islamic power in the Levant. More recently, they have been cast as the prototype of Western aggression in the discourses of Arab nationalists and Muslim activists.

Although the Crusades have been extensively studied in the West, even the best of innumerable works are somewhat lacking in their treatment of Muslim warfare. This disparity derives from several factors, including scholarly predisposition, translation problems, and source deficiencies. Whereas the Crusaders' memoirs are relatively informative regarding their own force composition, they are not so regarding the Muslims'. Moreover, both Muslim and Christian sources tend toward generality in their designation of the "enemy." Medieval Muslim historians usually refer to the Crusaders as Franks (*al-Afrānj*), which probably connotes Western Europeans. Christian historians refer to the Crusaders' foes as Saracens. This obscurity deprives us of external evidence on the manning of Muslim armies. Even when the Islamic sources afford clues, modern scholars have been remiss in studying the correlation between Muslim force composition and battlefield performance. Existing campaign analyses should be reassessed on this basis. The relevant point is that the Christian armies of the early Crusades encountered a diversity of enemy forces—the Turcoman tribal warriors of Anatolia, the Arab militias of Syrian towns, and the multiethnic standing forces of the Seljuk and Fatimid regimes.

NOTES

1. See E32 and J665 in A.F.L. Beeston, *Warfare in Ancient South Arabia* (in Chap. 1, Bibliog. 3).
2. See Gunnar Olinder, *The Kings of Kinda* (in Chap. 1, Bibliog. 3), p. 73.
3. See David Nicolle and Angus McBride, *The Armies of Islam* (in Bibliog. 1), p. 14; H.A.R. Gibb in K. M. Setton, ed., *History of the Crusades*, vol. 1 (in Bibliog. 5), pp. 81–98; and also Marshall G. S. Hodgson, *The Venture of Islam* (Chicago: University of Chicago Press, 1974), vol. 1, p. 478, especially n. 1.
4. See Bibliog. 1, works by Claude Cahen (*EI* 1); Nicolle and McBride, pp. 19–20; and Y. Lev (1982).
5. See discussion in chapter 1.

BIBLIOGRAPHY

1. The Abbasid and Fatimid Armies

Beshir, B. J. ''Fatimid Military Organization.'' *Islam* 55 (1978): 37–56.

Bosworth, C. E. ''Istiʿrāḍ, ʿArḍ.'' *EI* 3 (new ed.): 265–69.

———. ''Military Organization under the Būyids of Persia and Iraq.'' *Oriens* 18–19 (1965–1966): 143–67.

———. ''Recruitment, Muster, and Review in Medieval Islamic Armies.'' In *WTS*.

Cahen, Claude. ''Aḥdāth.'' *EI* 1 (new ed.): 256.

———. ''Djaysh I.'' *EI* 2 (new ed.): 504–9.

Hamblin, William J. ''The Fatimid Army during the Early Crusades.'' Ph.D. diss., University of Michigan, 1985.

Hoenerbach, W. ''Zur Heeresverwaltung der ʿAbbāsiden: *Diwān al-ǧaiš*.'' *Islam* 24 (1950): 257–90.

Nicolle, David, and Angus McBride. *The Armies of Islam 7th–11th Centuries*. Men-at-Arms Series, no. 125. London: Osprey Publishing, 1982.

Lev, Y. ''The Fāṭimid Army, A.H. 358–427/968–1036 C.E.: Military and Social Aspects.'' *Asian and African Studies* (Haifa) 14 (1980): 165–92.

———. ''The Fāṭimid Conquest of Egypt: Military, Political, and Social Aspects.'' *Israel Oriental Studies* 9 (1979): 315–28.

———. ''Fāṭimid Policy towards Damascus (358/968–386/996): Military, Social, and Political Aspects.'' *JSAI* 3 (1981–1982): 165–83.

———. ''The Fāṭimids and the Aḥdāth of Damascus 386/996–411/1021.'' *Welt des Orients* 13 (1982): 97–106.

Saidi, A. ''L'Armée Abbaside.'' Ph.D. diss., University of Paris, 1972.

Vasiliev, A. A. et al. *Byzance et les Arabes*. 2 vols. Brussels: Institut de Philologie et d'Histoire Orientales, 1935–1950.

2. The Slave-Soldier Phenomenon

Ayalon, David. "Aspects of the *Mamlūk* Phenomenon." *Islam* 53 (1976): 196–225; 54 (1977): 1–32.
———. *Islam and the Abode of War: Military Slaves and the Adversaries of Islam.* Aldershot, England: Variorum, 1994.
———. "The Military Reforms of the Caliph al-Muʿtaṣim—Their Background and Consequences." Mimeograph. Jerusalem, 1963.
———. "Preliminary Remarks on the *Mamlūk* Military Institution in Islam." In *WTS*.
Bacharach, J. L. "African Military Slaves in the Medieval Middle East: The Cases of Iraq (869–955) and Egypt (868–1171)." *International Journal of Middle East Studies* 13 (1981): 471–95.
Crone, Patricia. *Slaves on Horses: The Evolution of the Islamic Polity.* Cambridge, England: Cambridge University Press, 1980.
Forand, P. G. "The Development of Military Slavery under the Abbasid Caliphs of the Ninth Century A.D. (Third Century A.H.) with Special Reference to the Reigns of Muʿtaṣim and Muʿtaḍid." Ph.D. diss., Princeton University, 1962.
Pipes, Daniel. *Slave Soldiers and Islam: The Genesis of a Military System.* New Haven, Conn.: Yale University Press, 1981.
———. "Turks in Early Muslim Service." *Journal of Turkish Studies* 2 (1978): 85–96.
Sourdel, Dominique. "Ghulām I." *EI* 2 (new ed.): 1079–81.

3. Muslim Armament and Military Methods

Works on this topic as it specifically relates to the Mamluks of Egypt are cited in Chap. 6, Bibliog. 3.

Ayalon, David. "A Reply to Professor J. R. Partington." *Arabica* 10 (1963): 64–73.
Cahen, Claude. "Les Changements Techniques Militaires dans le Proche Orient Médiéval de leur Importance Historique." In *WTS*.
Canard, Marius. "Textes relatifs à l'Emploi du Feu Grégeois chez les Arabes." *Bulletin des Études Arabes* 26 (January–February 1946): 3–7.
Creswell, K.A.C. *A Bibliography of Arms and Armour in Islam.* London: Royal Asiatic Society, 1956.
———. "Fortifications in Islam before 1250." *Proceedings of the British Academy, London* 38 (1952): 89–125.
Faris, Nabih Amin, and Robert Elmer, trans. and eds. *Arab Archery.* Princeton, N.J.: Princeton University Press, 1945.
"Ḥiṣār (siege)," *EI* 2 (new ed.): 469–76. Pts. 1 and 4 are the most relevant.
Kolias, T. G. "The *Taktika* of Leo VI the Wise and the Arabs." *Graeco-Arabica* 3 (1984): 129–35.
Latham, J. D. and W. F. Paterson. "Archery in the Lands of Eastern Islam." In *IAA*.
———. *Saracen Archery: An English Version and Exposition of a Mameluke Work on Archery (c. A.D. 1368).* London: Holland Press, 1970.
Lot, Ferdinand. *L'Art Militaire et les Armées au Moyen Age en Europe et dans le Proche Orient.* 2 vols. Paris: Payot, 1946.
Nicolle, David. "Byzantine and Islamic Arms and Armour: Evidence for Mutual Influence." *Graeco-Arabica* 4 (1991): 299–325.

———. "The Impact of the European Couched Lance on Muslim Military Tradition." *Journal of Arms & Armour Society* 10 (1980–1982): 6–40.

———. "An Introduction to Arms and Warfare in Classical Islam." In *IAA*.

———. "The Military Technology of Classical Islam." Ph.D. diss., Edinburgh University, 1982.

———. "Wounds, Military Surgery and the Reality of Crusading Warfare: The Evidence of Usamah's Memoires." *Journal of Oriental and African Studies* 5 (1993): 33–46.

Nicolle, David, and Christa Hook. *Saracen Faris: 1050–1250.* Warrior Series, no. 10. London: Osprey Publishing, 1994.

North, Anthony. *An Introduction to Islamic Arms.* Owings Mills, Md.: Stemmer House, 1986.

Paterson, W. F. "The Archers of Islam." *Journal of the Economic and Social History of the Orient* 9 (1966): 82–85.

Quatremère, M. E. "Observations sur le Feu Grégeois." *Journal Asiatique*, VIe série, 15 (1850): 214–74.

Reinaud, Joseph Toussaint. "De l'Art Militaire chez les Arabes au Moyen Âge," *Journal Asiatique* VIe série, 12 (1848): 193–237.

———. "Nouvelle Observations sur le Feu Grégeois et les Origines de la Poudre à Canon." *Journal Asiatique* VIe série, 15 (1850): 371–76.

Ritter, H. "La Parure des Cavaliers und die Literatur über die Ritterlichen Künste." *Islam* 18 (1929): 116–54.

Scanlon, George T., ed. and trans. *A Muslim Manual of War, being Tafrīj al-Kurūb fī Tadbīr al-Ḥurūb by ʿUmar ibn Ibrahim al-Awsī al-Ansarī.* Cairo: American University, 1961.

Schwarzlose, Friedrich Wilhelm. *Die Waffen der Alten Araber.* Leipzig, Germany: J. C. Hinrichs, 1886.

Smith, G. Rex. *Medieval Muslim Horsemanship: A Fourteenth Century Arabic Cavalry Manual.* London: British Library, 1979.

Tantum, Geoffrey. "Muslim Warfare: A Study of a Medieval Muslim Treatise on the Art of War." In *IAA*.

Zaky, Abdel Rahman. "Medieval Arab Arms." In *IAA*.

4. Muslim Maritime Warfare

Barnard, J. B. "The Arab Conquest" (of Malta). *Journal of the Faculty of Arts, Malta* 6 (1975): 161–71.

Christides, V. "Naval Warfare in the Eastern Mediterranean (6th–14th Centuries): An Arabic Translation of Leo VI's *Naumachica.*" *Graeco-Arabica* 3 (1984): 137–48.

———. "Two Parallel Naval Guides of the Tenth Century: Qudama's Document and Leo VI's *Naumachica*: A Study on Byzantine and Moslem Naval Preparedness." *Graeco-Arabica* 1 (1982): 51–103.

Kubiak, W. B. "The Byzantine Attack on Damietta in 853 and the Egyptian Navy in the 9th Century." *Byzantion* 40 (1970): 145–66.

Lev, Y. "The Fātimid Navy, Byzantium and the Mediterranean Sea 909–1036 C.E./297–427 A.H.," *Byzantion* 54 (1984): 220–252.

Lewis, Archibald R. *Naval Power and Trade in the Mediterranean, A.D. 500–1100.* Princeton, N.J.: Princeton University Press, 1951. See chaps. 4–7.

Pryor, John H. *Geography, Technology, and War: Studies in the Maritime History of the Mediterranean, 649–1571.* Cambridge, England: Cambridge University Press, 1988. See chaps. 4 and 5.

Setton, K. M. "On the Raids of the Moslems in the Aegean in the Ninth and Tenth Centuries and Their Alleged Occupation of Athens." *American Journal of Archeology* 58 (1954): 311–19.

5. Crusading Warfare, Overview

There are many Western works that offer comprehensive views of Crusading warfare. Only a few of these consider the Muslim forces with any degree of objectivity and genuine interest. The works cited below are among the best of this subset. No single work on the Crusading era fully addresses Muslim military techniques, that is, the correlation of weaponry, battle drill, and campaign strategy.

Finucane, Ronald C. *Soldiers of the Faith: Crusaders and Moslems at War.* New York: St. Martin's Press, 1983.

LaMonte, John L. "Crusade and Jihād." In *The Arab Heritage*, edited by Nabih Amin Faris. Princeton, N.J.: Princeton University Press, 1944.

Marshall, Christopher. *Warfare in the Latin East, 1192–1291.* Cambridge, England: Cambridge University Press, 1992.

Nicolle, David. *The Arms and Armour of the Crusading Era 1050–1350.* 2 vols. New York: Kraus International, 1988.

Nicolle, David, and Angus McBride. *Saladin and the Saracens.* Men-at-Arms Series, no. 171. London: Osprey Publishing, 1986.

Runciman, Steven. *A History of the Crusades.* 3 vols. Cambridge, England: Cambridge University Press, 1951–1954.

Setton, K. M., ed. *A History of the Crusades.* 3 vols. Madison: University of Wisconsin Press, 1969–1974. See vol. 1: *The First Hundred Years*, edited by M. W. Baldwin; and vol. 2, *The Later Crusades, 1189–1311*, edited by R. L. Wolff and H. W. Hazard.

Smail, R. C. *Crusading Warfare (1097–1193).* Cambridge, England: Cambridge University Press, 1956.

5

The Defeat of the Infidels

The story of the Crusades from the Western perspective has been recounted in a great many scholarly and popular works. There is no doubt, even from the Muslim perspective, that the disunity of the Islamic world abetted the early Crusader successes at Dorylaeum, Antioch, and Jerusalem from 1097 to 1099. However, that very disunity was brought about by forces that were yet to have a salutary impact on the Sunni ("orthodox" Muslim) communities of the Levant. Most of these communities had been under Shiite rule since the mid-10th/4th century. The Seljuk invasion of Syria signified the restoration of Sunni rule. The Seljuks themselves did not remain in power long enough to be an enduring influence, but their successors gave permanence to this change.

During the late 11th/5th century, Syria had become an arena of conflict between the rising Seljuk power in the north and the decaying Fatimid power in the south. Native Arab leaders, who were caught in this confrontation, vacillated in their loyalties, as the local balance of power fluctuated. The Crusaders, once they estalished the Latin states of the Syrian littoral, became yet another factor in this complex struggle. The result was a successive realignment of forces, which often resulted in an alliance of Muslims and Christians and war between one such alliance and another. In their efforts to drive back the Frankish invaders, some of the Muslim war leaders called for a jihad. However, such appeals were not very effective means of mobilizing Muslim manpower.[1]

Distant Muslim potentates were usually unwilling or unable to commit their standing forces to the struggle at hand. However, they sometimes encouraged or assisted warriors from their region to serve at the front. These fighters for the faith joined with local volunteers and militiamen to swell the ranks of Muslim armies. Like the "peasant Crusaders," the Muslim auxiliaries were highly motivated but poorly armed. They could not fight effectively against heavily armed, regular troops. In many engagements, it was their fate to be slaughtered, as it was with their Christian counterparts. Their story would not be told in the contemporary histories, which in general merely observed their presence in campaigns.[2]

Both Muslim and Christian historiography of the Crusading era focus on the leaders and on their immediate circles of nobles and elite troops. This is the usual perspective in medieval times. However, the reportage in the Muslim case is rather unusual in its degree of detail. The events of the Crusading era are relatively well documented in comparison to earlier periods of Islamic history. Moreover, many of the relevant sources are available in translation. The abundance of sources affords both specialist and generalist scholars with insights that are not attainable for earlier periods of Arab-Islamic history.

The period under review (12–13th/6–7th centuries) was one of high literary activity in Egypt and the Levant. The events of the time inspired both historical and fictional writing. They were recorded in chronicles of both local and dynastic scope and reflected in topographic works, biography, including Usāma's observations on Crusader culture, and treatises (advice for rulers) on statecraft and war.[3] They were also reflected in folk epic (the Romance of Baybars) and historical romance (the pseudo-futūḥ works, which were discussed in chapter 2). This output, however, was offset by the considerable cultural loss that occurred during the same period. The Crusading wars brought about the destruction of al-Fusṭāṭ and Tripoli, which had become a great city under the Fatimids. To the east, the advance of the Mongols led to the destruction of Baghdad. From descriptions of those cities, we can safely conjecture that many archives and libraries, both great and small, were consumed in flames or buried in rubble.

Apart from the destruction of human works, the Crusading wars apparently added a new dimension to the brutality of conflict in the Near East. It was a common practice of the time for victorious troops to dispatch wounded or exhausted foes, particulary those who offered no prospect of ransom. When the killing ended, the victors decapitated or scalped the corpses of their enemy. They took the severed heads and scalps to display as trophies when they returned to their base of operations. Noncombatants were subjected to the same sort of brutality. The Crusaders in particular were apt to engage in mass slaughter after taking towns by storm. Such brutality was seemingly more remarkable to contemporary Muslim, vice Christian, historians. However, their perception may have been shaped by the relative lack of comparative historical evidence, for example, detailed accounts of earlier civil wars and insurrections in the Islamic heartland.

As is usual in such cases, it is difficult to determine which side committed the first atrocity. It is likewise difficult to trace the source of practices common to both of the warring sides. Muslim and Christian siege weaponry and techniques were virtually the same. However, despite the recurring conflict between Muslims and Crusaders, there was little cross influence regarding battle drill. In maneuver warfare, as opposed to siege warfare, the Crusaders based their tactics and operational art on the shock effect of heavy cavalry charges. The Muslims, in contrast, relied more on countershock measures—standoff and attrition through mobility and missile attack, and deception by feint or other ruse. Muslim war leaders did employ Christian soldiers, renegades, or paroled captives in their armies; however, they did not, and probably could not, emulate the Western offensive shock approach to war. Indeed, shock warfare became less feasible for the Crusaders because of the increasing scarcity of horses sturdy enough to carry heavily armored knights. To conserve military resources, the Crusaders eventually adopted a defensive strategy. Some of their mutually supporting castles have survived to this day.

The influence of the Crusaders can be seen in the military achitecture of Syria and Egypt. Otherwise, the traces of their former presence in those lands are not noticeable. They are remembered in Arab historical consciousness as barbarous, but valorous, fighters who temporarily devastated Syro-Egyptian society. None of their leaders has a prominent place in Arabic historiography. Conversely, the figure of Ṣalāḥ al-Dīn Yūsuf ibn Ayyūb (known in the West as Saladin) looms large in both Arab and Western historical works. For contemporary and near contemporary historians, Muslim and Christian alike, he is a paragon of virtue. For the Christians, he is a most chivalrous foe; for the Muslims, he is a great counter-Crusading hero. For Sunni Muslims in particular, Saladin represents the overthrow of Fatimid Shiite rule in Egypt. Among modern historians, Arab writers generally sustain the hero image. Some Western writers, though, examine his career in more critical terms.

Saladin's rise to power was linked to the ascendancy of the Zangid dynasty. This turning point for the Muslim war effort came in 1127/521, when the Seljuk sultan appointed the Turkish officer ʿImād al-Dīn Zangī as *atabeg* at Mosul. (The *atabeg* institution involved the apppointment of a senior officer as guardian-educator of a minor-age Seljuk prince who was the nominal ruler of a city or province. Depending on personalities, the *atabeg* might remain the real ruler well beyond the minority years of his protégé suzerain.) From his base at Mosul, Zangī initiated the conquest movement that became a viable counter-Crusade. He advanced across northern Syria and took Aleppo in 1128/522. He consolidated his hold on

Plate 4. The Citadel of Cairo, built by Saladin. This structure has many similarities with Crusader castles of the same era. (Author's photograph)

that region and eventually captured al-Ruhā', the capital of the Crusader state of Edessa, in 1144/539. After Zangī's death in 1146/541, the war effort was sustained by his son Nūr al-Dīn Maḥmūd. Nūr al-Dīn, an equally capable war leader, completed the conquest of the county of Edessa, took part of the principality of Antioch, wrested control of Damascus from a rival Turkish officer, and unified Islamic (inner) Syria against the Crusaders.

A Kurdish officer named Shīrkūh led the Zangid war effort in Egypt. There, an internecine rivalry for control of the government resulted in the Crusaders' intervening three times in the period from 1163 to 1168. In the end, Shīrkūh saved Cairo and attained the office of vizier (*wazīr*) in 1169/564, whereby he became the effective ruler of Egypt. Among the officers serving under Shīrkūh was his brother's son Saladin. When Shīrkūh died two months after his accession, Saladin succeeded him as vizier. Two years later, Saladin brought an end to the nominal Fatimid rule in Egypt. He accomplished that coup by substituting the name of the Abbasid caliph in Friday prayers at the capital mosque. The reigning Fatimid caliph was on his death bed, and there was apparently no open opposition.

Saladin had already taken Ayla (on the Gulf of ʿAqaba) and had driven back the Crusaders at the Palestinian frontier. Having secured Egypt, he next sought to impose his rule over other former Fatimid territories in

North Africa, Arabia, and Syria. His ambitions regarding Syria led to strained relations with his suzerain Nūr al-Dīn. Upon Nūr al-Dīn's death, Saladin declared his independence. He subsequently defeated the forces of the Zangid successor Ismāʿīl at Ḥamā and took Damascus in 1174/569. For the next twelve years, he concentrated his war effort against the Zangids and other Muslim rivals in Syria and upper Mesopotamia. He captured Aleppo in 1183/579 and took much of the territory of Mosul in 1186/582. These deeds, although censured by contemporary pro-Zangid writers, became part of the Saladin legend. Meanwhile, in 1175/570, the Abbasid caliph had bestowed on Saladin the title of sultan with the right to govern the lands under his control.

While he fought to unite inner Syria, Saladin avoided decisive engagement with the Crusaders. With his victories in upper Mesopotamia, he attained an optimal situation for military action against them. Even then, Saladin respected the existing truce between himself and the Latin Kingdom of Jerusalem until the raiding activity of the notorious Reynald of Chatillon afforded a pretext for waging war. Saladin's strategy was to lure the Crusader forces from their defenses to engage them in the open. To achieve that situation, he first carried out raids in the Trans-Jordan area and then opted for a move against the city of Tiberias in Galilee.

The Crusader effort to relieve Tiberias resulted in the famous battle at the Horns of Ḥaṭṭīn (variant Ḥiṭṭīn). The Muslims' victory there was due largely to their advantageous use of terrain and weather conditions. Saladin deployed his forces to block the Crusaders' access to drinking water, and he increased their misery by employing fire and smoke to foul the air around them. With their stamina and morale thus broken, the Crusaders could not maintain cohesion in their ranks. In the end, Saladin's numerically superior force killed or captured most of the Christian troops. Consequently, most of the towns and outposts of Latin Syria, having lost their soldiery at Ḥaṭṭīn, easily fell to the victorious Muslims. Jerusalem (Arabic al-Quds) capitulated after a week's siege, and the Crusaders were left holding little more than the districts of Antioch, Tripoli, and Tyre.

There is no "decisive battles" genre in Arabic historiography. Nonetheless, the battle of Ḥaṭṭīn has a prominent place in Arab history. It is seen as a victory of Sunni Syria–Egypt over Christian Europe. By extension, it is a victory for the Arab people, although neither Saladin nor the elite troops under his command were ethnic Arabs. Ḥaṭṭīn is one of the very few great battles of the Arab-Islamic world for which we have considerable detail.

Saladin's victories shocked Christian Europe, which responded with another Crusade. The forces of this famous Third Crusade joined with the surviving troops of the Latin states of Syria in a concerted effort against Acre (ʿAkka). After a two-year siege, the Crusaders finally captured that port city and made it their main military base. However, they were unable

Map 5.1
Saladin's Empire, circa 1192/588

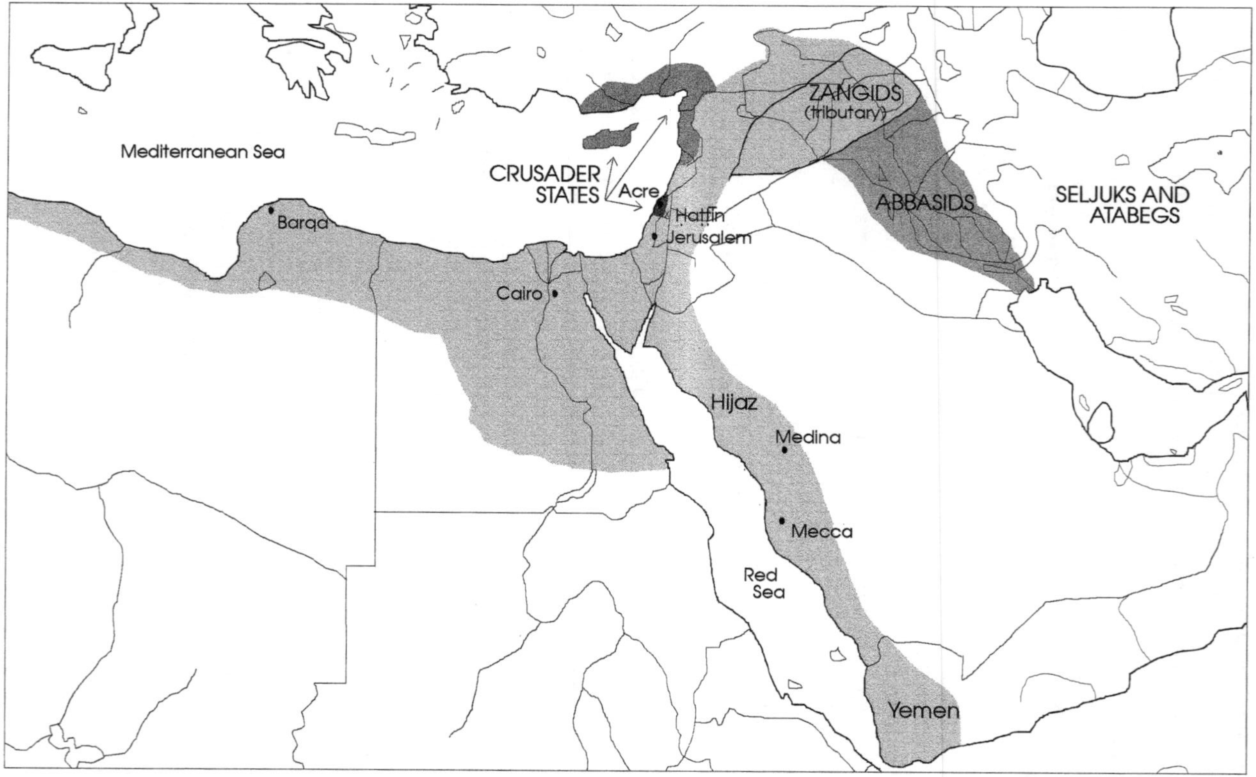

to make further headway against the Muslims and agreed to a peace treaty with Saladin in late 1192/588. Saladin himself took ill and died shortly thereafter; his sultanate was divided among his brother and confidant al-ʿĀdil Ṣafāʾ al-Dīn (Saphadin of Crusader lore) and his own sons. Al-ʿĀdil eventually gained control of Egypt and most of Syria, and his line became the dominant branch of the Ayyubid House. The Crusaders, meanwhile, recovered several cities that had been lost to Saladin, including Jerusalem itself. However, they could not hold these for long, as Muslim supremacy was restored by the Mamluks of Egypt.

Ayyubid rule at Cairo came to an end with the death of Sultan al-Ṣāliḥ in 1249/647. The mamluks of al-Ṣāliḥ's guard corps rejected his son Tūrān-Shāh's claim to the sultanate and killed him. They acclaimed instead al-Ṣāliḥ's widow, Shajar al-Durr. The Abbasid caliph, who was dissatisfied with this arrangement, prevailed on the senior military officers of Egypt to elect a new sultan. They consequently chose one of their own number, ʿIzz al-Dīn Aybeg, who had once been a slave of al-Ṣāliḥ. Aybeg married Shajar al-Durr to secure his position and successfully checked the Ayyubid legitimists in Syria. However, he was unable to cultivate the allegiances necessary to perpetuate his rule. In the spring of 1257/655, he was murdered at the behest of Shajar al-Durr, who herself was killed shortly thereafter.

After Aybeg's murder, his son ʿAlī became the nominal successor. Real power, though, was in the hands of Quṭuz, the commander of Aybeg's mamluks. Quṭuz, who was an ex-slave like Aybeg, deposed ʿAlī in 1259/657 and claimed the sultanate for himself. He ruled as sultan for less than a year before he too was murdered. Quṭuz was succeeded by the famous Baybars, yet another former slave. These sanguinary events constituted the genesis of the Mamluk dynasty of Egypt, which ruled from 1250/648 to 1517/922. This dynasty has by convention been divided into Baḥrī (until 1390/792) and Burjī lines—the ascriptions indicating the garrison locations of the elite units from which the sultans emanated. The Baḥrī Mamluks were mostly Turks and Mongols by origin; the Burjī Mamluks were mostly Circassians.

Due to its origin and nature, the Mamluk dynasty has evoked curiosity at best, but little objectivity, in Western historical works. Its record in government was apparently uneven, as Egypt and Syria were adversely affected by regional developments during the 15th/9th century. Nonetheless, the culture and commerce of those lands prospered during the first 150 years of Mamluk rule. Arabic historiography has commended the sultans for their endowments and their building of mosques, schools, hospitals, and other public works. Yet, it has generally overlooked the fact that a military institution was the bedrock of Mamluk society. The Mamluks' performance as soldiers has not been well recorded nor extensively studied.[4] The contemporary historians did not leave detailed accounts of their campaigns, but a number of extant training manuals afford insights into their methods of war.

By any standards, the corps of mamluks was an exquisite "fighting machine," which included shock effect, deadly archery, mobility, and force sustainability. Each warrior had an extensive panoply of armor and weapons which contributed to these various combat capabilities. The mamluk horsemen probably rated higher than Frankish knights in all but shock effect. They had less armor and lighter horses; therefore, their charge had less impact upon hitting an enemy formation. Otherwise, they were well equipped to close on any enemy force. The mamluks were trained to shoot arrows from both static and moving formations. Their archery technique gave greater penetrating force than "shower-shooting," which was commonly used by Sassanian and later Muslim Iranian horse archers. (Shower-shooting involved the rapid discharge of numerous arrows in succession. The bow had to be handled in such a way that the penetration power of the arrows was considerably reduced. The combat application of this technique was to create a barrage of arrows that covered assault forces as they closed with the enemy.) Being trained primarily as horsemen, the mamluks had excellent mobility. However, unlike enemy cavalrymen, they were also trained to fight on foot. Such capability would have been particularly advantageous when cavalry attack formations were broken. The usual recourse for horsemen of that era was to flee the combat area to escape pursuing enemies. The mamluks, though, ostensibly had some chance of sustaining the fight by deploying as infantry. According to the historical record, the Mamluk army was equally adept at field and siege operations.

It was the destiny of the Mamluks to expel the last of the Crusaders from the Levant and to check the Mongol threat from the east. In the course of attaining these ends, they had to reunite Islamic Syria by force, as had ʿImād a-Dīn Zangī and Saladin before them. Under Tūrān-Shāh, Mamluk forces defeated the Sixth Crusade, led by Louis IX of France. Under Quṭuz, they repelled an Ayyubid invasion of Egypt and checked a Mongol advance at ʿAyn Jālūt (the Spring of Goliath) in Palestine. These victories evolved as defensive reactions to enemy moves against Egypt. Under Baybars, the Mamluk regime went onto the offensive in Syria. Baybars successfully waged war against the Ayyubids, Franks, and Armenian allies of the Mongols, taking Caesarea, Jaffa, and Antioch, among numerous other towns. These victories, although not climactic, added to his legendary fame.

In contrast to his place in Crusader lore, Baybars' renown in Arabic-Islamic culture has exceeded that of Saladin. Baybars was first and foremost a warrior. Before his accession to the sultanate, he had important roles in the Mamluk victories over the Crusaders at Gaza (1244/642) and over the Mongols at ʿAyn Jālūt. As sultan, he extended the Mamluk dominion into Nubia and Libya as well as Syria. Baybars also established a protectorate over the Hijaz. Consequently, he was able to broaden his prestige in the Islamic world by assuming the title *Khādim al-Ḥaramayn* (servant of the two holy places, i.e., Mecca and Medina). Apart from his military exploits, Baybars initiated many new public works and services in his realm. He even restored the Abbasid caliphate, which the Mongols had terminated, but as a ceremonial office only, with new residence at Cairo. Baybars' many deeds have been commemorated and aggrandized both as an historical romance and as popular folklore.[5] His hero image was not tarnished by his part in the assassination of Tūrān-Shāh and Quṭuz and in the massacre of the Crusaders who surrendered at Ṣafad and Antioch.

As for ʿAyn Jālūt, it has acquired a higher renown than many larger engagements of the early Mamluk period. Accounts of the battle have conveyed a fairly simple scenario. The encounter evolved as Kitbuga Noyon led at most some 10,000 of his Mongol and allied troops into Palestine in what was seemingly a reconnaissance in force. The Mamluks, who had arranged to march through Crusader territory, monitored the Mongol moves to their east. Being numerically stronger, the Mamluks intercepted the Mongol force, lured it into battle, and overwhelmed it. Some of the fame of ʿAyn Jālūt among the Arabs has derived from its inclusion in the Baybars legend. However, the preeminence of the battle has been further established by Western and Arab historians in modern times.

In the military historiography of the West, ʿAyn Jālūt has, with some dissent, been listed among the decisive battles of world history. The relevant point is that the Mamluk victory there checked the Mongols at the high tide of their conquest movement in the Near East. Although the Mongol threat to Syria was not eliminated, the Mongol threat to Egypt was. Modern Arab historians have seized on this significance and have added another. For them, ʿAyn Jālūt complemented Ḥaṭṭīn in symbolizing a decisive defeat of the infidels. These two victories—one over the Crusaders, the other over the Mongols and their Armenian and Georgian allies—seemingly correlated with those of al-Yarmūk and al-Qādisīya in the early Islamic conquest era (chapter 2).

After the short reigns of two sons of Baybars, Qalawun (Qalā'ūn), the seventh Baḥrī sultan, continued the struggle for Syria. In 1280/679, he defeated the Mongols and their allies in a great battle near Homs. He extended Mamluk control in Islamic Syria and then turned against the Crusaders. In 1289/688, Qalawun captured the great, fortified port city of Tripoli, which had been the largest Crusader-held town. He made preparations to besiege Acre, the Crusader capital, but died before he could commence operations against it. That task was left to his son and successor al-Ashraf Khalīl, who took the town by storm in 1291/690. The few remaining Crusader possessions in the Levant were subsequently taken with relative ease. To discourage the Franks from returning, the Mamluks selectively destroyed castles and fortifications, demolished cities too exposed to the sea, and settled Kurdish and Turcoman bands where the loyalty of the population was suspect. Beyond that, they imposed various discriminatory restrictions on Christians and Jews throughout their realm.

The people of Damascus celebrated for an entire month at the final departure of the Crusaders. However, they would not have complete security for yet another twelve years. Although the Il-Khanid Mongols of Persia were converting to Islam, they continued to threaten the Mamluk realm. In 1299/699, the Īl-Khān Ghāzān crossed the Euphrates with a large army, captured Aleppo, defeated the Mamluks near Homs, and occupied Damascus. Upon his return to Persia, the Mamluks recovered their losses. They further secured their hold on Syria by suppressing the militias of the autonomy-minded Alawite, Druze, and Maronite communities. Another major conflict ensued when Il-Khanid forces again invaded Syria in 1303/702. This time, the Mamluks decisively defeated them at Marj al-Ṣuffar near Damascus, permanently ending the Il-Khanid Mongol threat to Syria. That great battle has not been well commemorated in historical literature—perhaps because it does not fit the theme of Muslims versus infidels.

The 14th/8th century was for the most part a period of peace and prosperity for the Mamluk domain. Beginning with Baybars' reign, the Mamluks had extended their authority or influence into the lands along the Red Sea. They encouraged and protected trade between the Indian Ocean world and Egypt. Syria was also linked to the Mamluk commercial network. The fortunes of Mamluk Syria changed, however, when Tīmūr's Turco-Mongol hordes appeared on the eastern frontier in 1387/789. Tīmūr waited three years, while local governors rebelled against the sultan's authority, and then invaded. His forces swept from Aleppo to Damascus, taking several other towns and crushing the Mamluk army along the way. They wrought great destruction of life and property. This invasion was followed by outbreaks of disease and pestilence, pirate attacks, the breakdown of order, and economic ruin. Egypt too was adversely affected. Its financing of the war with Tīmūr led to economic strains. The country was further beset by famine and plague, which devastated the populace and the army.

Meanwhile, the center of gravity in world events was shifting to the Indian Ocean. Chinese efforts to reach markets in the West led to a commercial boom in that area during the 15th/9th century. The Mamluk regime in Cairo gained from this situation by channeling more trade through the Red Sea. Its efforts to control the littoral areas, however, were not always acceptable to local rulers. Eventually, the Portuguese rounded Africa and became a threat to Muslim shipping in Indian waters. The Mamluks, being outclassed in ship design and naval armament, could not check

Plate 5. The Citadel of Aleppo, as rebuilt by the Mamluks. This fortress is one of the best surviving examples of Mamluk military construction. (Photograph by Garbis)

this incursion without help. They looked for assistance to the Ottoman Turks, who were then becoming the premier power of the Islamic world. In the early years of the 16th/10th century, the Ottomans helped launch naval expeditions against the Portuguese. Through these undertakings, they were alerted to the weakness of the Mamluks and the new direction of Christian aggression. This awareness may have spurred them to the conquest of the Mamluk realm.

Relations between the Mamluks and Ottomans had been fairly amicable except for one war, which lasted from 1485/890 to 1490/896. However, the rise of Safavid Persia brought new pressure on the two neighboring states. During a confrontation with the Safavids, the Ottomans were impelled to strike at the Mamluks when their neutrality became suspect. In the late summer of 1516/922, Sultan Selīm's army advanced against the Mamluk forces that had deployed near the Anatolian frontier. It engaged and defeated them at Marj Dābiq, north of Aleppo. The Mamluk sultan Qānṣawh al-Ghawrī died of apoplexy during the battle, and his forces retreated into Egypt. The senior Mamluks chose a new sultan, Tūmān-Bāy, who had little time to plan a defensive campaign. The Ottoman forces pushed on into Egypt and defeated the Mamluks at Raydānīya, near Cairo, toward the end of January 1517/Dhū al-Ḥijja 822. They thus brought about an end to the Mamluk sultanate, having prevailed through better employment of artillery and musket fire—technology the Mamluks had been loathe to adopt.[6]

The Ottomans gradually expanded their domain to include most of the lands that are now considered the Arab world. Although they assumed the burdens of territorial defense, their military endeavors have not been commemorated in Arab culture. The native historians and litterateurs of Syria-Egypt apparently had far less enthusiasm for the Ottoman and later Mamluk regimes than they did for the early Mamluk sultanate. Their attitude was shaped by the changing fortunes of their own social class. Under the later Mamluks, they watched and recorded the gradual ruin of their society. Under the Ottomans, they saw the status of Cairo degraded from seat of empire to provincial capital. Their views still stand without revision, since Arab nationalist ideologues have denigrated the Ottoman era of Arab history.

It may seem odd that modern Arab historians have claimed the early Mamluk sultans as heroes. The Mamluks were indeed non-Arabs, and the military culture of Mamluk society was largely Turkish. However, the more relevant point is that the bureaucratic culture of Mamluk society remained Arabic. In this sense, there was still an "Arab" influence in Mamluk government. One should note, though, that ethnic identities were not then what they are today. Mamluk historians belonged to a Sunni urban elite who spoke Arabic. They did not identify with the bedouin Arab tribes which were subject to the sultans. Although the bedouins provided auxiliary cavalry for the Mamluk army, their service in war was not acclaimed in contemporary Arabic works. Nor has it been extolled in modern ones. For all the above reasons, Arabic historiography has generated a somewhat limited picture of Muslim military endeavors in late medieval times.

NOTES

1. See discussion and Bibliog. 4 in Chapter 3, especially works by Albrecht Noth (1966 and 1986) and Emmanuel Sivan.
2. The mobilization of Arab urban militiamen (*aḥdāth*) and tribal auxiliaries is well attested to in Ibn al-Qalānisī's Chronicle (in Bibliog. 1); see pp. 70, 115, 140, 145, 175, 196–198, 203, 257, 259, 306–7, 333, and 339.
3. Concerning the last-mentioned category, see works by Claude Cahen, William J. Hamblin, and Janine Sourdel-Thomine in Bibliog. 2.
4. The seminal works on this topic are those of David Ayalon (1980) and David Nicolle and Angus McBride (1993) in Bibliog. 3.
5. The folktale version of the Baybars' romance is summarized in Edward William Lane, *An Account of the Manners and Customs of the Modern Egyptians* (London: East-West Publications, 1978), vol. 2, chap. 9.
6. This theory of the Mamluk defeat, which has been generally accepted, is presented in David Ayalon, *Gunpowder and Firearms in the Mamluk Kingdom* (in Bibliog. 5).

BIBLIOGRAPHY

1. Crusades, Muslim Perspective

Abu Shama (Abū Shāma, ʿAbd al-Raḥmān ibn Ismāʿīl). *Le Livre des deux Jardins*. In *RHC, Hist. Or.* 4, 5.

———. *Arabische Quellenbeiträge zur Geschichte der Kreuzzüge*, edited and translated by E. P. Georgens. Reprint of 1879 edition. New York: Olms, 1975.

Beha ed-Din (Bahā' al-Dīn Ibn Shaddād). *Anecdotes et Beaux Traits de la Vie du Sultan Youssof (Salah ed-Din)*. In *RHC, Hist. Or.* 3: 3–370.

Gabrieli, Francesco, ed. and trans. *Arab Historians of the Crusades*. Translated from the Italian (*Storici Arabi Delle Crociate*) by E. J. Costello. Berkeley: University of California Press, 1969.

Haddad, Wadiʿ Z. "The Crusaders through Arab Eyes." *Muslim World* 73 (1983): 234–52.

Ibn al-Athir (Ibn al-Athīr, ʿIzz al-Dīn). *Histoire des Atabecs de Mosul*. In *RHC, Hist. Or.* 2, 2ème partie: 5–375.

Ibn al-Qalānisī. *The Damascus Chronicle of the Crusades*. Extracted and translated from the Chronicle of Ibn al-Qalānisī by H.A.R. Gibb. London: Luzac, 1932.

Kemal ed-Din (Kamāl al-Dīn). *Extraits de la Chronique d'Alep*. In *RHC, Hist. Or.* 3: 577–690.

Maalouf, Amin. *The Crusades through Arab Eyes*. Translated by Jon Rothschild. New York: Schocken Books, 1985.

Usamah Ibn Munqidh. *An Arab Syrian Gentleman and Warrior in the Period of the Crusades: Memoirs of Usamah Ibn Munqidh*. Translated by Philip K. Hitti. Princeton, N.J.: Princeton University Press, 1987.

2. Saladin's Military Achievements

Blythe, E. "The Battle of Ḥaṭṭīn, July 1, 1187." In *Palestine Exploration Fund, Quarterly Statement*, 1922.

Cahen, Claude. "Un Traité d'Armurerie Composé pour Saladin." *Bulletin d'Études Orientales* 12 (1947–1948): 103–63.

Ehrenkreutz, E. S. "The Place of Saladin in the Naval History of the Mediterranean Sea in the Middle Ages." *Journal of the American Oriental Society* 65 (1955): 100–116.

Elbeheiry, Salah. "Les Institutions de l'Égypt au Temps des Ayyubides." Vol. I, "L'Organization de l'Armée et les Institutions Militaire." Ph.D. diss., Université de Paris, n.d.

Gibb, Hamilton A. R. "The Armies of Saladin." In *Studies on the Civilization of Islam*, edited by S. J. Shaw and W. R. Polk. Boston: Beacon Press, 1962.

Hackett, J. W. "Saladin's Campaign of 1188 in Northern Syria." Ph.D. diss., Oxford University, 1937.

Hamblin, William J. "Saladin and Muslim Military Theory." In *The Horns of Ḥaṭṭīn*, edited by Benjamin Z. Kedar. Proceedings of the Second Conference of the Society for the Study of the Crusades and the Latin East. Jerusalem: Ben-Zvi; London: Variorum, 1992.

Herde, Peter. "Die Kämpfe bei den Hörnern von Hittin und der Untergang des Kreuzritterheeres (3. und 4. Juli 1187)." *Römische Quartalschrift für Christliche Altertumskunde und Kirchengeschichte* 61 (1966): 1–50.

Imad ed-Din (al-Iṣfahānī, ʿImād al-Dīn). *Conquête de la Syrie et de Palestine par Ṣalāḥ al-Dīn*. Translated by Henri Massé. Paris: Paul Geuthner, 1972.

Kedar, Benjamin Z. "The Battle of Ḥaṭṭīn Revisited." In *The Horns of Ḥaṭṭīn*, edited by Benjamin Z. Kedar. Proceedings of the Second Conference of the Society for the Study of the Crusades and the Latin East. Jerusalem: Ben-Zvi; London: Variorum, 1992.

Lane-Poole, Stanley. *Saladin and the Fall of the Kingdom of Jerusalem*. Reprint of 1898 edition. New York: AMS Press, 1978.

Lyons, Malcolm C., and D.E.P. Jackson. *Saladin: The Politics of the Holy War*. Cambridge, England: Cambridge University Press, 1982.

Möhring, Hannes. *Saladin und der Dritte Kreuzzug*. Weisbaden, Germany: Steiner, 1980.

———. "Saladins Politik des Heiligen Krieges." *Islam* 61 (1984): 322–26.

Nicolle, David. *Hattin 1187: Saladin's Greatest Victory*. Campaign Series, no. 19. London: Osprey Publishing, 1993.

Pellat, C. "La Conquête de la Syrie et de la Palestine ou les Dernière Années de Saladin." *Mélanges E. R. Labande, Poitiers* (1975): 589–93.

Prawer, Joshua. "La Bataille de Ḥaṭṭīn." *Israel Exploration Journal* 14 (1964): 160–79.

Regan, Geoffrey. *Saladin and the Fall of Jerusalem*. London: Croom Helm, 1987.

Sourdel-Thomine, Janine. ''Les Conseils du Shayh al-Harawī à un Prince Ayyubid.'' *Bulletin des Études Orientales* 16 (1961–1962): 205–66.

3. The Mamluk Military Establishment

Ayalon, David. ''Baḥriyya, II. The Navy of the Mamlūks,'' *EI* 1 (new ed.): 945–47.
———. ''L'Esclavage du Mamlouk.'' Oriental Notes and Studies, No. 1. Jerusalem: Israel Oriental Society, 1951.
———. ''Mamlūk.'' *EI* 5 (new ed.): 314–21.
———. ''Mamlūkiyyat: A First Attempt to Evaluate the Mamlūk Military System.'' *JSAI* 2 (1980): 321–49.
———. ''Notes on the Furūsiyya Exercises and Games in the Mamlūk Sultanate.'' *Scripta Hierosolymitana* 9 (1961): 31–62.
———. *Studies on the Mamlūks of Egypt (1250–1517)*. London: Variorum Reprints, 1977. This volume contains reprints of several articles by this foremost student of Mamluk military society. The most relevant are the following:

''Studies on the Structure of the Mamluk Army.'' *BSOAS* 15 (1953): 203–28, 448–76; 16 (1954): 57–90.
''The Wafidiya in the Mamluk Kingdom.'' *Islamic Culture* 25 (1951): 81–104.
''Le Régiment Bahriya dans l'Armée Mamelouke.'' *Revue des Études Islamiques* 19 (1951), 133–41.
''The Circassians in the Mamluk Kingdom.'' *Journal of the American Oriental Society* 69 (1949): 135–47.
''The Plague and Its Effect upon the Mamluk Army.'' *JRAS* (1946): 67–73.
''The Mamluks and Naval Power—A Phase of the Struggle between Islam and Christian Europe.'' *Proceedings of the Israel Academy of Sciences and Humanities* 1 (1965): 1–12.
''The System of Payment in Mamluk Military Society.'' *Journal of the Economic and Social History of the Orient* 1 (1958), pp. 257–96.

Guémard, G. ''De l'Armament et de l'Equipement des Mamelouks.'' *Bulletin de l'Institut d'Égypte* 8 (1926): 1–19.
Humphreys, R. Stephen. ''The Emergence of the Mamlūk Army.'' *Studia Islamica* 45 (1977): 67–91; 46 (1978): 147–82.
Nicolle, David. ''14th Century Cavalry Warfare: The Mamluk Art of Furusiyya.'' *Military Illustrated* 60 (May 1993): 30–34.
———. ''The Reality of Mamluk Warfare: Weapons, Armour and Tactics.'' *al-Masāq* 7 (1994): 77–110.
Nicolle, David, and Angus McBride. *The Mamluks of Egypt 1250–1517*. Men-at-Arms Series, no. 259. London: Osprey Publishing, 1993.
Rabie, Hassanein. ''The Training of the Mamlūk Fāris.'' In *WTS*.

4. Mamluk Campaigns in Syria

Cathcart King, D. J. ''The Taking of Le Krak des Chevaliers in 1271.'' *Antiquity* 23 (1949): 83–92.
Ibn ʿAbd al-Ẓāhir Muḥyī al-Dīn. *Baybars I of Egypt (Sīrat al- Mālik al-Ẓāhir)*. Partly

edited and translated with historical introduction by S. F. Sadeque. Dacca, Bangladesh: Oxford University Press, 1956.
Ibn al-Furat (Ibn al-Furāt, Muḥammad ibn ʿAbd al-Raḥīm). *Ayyubids, Mamluks, and Crusaders: Selections from the Ta'rikh al-Duwal wa al-Muluk*. Text and translation by U. Lyons and M. C. Lyons. Introduction and notes by J.S.C. Riley-Smith. 2 vols. Cambridge, England: W. Heffer and Sons, 1971.
Irwin, Robert. "The Mamlūk Conquest of the County of Tripoli." In *C&S*.
———. *The Middle East in the Middle Ages: The Early Mamluk Sultanate, 1250–1382*. London: Croom Helm, 1986. See chaps. 3, 4, and 5.
Khowayter, A. A. (Khuwayṭir ʿAbd al-ʿAzīz). *Baibars the First: His Endeavors and Achievements*. London: Green Mountain Press, 1978.
———. "A Critical Edition of an Unknown Arabic Source for the Life of al-Malik al-Zahir Baybars." Vol. 2. Ph.D. diss., University of London, 1960.
al-Makrizi (al-Maqrīzī, Taqī al-Dīn Aḥmad). *Histoire des Sultans Mamlouks de l'Égypt*. Translated by M. E. Quatremère. 2 vols. Paris: Oriental Translation Fund, 1845. Recounts many Mamluk campaigns. For the Battle of ʿAyn Jālūt, see vol. 1, pt. 1, pp. 104–6.
Morgan, David O. "The Mongols in Syria." In *C&S*.
Raschid ed-Din (Rashīd al-Dīn Tabīb). *Histoire des Mongols de la Perse*. Edited and translated by M. E. Quatremère. Reprint of 1836 edition. Amsterdam: Oriental Press, 1968. On the Battle of ʿAyn Jālūt, see pp. 349–52.
Preiss, Reuven Amitai. *Mongols and Mamluks: The Mamluk-Ilkhanid War, 1260–1281*. Cambridge, England: Cambridge University Press, 1995.
Runciman, Steven. *A History of the Crusades*. Cambridge, England: Cambridge University Press, 1951–1954. See vol. 3, chaps. 3 and 4.
Smith, J. M. "ʿAyn Jālūt: Mamlūk Success or Mongol Failure?" *Harvard Journal of Asiatic Studies* 44 (1984): 307–45.
Thorau, Peter. "The Battle of ʿAyn Jalut: A Re-examination." In *C&S*.
Wiet, Gaston. "Baybars I." *EI* 1 (new ed.): 1124–26.

5. The Ottoman Conquest of the Mamluk Realm

Ayalon, David. *Gunpowder and Firearms in the Mamluk Kingdom: A Challenge to Medieval Society*. London: Mitchel, Valentine, 1956.
Dames, M. Longworth. "The Portuguese and the Turks in the Indian Ocean in the 16th Century." *JRAS* (1921): 1–28.
Edhem, Halil. *Sultan Selim's Aegyptischer Feldzug*. Weimar, Germany: n.p., 1916.
Har-el, Shai. *Struggle for Domination in the Middle East: The Ottoman-Mamluk War, 1485–1491*. Leiden, Netherlands: E. J. Brill, 1995.
———. "The Struggle for Southeastern Anatolia and the First Ottoman-Mamluk War, 1485–1491." Ph.D. diss., University of Chicago, 1993.
Hess, A. C. "The Evolution of the Ottoman Seaborne Empire in the Age of the Oceanic Discoveries, 1453–1525." *American Historical Review* 75 (1970): 1892–919.
Holt, P. M. et al., eds. *The Cambridge History of Islam*. London: Cambridge University Press, 1970. See vol. 1A, pp. 228–30 and 317–19.
Ibn Iyās. *An Account of the Ottoman Conquest of Egypt in the Year A.H. 922*. Translated by W. H. Salmon. London: Royal Asiatic Society, 1921.

Jansky, Herbert E. F. "Die Eroberung Syriens durch Sultan Selim I." In *Sonder-Abdruck aus Mitteilungen zur Osmanischen Geschichte*, Bd. II, 1923–1926.

Massé, Henri. "Selīm Ier en Syrie, d'après le Selīm-Nāme." *Mélanges René Dussaud* 2 (1939): 779–82.

Stripling, George William. *The Ottoman Turks and the Arabs*. Philadelphia: Porcupine Press, 1977.

Part III

Arab Armies in the Modern Age

6

The Break with the Ottoman Past

Following their conquest of the Mamluk dominion, the Ottomans took military action to secure their corridor to the Indian Ocean—the focal point of world trade. They pushed back the Persian frontier into the Tigris-Euphrates valley. They drove the residual Crusader forces from the eastern into the central Mediterranean. To ward off maritime threats from the south, the Ottomans established outposts at the head of the Persian Gulf and secured the entrance to the Red Sea. Consequently, warfare came to be of little or no concern to the people of Egypt and Syria. Their homelands had become insulated from the main conflicts of the Sunni-Islamic world. They themselves were generally exempted from conscription for military service.

The Ottomans did subject the former Mamluk provinces to military occupation. They established garrisons at strategic sites, but they seldom rotated their troops. As a consequence, the garrison units sustained their manning by enlisting the offspring of retired soldiers. Over time, the garrisons assimilated with the local populace and economy and lost much of their military character and competence. In Egypt, the Ottomans chose not to disestablish but to co-opt the slave-soldier institution. The self-sustaining mamluk units served as local security forces, and their leaders eventually gained the provincial governorship. The Ottomans even allowed the revival of the mamluk institution at Baghdad, the governmental center of Iraq. There, a dynasty of Georgian Mamluks ruled from 1749/

1162 to 1834/1247. Otherwise, Ottoman provincial governors often had to recruit private armies to enforce their authority and police their jurisdictions. From the perspective of most natives of the Arab provinces, soldiering was a job for "Turks"—the term applying as well to Bosnians, Albanians, and other alien troops.

Under Ottoman rule, Syria and Egypt witnessed a number of local power struggles. However, the native Sunni population was generally secure in its way of life until the Ottomans' regional hegemony was fractured from without. In 1798 French forces, led by Napoleon Bonaparte, invaded and occupied Egypt.[1] During their three-year stay, they brought to the native consciousness direct, and sometimes shocking, experience with the technology, institutions, and ideas of the modern West. This experience revealed the relative inadequacy of Ottoman society. Shortly after the French withdrew from Egypt, Wahhabi forces from the Najd (inner Arabia) captured Mecca and Medina and prevented the Ottoman pilgrim caravan from entering the Hijaz. Their success seemingly confirmed Wahhabi doctrine, which challenged the Ottomans' claim to the preeminent religious position within Islam. The events in Arabia raised doubts about the moral strength of the Ottoman regime; those in Egypt raised doubts about its material strength. Such doubts gave rise to disaffection, which grew in reaction to yet other events and contributed to the eventual genesis of an Arab consciousness movement.

The French venture in Egypt led to the rise of the famous Muḥammad ʿAlī Pasha, who made a remarkable but ill-fated effort to transform his domain into a modern state. Like many of his colleagues, Muḥammad ʿAlī (or Mehmet Ali) was highly impressed with the power of European society. He came to Egypt as an officer in the Ottoman expeditionary force that reoccupied the country in 1801. When the Ottoman-Mamluk elite of Egypt became embroiled in internecine conflict, Muḥammad ʿAlī emerged as the dominant power broker. He was appointed pasha of Cairo—in effect, viceroy of Egypt—in 1805 and, henceforth, pursued autocratic measures to secure his hold on power. Muḥammad ʿAlī moved against the ulema (religious and bureaucratic authorities) and the mamluk households, confiscated their wealth, and created state monopolies for certain commercial and agricultural activities. He also undertook reform of the government and the army according to Western models. The viceroy had not yet dealt with the mamluks, when Sultan Mahmud II called on him to restore Ottoman authority in the Hijaz.

The Wahabbi movement, which so unnerved the Ottoman regime, had originated in 1744/1157 as the result of an alliance between the religious reformer Muḥammad ibn ʿAbd al-Wahhāb and the tribal leader Muḥammad ibn Suʿūd.[2] Ibn ʿAbd al-Wahhāb was a proponent of the strict Ḥanbalī doctrine of Islam. He condemned the mystic (Sufi) and other alien influences that had corrupted the original teachings of the Prophet. His criticism of the state of Islamic worship was also criticism of the Ottoman and Persian regimes, which had sanctioned the popular practices among Sunnites and Shiites, respectively. Ibn ʿAbd al-Wahhāb had no means of reaching all the people of Islam; however, he was able to convert the Arab clans that dwelt near his home. With Ibn Suʿūd's help, his teachings spread to ever wider circles.

As for Ibn Suʿūd, he was apparently intent on expanding the authority of his house, which ruled an oasis settlement in the Wādī Ḥanīfa (near modern Riyadh). That settlement was capable of exerting a region-wide influence owing to its location. It was situated near the intersection of the trade routes that linked lower Iraq with Yemen and Baḥrayn (Bahrain) with Jidda. Although the site was probably coveted by neighboring tribes, it could not be easily taken. Ibn Suʿūd's people could defy aggression from the safety of their town, known as al-Dirʿīya, which had natural and man-made defenses and constant sources of water and food. From this same stronghold, they dominated the surrounding area and controlled the transit trade. Because the life of Muḥammad ibn Suʿūd was not well documented, it is difficult to assess his motives. Whatever they were, his adherence to Wahhabism afforded a religious sanction and a militant quality to his expansionist efforts. His immediate successors ruled as Wahhabbi imams, while their tribal forces encroached on and eventually overran the Ottoman outposts in northern and western Arabia. The Wahhabi westward drive continued until Suʿūd ibn ʿAbd al-ʿAzīz brought an end to Ottoman authority in the Hijaz in the early years of the 19th century.

In response to the sultan's request, Muḥammad ʿAlī organized an expeditionary force to recover the holy sites of Arabia. Excluding the mamluks, the majority of troops then available to him were Turkish, Albanian, and North African infantry and Turkish cavalry. He committed over 10,000 of these soldiers to the expedition and placed his son Ṭūsūn in command. At their departure, the viceroy had his guards massacre the mamluk leaders at Cairo and drive their subordinates into hiding. Ṭūsūn's troops marched or sailed by way of Suez and arrived at Yanbūʿ in the latter part of 1811. This army's initial advance was repulsed, but after regrouping and refitting, it secured Medina, Mecca, and Jidda during the winter of 1812–1813. The war in Arabia would, however, continue for years, as Muḥammad ʿAlī sought to force the Wahhabi-Saudi regime onto the defensive. He deployed forces into the mountainous Sarāt lands south of the Hijaz, where many of the native tribesmen were devoted Wahhabis. He even took personal charge of operations there for a while during 1814. Although the struggle in the Sarāt lands was inconclusive, the troops of Egypt eventually vanquished the Saudis in their own homeland.

In 1816 Muḥammad ʿAlī undertook yet another campaign in Arabia. He sent an expedition under his eldest son, who would become renowned as Ibrāhīm Pasha, to reduce the Saudi stronghold of al-Dirʿīya. Ibrāhīm's force was similar in composition to the one Ṭūsūn had led. It was augmented by tribal contingents as it advanced eastward across central Arabia. Ibrāhīm's troops closed on al-Dirʿīya in late winter 1817–1818 and laid siege to the town. His regular units then included several thousand infantry, about 2,000 cavalry, over 200 engineers, and at least 13 field pieces with crews.[3] After a seven-month struggle, the defenders surrendered, the Saudi leaders were taken captive, and the town was destroyed. Ibrāhīm returned to a hero's welcome in Egypt the following year. The Cairo regime withdrew its troops from the Najd in 1824, although it reoccupied that region in 1837.

In the midst of his war against the Wahhabis, Muḥammad ʿAlī made his first attempt to institute reforms among the armed forces of Egypt. He planned to have his troops train under European officers who would instruct and advise them in modern military tactics and techniques.[4] Some of his soldiers, however, were not receptive to his ideas and revolted against the order to train. This experience prompted the viceroy to recruit new soldiers, who might be more willing to assimilate Western ways. Because of the Russian expansion in the Caucasus, that traditional source of military manpower was eliminated. However, the Sudan had high potential as a source of both manpower and wealth, and so the viceroy opted for a military venture there. Meanwhile, to offset troop shortages, Muḥammad ʿAlī allowed for the parole and enrollment of former mamluks in regular units.[5]

Muḥammad ʿAlī appointed yet another son, Ismāʿīl, to lead one of the two expeditions he sent across the southern frontier. Ismāʿīl's force conquered Nubia and Sennar in 1820–1821, and the other force took control of Kordofan. The viceroy's officers enrolled thousands of Sudanese captives and slaves into the regular army, which until then had consisted mainly of Turks, North Africans, and ex-mamluks. The Sudanese were taken to Aswan for military training. However, the majority of them died there because of their low resistance to local diseases. Meanwhile, Muḥammad ʿAlī applied resources toward the reconstitution of a naval arm to complement the land forces.

To compensate for the loss of the Sudanese soldiers, Muḥammad ʿAlī took the seemingly unprecedented step of conscripting the young men of the agrarian population of Egypt. For many centuries prior, only the bedouins of Egypt had been called up for military campaigns, in which they served as auxiliary light cavalry. The viceroy's recruiting innovation was in reality the birth of the modern Egyptian army; however, it has not been favorably commemorated for a number of reasons. His impressment of peasant youths was highly unpopular at the time. It led to several peasant revolts and flight from the countryside to the towns or beyond the border to Syria. The native Egyptians were not allowed into the officer class; their units were for the most part commanded by Turks and Circassians (ex-

Plate 6. The ruins of the Saudi stronghold of Dirʿīya. The desert approaches to these once imposing mud palaces and residences were protected by outlying walls and towers. (Author's photograph)

mamluks). Besides, the troops of Egypt, irrespective of ethnicity, still technically belonged to the Ottoman army. Indeed, they were among the best troops available to the sultan.

As he did earlier in the case of Arabia, Sultan Mahmud II called on Muḥammad ʿAlī for military assistance in suppressing the Greek insurrection. Thus, in 1822–1823, troops of Egypt squelched the revolt on Crete. Early in 1825, Ibrāhīm Pasha landed in the Morea at the head of a well-equipped, well-trained army. He had succeeded in reducing the insurgent strongholds on the Peloponnesian peninsula when the European powers intervened on the side of the Greeks. The combined fleets of Great Britain, France, and Russia destroyed most of the Turkish-Egyptian fleet in the Battle of Navarino in October 1827. A subsequent show of force by the British navy at Alexandria pressured Muḥammad ʿAlī into recalling his expeditionary force from the Morea.

Within a few years, the viceroy of Egypt had a falling out with the sultan regarding his reward for assisting in the Greek war. When he was denied the governorship of Syria, Muḥammad ʿAlī contrived to take that province by force. He turned a dispute with the ruler of Acre into a pretext to invade. He again chose Ibrāhīm to lead the war effort. Ibrāhīm Pasha moved his forces into Palestine in November 1831 and laid siege to Acre. By mid-summer 1832, he had defeated Ottoman loyalist forces south of Homs, received the capitulation of Acre, and won another battle near Homs against the advance guard of the main Ottoman army. On 29 July, Ibrāhīm engaged and defeated the Ottoman main force in the pass of Baylān near Alexandretta. He led his troops on into Anatolia, attained a decisive victory at Konya in December, and advanced toward Istanbul. At his father's order, Ibrāhīm halted at Kutahiya (Kütahya)—about 150 kilometers from the Sea of Marmora.

Faced with the military catastrophe in Anatolia and the subsequent death of Sultan Mahmud, the Ottoman government negotiated for peace. In May 1833 it conceded to Muḥammad ʿAlī the right to rule Syria and Adana. That same year, troops of Egypt conquered part of the Yemen. With those territorial gains, Muḥammad ʿAlī, in effect, reconstituted the Ayyubid-Mamluk realm of medieval times. Some intellectuals in Syria took note of this historic correlation, as they had taken note of the contemporary, nationalist movements in Europe. They had also heard Ibrāhīm Pasha's war propaganda about liberation from the Turkish yoke. These influences prompted them to contemplate an Arab resurgence under the leadership of the Cairo regime.

Other segments of the Syrian population were not so favorably inclined toward the Egyptian administration. In time, people came to resent the implementation of efficient taxation, forced labor, religious equality, and, particularly, disarmament and conscription. Besides, they were not convinced that the authority of the Cairo regime was as legitimate as that of

Map 6.1
Muḥammad ʿAlī's Empire, Early 19th Century

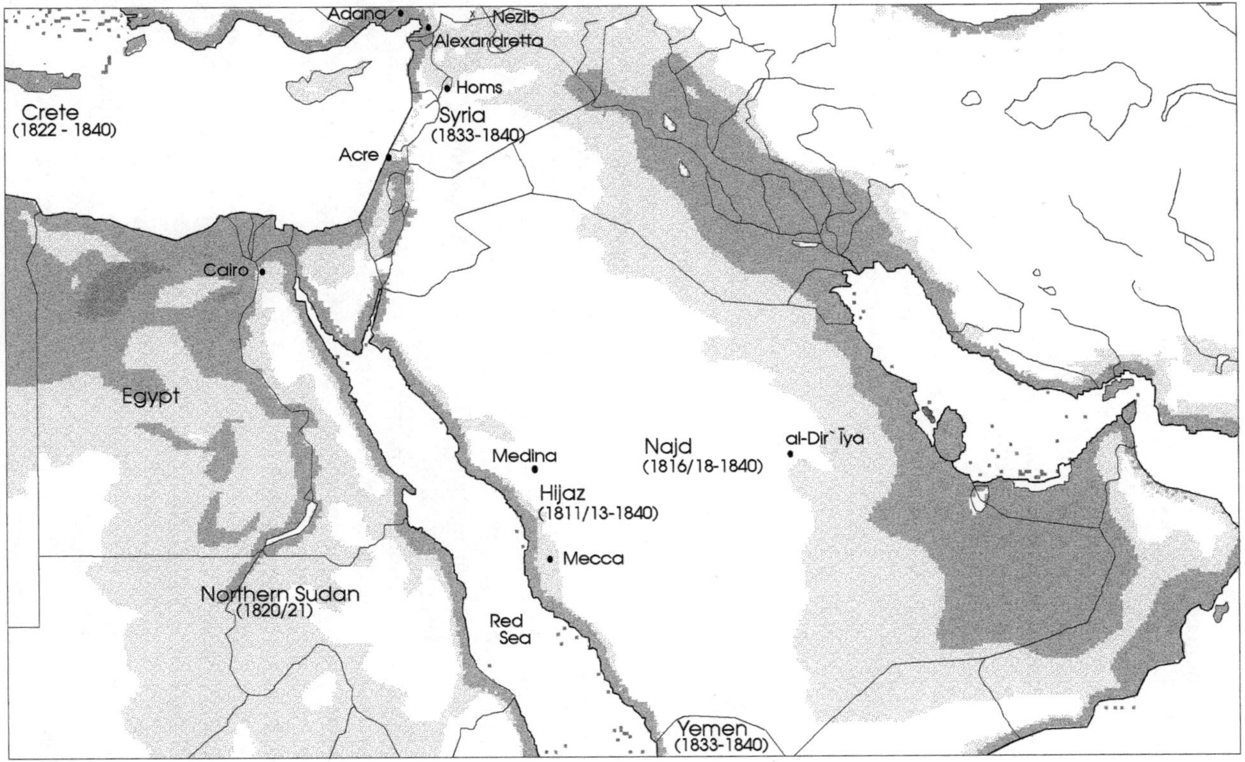

the Sublime Porte (i.e., the Ottoman central government). The consequence was the outbreak of sporadic revolts, which, as they increased in severity, raised the prospects of an Ottoman restoration. The Ottomans recommenced hostilities in 1839, only to incur yet another major defeat at Nezib (Nizip) to the north of Aleppo. Their army was beaten; their fleet defected to Muḥammad ʿAlī. The Sublime Porte was again humbled by its own servant. However, the European powers intervened to retrieve the situation for the Ottomans. They brokered a treaty by whose terms Muḥammad ʿAlī was to relinquish control of Syria in return for hereditary rule in Egypt only. The viceroy rejected those terms, and his fortunes took a turn for the worse.

With France abstaining, the powers determined to force Muḥammad ʿAlī to comply with the Treaty of London. They blockaded the coasts of Syria, landed forces, and incited and supported uprisings among the populace. After the British captured Acre, they persuaded Muḥammad ʿAlī to evacuate Syria. His forces returned to Egypt at the end of 1840. That same year, the viceroy withdrew his troops from Crete, Yemen, and central and western Arabia. Many units were subsequently disbanded in compliance with an Ottoman decree, which the powers backed as part of the overall peace process. That dictate limited the size of the viceroy's army to 18,000 men; at peak strength, it had probably been ten times that number, including both regular and auxiliary troops. The militarism at Cairo abruptly ended and remained dormant until Egypt undertook further ventures in the Sudan and Horn of Africa in the 1860s and 1870s. In 1848 Muḥammad ʿAlī succumbed to senility and relinquished the viceroyalty of Egypt to his son Ibrāhīm. He had at least attained the privilege of hereditary rule for his family. The House of Muḥammad ʿAlī would continue to rule at Cairo until 1952.

Egypt's experience with military modernization was cut short by strength and budget reductions and the dismissal of European officers. Nonetheless, Muḥammad ʿAlī's efforts had many immediate and future effects on Egyptian society at large. To provide modern education for the military and governmental establishments, Muḥammad ʿAlī sent numerous student missions to Europe, particularly Italy and France. He also established in Egypt several new schools and staffed them with European instructors. On the military side, the most famous of the European trainers was the French Colonel Sèves, who eventually converted to Islam and married into the native nobility. To support these educational programs, Muḥammad ʿAlī established a governmental translation and publication bureau. Purely military manuals were published in Turkish. However, medical and veterinary source books were published in Arabic; that effort helped prompt the revival of Arabic as a medium of modern, scientific knowledge.

Since Bonaparte's expedition in 1798, Britain and France had been contending for dominant influence in Egypt. Britain's aim was to secure trade routes and lines of communication between India and the Mediterranean. France's aim was to counter the British while it expanded its own control or influence along the southern and southeastern Mediterranean littoral. However, by the mid-1870s, the two rivals overcame their differences in an effort to reverse the reckless economic policies of the Cairo regime. They acted jointly to take over the financial management, and hence the effective government, of Egypt. Resentment of both this foreign interference and the prerogatives of the Turco-Circassian ruling class spurred an emerging nationalist movement among ethnic Egyptian elites.

With considerable support from the army, and particularly from ʿUrābī Pasha, the nationalists began to press for a greater share in government. They eventually took over key ministerial posts, undermined the authority of the titular ruler Muḥammad Tawfīq, and challenged the British-French Dual Control. Tensions led to antiforeigner rioting in the summer of 1882, which in turn induced forceful intervention. The British navy bombarded Alexandria and landed an expeditionary force at Suez. This force defeated ʿUrābī's troops at Tall al-Kabīr on 13 September, entered Cairo the next day, and put the country under military occupation. Britain subsequently placed Egypt in protectorate status at the onset of World War I. Although the nationalist revolt failed, the Egyptian veterans of Tall al-Kabīr attained a heroic status. For the nationalist historians of Egypt, this event greatly overshadowed the past deeds of native troops.

Meanwhile, in Arabia, the Saudis recovered from the defeat that Ibrāhīm Pasha had inflicted on them in 1818. They gradually regained control of the towns and tribes of central Arabia and established a new capital at al-Riyāḍ (Riyadh). They extended their rule to the Persian Gulf and exacted tribute from the rulers of Baḥrayn and Masqaṭ. Otherwise, their eastward expansion was checked by the British, who were the police power in the Persian Gulf. Although the Saudis had no navy, they maintained an effective land force. The mainstay of their army consisted of a small, standing unit of guards and the town militias of the core districts of the state, which were mobilized as required.[6] The warriors of subject bedouin tribes sometimes served in campaigns as auxiliary troops.

An internal power struggle led to a second Saudi collapse in 1871. One of the contending parties called in the Ottomans, who reoccupied al-Ḥasā (now commonly known as the Eastern Province). The House of Rashīd, which ruled at Ḥā'il, supplanted the House of Suʿūd as the dominant power in inner Arabia. The Saudis supported an unsuccessful revolt against the Rashidi regime. After the battle of Mulayda in early 1891, the Saudi noble families and their retainers fled the Najd and eventually took refuge in Kuwait. There, the young ʿAbd al-ʿAzīz ibn ʿAbd al-Raḥmān (now renowned as Ibn Suʿūd) developed the traits and skills that would help him become the foremost scion of the House of Suʿūd.

In late 1901, ʿAbd al-ʿAzīz set out with forty followers on a daring venture to regain his family's realm. With a picked group of fifteen men, he seized Riyadh in mid-January. ʿAbd al-ʿAzīz fought for some years to secure his position against the Rashidis and their local Ottoman allies. In 1906 he decisively defeated the House of Rashīd and induced the Turks to withdraw from central Arabia, although he acceded to nominal Ottoman suzerainty. ʿAbd al-ʿAzīz then set about reclaiming the territories that had formerly been part of the Wahhabi-Saudi state. He eventually departed from the traditional methods of recruiting and mobilizing military forces. In 1912 he founded a prototype colony at al-Arṭāwīya, where bedouins were settled and trained to be agriculturalists, soldiers, and Wahhabi zealots. Within a decade, the Saudi leader established throughout central Arabia almost 100 settlements of this kind, whose fierce militiamen became known as Ikhwān (Brethren). ʿAbd al-ʿAzīz took and then lost al-Ḥasā just before the advent of World War I. Caught between conflicting British and Ottoman objectives, he maintained a virtual neutrality throughout the war.

An important chapter in the story of modern Arab militarism was lost as a coincidence of the Ottoman collapse in World War I. Toward the end of the 19th century, the Ottoman government changed its military recruiting policy relative to the Arab population of the empire. Many traditional recruiting grounds in the Balkans had been lost due to successful nationalist revolts. To compensate, the Sublime Porte began to draft the male youth of the Syrian and Iraqi provinces. Some of those conscripts became officers and attended Ottoman military schools. There they learned two ideals that would significantly influence later Arab political practice: (1) the armed forces are guarantors of the survival of the state, as distinct from the governing regime; and (2) they have an important role in the modernization of society.

The loyalties of the Ottoman Arab elite became strained, however, because of the ethnocentric "Young Turk" government which took over in 1908. A minority within the Arab leadership saw the outbreak of war as an opportunity to break with Istanbul. There was growing resentment against the inevitable military drafts in the Arab provinces. Still, there was minimal support for a popular uprising. Many Arabs went to war to fight for the Ottoman state, but their service was not commemorated by any of the successor regimes.

The so-called Arab Revolt (against the Ottomans) was to a large extent brought about by the British. Their agents in the Near East knew that Sharīf Ḥusayn ibn ʿAlī of Mecca had been for some time contemplating separatist designs and that he was in communication with dissident leaders in Syria. The sharif, however, lacked the means to sustain an effective regionwide revolt. The British provided him with money and arms. They also helped him muster an all-Arab force by facilitating the parole and transfer of Ottoman Arab prisoners of war, who had been captured during the Gallipoli campaign. These former Ottoman veterans enlarged the sharif's army, which otherwise consisted of a guard force, loyal militias, and allied bedouin tribesmen of the Hijaz.

Arab military involvement in World War I was not quite what the Western legend of T. E. Lawrence represents. The sharif's regular forces fought mainly to defeat or neutralize the local Ottoman garrisons; few of them deployed beyond the Hijaz. The sharifian force that struck north consisted mostly of tribal auxiliaries. As commemorated in the Lawrence legend, these warriors raided the Hijaz railway, captured ʿAqaba, and screened the right flank of the British advance through Palestine. In Arabic historiography and folklore, these deeds have been ascribed to the perseverence of the sharifian regime, whereas the contributions of Lawrence and other British liaison officers have been minimized or ignored.

The war in the Near East concluded with the breakup of the Ottoman Empire and the establishment of mandatory rule—French in Syria and Lebanon and British in Palestine, Transjordan, and Iraq. Only Arabia became fully independent. However, Sharīf Ḥusayn did not attain any long-term benefit from the Ottoman demise. In 1919 the Saudis resumed their expansionist activity in Arabia. They attacked the Hijaz and Sarāt lands and then took the Rashidi stronghold of Ḥā'il and with it all of northern Arabia. By the end of 1925, they had ousted the sharifian regime from the Hijaz. Meanwhile, their fighters continued to press northward against Transjordan and Iraq, where the sons of Sharīf Ḥusayn were the titular rulers. Saudi raiding along the frontier prompted the British mandate authorities to mobilize and train local forces for border defense. The same authorities also had to ensure the internal security of the mandated states.

The British, like the French in Syria, followed judicious recruiting and force management policies. Many Sunni Arabs among the sedentary population resented the foreign occupation and were ill disposed to serve under infidels. It was unwise, and actually unnecessary, to recruit heavily from this potential source of manpower. The mandate authorities found willing soldiers and militiamen among the minorities. The French enrolled many Alawite Shiites in the army of Syria. The British made soldiers of bedouin tribesmen in Transjordan. They employed Assyrian and Kurd militias to suppress rebellions in Iraq.[7] The Western powers relied on their own forces to ensure regional security and so obviated the need to create large, native armies for territorial defense.

The British succumbed to native popular demands and granted full independence, albeit with treaty ties, to Egypt in 1922 and Iraq in 1932. They brought back their forces to reoccupy both countries during World War II. The British stayed on in Palestine and Transjordan, as the French stayed on in Syria and Lebanon, until shortly after the war. A number of the military advisors and liaison officers who served with the mandate regimes have left memoirs of their experiences. However, as much of their writing recorded personal challenges and frustrations, it conveyed few objective observations on native military capabilities. Still, the works of John Bagot Glubb and his colleagues (in Bibliog. 4) have afforded solid insights on the native soldiery in Jordan. This is no coincidence, since British military influence was more consistent and welcome there than in other Western mandates in the Near East.

One might use works on the Arab Legion of Jordan to attain some understanding of Arab military thought and practice in the decades prior to the 1948 war over Palestine. Apart from these sources, the Western historical record is rather meager. The Arabs themselves generally do not look favorably on the mandate period of their history, and so their historians have not recorded the native military undertakings of this era. The resultant lack of historical insight has bred and still breeds misperceptions regarding the Arab militarism of our own time.

NOTES

1. There was a precursor to the French action during the Russo-Turkish War of 1768–1774. A tsarist fleet sailed into the Mediterranean, defeated the Ottomans at sea, and coordinated operations with rebel forces in Egypt and Syria.

2. The currently ruling dynasty of Arabia traces its origin to Ibn Suʿūd, hence the name Suʿūdī, which by linguistic transfer has become Saudi in English.

3. For estimates of this force, see works in Bibliog. 1 by Maxime Weygand, vol. 1, pp. 96 ff.; G. Forster Sadleir, p. 488; and John Sabini, p. 166, who apparently follows Sadleir; and in Bibliog. 2. by R. Bayly Winder, p. 18.

4. Muḥammad ʿAlī at first employed mostly Italians, but his later preference was to hire Frenchmen. Many European adventurers left memoirs of their service in the army of Egypt, and so there exists considerable source material for reconstructing the military undertakings of Muḥammad ʿAlī's regime.

5. The viceroy also established a new corps of 300 of his own mamluks, which became part of the modernization cadre of the army.

6. This manpower sourcing scheme is not in evidence today because the demography of the Saudi heartland changed considerably during the 20th century. Many towns were abandoned when their populations migrated to Riyadh.

7. In a later similar development, Amīr ʿAbdullah's regime at ʿAmmān revived the medieval practice of employing "aliens" as soldiers. To man the royal guard, the court recruited from among the Circassian and Chechen communities, which the Ottomans had settled in Jordan in the late 1800s.

BIBLIOGRAPHY

1. The Military Achievements of Muḥammad ʿAlī Pasha

Bankes, W. J., ed. *Narrative of the Life and Adventures of Giovanni Finati . . . Who Made the Campaigns against the Wahabees.* 2 vols. London: J. Murray, 1830.

Cameron, Donald A. *Egypt in the Nineteenth Century*. London: Smith, Elder, 1898.

Dehérain, Henri. *Le Soudan Égyptien sous Mehemet Ali*. Paris: Georges Carré et C. Naud, 1898.

Dodwell, Henry Herbert. *The Founder of Modern Egypt: A Study of Muhammad Ali*. New York: AMS Press, 1977.

Douin, Georges. *Mohamed Aly et l'Expédition d'Alger (1829–1830)*. Cairo: IFAOC, 1930.

———. *La Première Guerre de Syrie*. Cairo: IFAOC, 1931.

———. *Les Premières Frégates de Mohamed Aly (1824–1827)*. Cairo: IFAOC, 1926.

Driault, Édouard. *La Formation de l'Empire de Mohamed Aly de l'Arabie au Soudan (1814–1823)*. Cairo: IFAOC, 1927.

Durand-Viel, Georges. *Les Campagnes Navales de Mohammed Aly et d'Ibrahim*. 2 vols. Paris: Imprimerie Nationale, 1935.

Kahle, P. "Ibrāhīm Pasha." *EI* 3 (new ed.): 999–1000.

Lawson, Fred H. *The Social Origins of Egyptian Expansionism during the Muhammad 'Ali Period*. New York: Colombia University Press, 1992.

Marsot, al-Sayyid Afaf Lutfi. *Egypt in the Reign of Muhammad Ali*. Cambridge, England: Cambridge University Press, 1984. See chap. 9.

Napier, Charles. *The War in Syria*. London: J. W. Parker, 1842.

Nicolle, David. "Nizam: Egypt's Army in the 19th Century." *Army Quarterly and Defence Journal* 108 (1978): 69–78, 177–87.

Politēs, Athanasios G. *Le Conflit Turco-Égytien de 1838–1841 et les Dernières Années du Regne de Mohamed Aly*. Cairo: IFAOC (for the Royal Geographic Society of Egypt), 1931.

Rifaat, Mohammed. *The Awakening of Modern Egypt*. London: Longmans, Green, 1947. See chaps. 2–4.

Rustum, Asad Jibrail. "Syria under Mehemet Ali." Ph.D. diss., University of Chicago, 1923.

Sabini, John. *Armies in the Sand: The Struggle for Mecca and Medina*. New York: Thames and Hudson, 1981.

Sadleir, G. Forster. "Account of a Journey from Katif on the Persian Gulf to Yamboo." *Transactions of the Literary Society of Bombay* 3 (1823): 449–93.

Weygand, Maxime. *Histoire de Mohammed Aly et ses Fils*. 2 vols. Paris: Imprimerie Nationale, 1936.

2. Saudi Expansionism in Arabia

Almana, Mohammed. *Arabia Unified: A Portrait of Ibn Saud*. London: Hutchinson Benham, 1980.

Burckhardt, Johann Ludwig. *Notes on the Bedouins and Wahabys*. Reading, England: Garnet Publishing, 1992. See vol. 2, pp. 95 ff.

Corancez, Louis Alexandre Olivier de. *Histoire des Wahabis: depuis leur Origine jusqu'à la fin de 1809*. Paris: Chez Crapart, 1810.

Elgood, Robert. *Arms and Armour of Arabia in the 18th, 19th, and 20th Centuries*. London: Scholar Press, 1993.

Glubb, John Bagot. *War in the Desert: An R.A.F. Frontier Campaign*. 1st American ed. New York: W. W. Norton, 1961.

Goldrup, Lawrence P. ''Saudi Arabia: 1902–1932: The Development of a Wahhabi Society.'' Ph.D. diss., University of California at Los Angeles, 1971.

Habib, John S. *Ibn Sa'ud's Warriors of Islam: The Ikhwan of Najd and Their Role in the Creation of the Sa'udi Kingdom, 1910–1930*. Leiden, Netherlands: E. J. Brill, 1978.

Howarth, David Armine. *The Desert King: The Life of Ibn Saud*. London: William Collins and Sons, 1965.

Kelly, John Barrett. *Eastern Arabian Frontiers*. New York: Praeger, 1964.

Kostiner, Joseph. *The Making of Saudi Arabia, 1916–1936: From Chieftaincy to Monarchical State*. New York: Oxford University Press, 1993.

Philby, H. St. John. *Arabia of the Wahhabis*. London: Constable, 1928.

———. ''The Triumph of the Wahhabis.'' *Journal of the Central Asian Society* 13 (1926): 293–319.

Rentz, George. ''al-Ikhwān'' *EI* 2 (new ed.): 1064–68.

———. ''Dirʿiyya.'' *EI* 2 (new ed.): 320–22.

———. ''Muḥammad ibn ʿAbd al-Wahhâb (1703/04–1792) and the Beginnings of Unitarian Empire in Arabia.'' Ph.D. diss., University of California at Berkeley, 1948.

Rosenfeld, Henry L. ''The Social Composition of the Military in the Process of State Formation in the Arabian Desert.'' *Journal of the Royal Anthropological Institute* 95 (1965): 75–86, 174–94.

Smalley, W. F. ''The Wahhabīs and Ibn Sa'ud.'' *Muslim World* 22 (1932): 227–46.

Wiet, Gaston. ''Les Révoltes en Arabie.'' *Bulletin du Comité de l'Asie Française* 9 (1909): 291–97.

Winder, R. Bayly. *Saudi Arabia in the Nineteenth Century*. London: Macmillan; New York: St. Martin's Press, 1965.

3. The Arabs and World War I

Bell, Gertrude. *The Arab War*. London: Golden Cockerell Press, 1940.

Brémond, Édouard. *Le Hejaz dans la Guerre Mondiale*. Paris: Payot, 1933.

El-Edroos, S. A. *The Hashemite Arab Army 1908–1979: An Appreciation and Analysis of Military Operations*. Amman, Jordan: Publishing Committee, 1980. An exceptional work authored by a Pakistani general officer; Western method applied to Arab History. See chap. 3 for rare details about World War I.

Ende, W. ''Iraq in World War I: The Turks, the Germans, and the Shiʿite Mujtahids' Call for Jihād.'' In *Proceedings of the Ninth Congress of the Union Européene de Arabisants et Islamisants, Amsterdam, 1978*. Edited by R. Peters. Publications of the Netherlands Inst. Cairo, 4. Leiden, Netherlands: E. J. Brill, 1981.

Falls, Cyril. *Military Operations, Egypt & Palestine, Pt. II*. London: Government of Great Britain, 1930. See references to Arab Campaign in the index.

Hurgronje, C. Snouck. *The Revolt in Arabia*. New York: G. P. Putnam's Sons, 1917.

Jarvis, C. S. *Arab Command*. London: Hutchison & Co., 1942. See chaps. 3–5.

Lawrence, Thomas Edward. *Revolt in the Desert, by T. E. Lawrence*. New York: George H. Doran Company, 1927.

———. *Seven Pillars of Wisdom*. Garden City, N.Y.: Doubleday, Doran, 1935.

Nicolle, David, and Richard Hook. *Lawrence and the Arab Revolts*. Men-at-Arms Series, no. 208. London: Osprey Publishing, 1989.

Parker, Alfred Chevallier. *The Diaries of Parker Pasha: War in the Desert 1914–18 Told from the Secret Diaries of Colonel Alfred Chevallier Parker.* Edited by H.V.F. Winstone. London: Quartet Books, 1983. See chap. 6.

Ta'uber Eliʿezer. *The Arab Movements in World War I.* London: Frank Cass, 1993.

Young, Hubert. *The Independent Arab.* London: J. Murray, 1933.

Zeine, Zeine N. *The Struggle for Arab Independence.* 2d ed. New York: Caravan Books, 1977. See chap. 2.

4. The Defense Forces of the Ottoman Successor States

Berger, Morroe. *The Military Elite and Social Change in Egypt since Napoleon.* Princeton, N.J.: Princeton University Press, 1960.

El-Edroos, S. A. *The Hashemite Arab Army.* (see Bibliog 3). See chaps. 4–5.

Glubb, John Bagot. *A Soldier with the Arabs.* New York: Harper, 1957.

———. "Transjordan and the War." *Journal of the Royal Central Asian Society* 32 (1945): 24–33.

Harvey, John. *With the French Foreign Legion in Syria.* London: Greenhill Books, 1995. These memoirs afford insights into the internal security problems in Syria during the mid-1920s. See references to the employment of bedouin and Circassian irregular forces, pp. 100–102, 125.

Jarvis, C. S. *Arab Command.* (see Bibliog 3). See chap. 8.

Khoury, Philip S. *Syria and the French Mandate: The Politics of Arab Nationalism, 1920–1945.* Princeton, N.J.: Princeton University Press, 1987. See references to army in the index.

Kirkbride, Alec Seath. *A Crackle of Thorns.* London: J. Murray, 1956.

Lias, Godfrey. *Glubb's Legion.* London: Evans Bros., 1956.

Lockhart, L. K. "The Transjordan Frontier Force." *Journal of the Royal Artillery* 56 (1929): 77–84.

Perowne, Stewart. "The Arab Legion." *Geographical Magazine* 27 (1954): 352–58.

al-Qazzaz, A. "The Iraqi-British War of 1941: A Review Article." *International Journal of Middle East Studies* 7, no. 4 (October 1976): 591–96.

Rostow, Dankwart A. "Political Ends and Political Means in the Late Ottoman and Post-Ottoman Middle East." In *WTS.*

Silverfarb, Daniel. *The Twilight of British Ascendancy in the Middle East: A Case Study of Iraq, 1941–50.* New York: St. Martin's Press, 1994. See chaps. 1 and 8.

Sinclair, J. M. "Trans-Jordan and the Trans-Jordan Frontier Force." *Journal of the Royal Artillery* 60 (1934): 471–85.

Tarbush, Mohammad A. *The Role of the Military in Politics: A Case Study of Iraq to 1941.* Foreword by H. A. Hourani. London: Kegan Paul International, 1982.

Vatikiotis, P. J. *Politics and the Military in Jordan: A Study of the Arab Legion, 1921–1957.* New York: Praeger, 1967. See chaps. 1–4.

Young, Peter. *Bedouin Command: With the Arab Legion in 1953–1956.* Foreword by Sir John Glubb. London: W. Kimber, 1956.

7

The Struggle with Israel

When the Arab states of the Middle East were confronted with the Palestine crisis of 1948, they were ill-prepared to respond militarily. Under the mandate regimes that governed the Ottoman successor states, advanced military methods and thought had generally not been inculcated among the native soldiery. At the termination of the mandates, indigenous forces had only rudimentary soldier skills and some experience in border defense and internal security operations. The armies of the new Arab states had little or no capability to wage cross-border war. Moreover, there was no reason for any local regime to organize and train forces for large-scale operations so long as British and French power ensured the security and stability of the region. With the British reoccupation of Iraq, their victory at al-ʿAlamayn (el-Alamein), and the Free French ascendancy in Syria-Lebanon, the region was insulated from further involvement in World War II. The military men of the Arab East were generally passive observers of that great conflict.[1] In contrast, some 20,000 Israelis saw service in combat and support units, which were subordinate to British or Allied command.

Among the consequences of World War II, Britain and France agreed to terminate the mandates in Syria, Lebanon, Transjordan, and Palestine and to withdraw forces from those countries as well as from Iraq and Egypt. The termination of the Palestine mandate brought to a head the sectarian animosities that had been growing over the decades. The Arabs' anxiety about the destiny of their country had led to minor outbreaks of violence in the early 1920s and one major incident in 1929. Then a surge in Jewish immigration sparked the so-called Arab rebellion of 1936–1939. Militant Palestinians took up arms and struck against the Jewish settlers and the regime that protected them. However, British troops and Jewish constabulary units effectively contained the insurgency until it subsided. The wartime British military buildup in the Middle East was a further, albeit temporary, deterrence to Palestinian militancy.

Faced with the conflicting aims of the Palestinian Arabs and the Jews, the British government deferred decision on the future of the mandated territory to international arbitration. On 29 November 1947, the United Nations announced the partition of Palestine into two independent Arab and Jewish states. Following that announcement, the mufti of Jerusalem, Amīn al-Ḥusaynī, called for jihad against the Jews. Sporadic violence erupted throughout the country. Disparate Palestinian militias rallied to the mufti, who attempted to organize them as the Arab Army of Salvation. Other volunteer fighters from Palestine as well as from Syria, Lebanon, Iraq, and elsewhere joined the so-called Arab Liberation Army, with headquarters at Damascus. The effective strength of these two volunteer "armies" fluctuated considerably over time. They both deployed about 1,000 men when they initiated hostilities in January 1948. At peak strength in April and May, each had less than 10,000 men under arms.

Considering manpower alone, the Palestinian-Arab irregular forces had virtually no chance of winning a civil war. Their Jewish opponents had about 30,000 men in standing units and over 30,000 more in reserve status. Logistics was another major weakness of the Palestinian-Arab war effort. A full study of this deficiency has not been undertaken and probably never will be, as too many firsthand observers have either died or chosen to keep silent about negative experiences. However, allusions to it have survived in various sources, such as Gamal Abdul Nasser's treatise on *Egypt's Liberation*. Reflecting on the defective weapons scandal and on the handling of the Palestine War, he wrote, "Here we are in these foxholes, surrounded, and thrust treacherously into a battle for which we were *not ready*, our lives the playthings of greed, conspiracy and lust, which have left us here *weaponless* under fire (p. 23, italics are the author's)." Many similar observations have been passed along in random conversation within Middle East military circles. Among the stories related to this author was that the money that some Palestinian communities gave for the war effort was never spent to purchase arms because the solicitors or their bosses absconded with it.[2] Such likely incidents reflect on the Palestinians' lack of solidarity, which was one of the great strengths of the Jews.

In some cases, the lack of serious preparation for combat may have been due to overzealousness to fight the infidels. Indeed, the designations chosen for units of the Arab Liberation Army suggest that the conflict at hand was seen to be part of the historic struggle of Islam. Among the battalion designations were the First Yarmūk, Second Yarmūk, Ḥaṭṭīn, Ajnādayn, and Qādisīya. These names had long been prominent in Arab-Islamic culture as symbols of God-given victory over infidel armies.[3] Oral accounts of the Palestine conflict further reveal that many of the Arab militiamen and volunteer fighters went to war expecting an easy victory. They associated the contemporary Jewish settlers of Palestine with the historic Jewish communities that had lived for centuries under Muslim rule as an inferior, protected people, exempt from military service. This view ignored reality.[4] The Jews of Palestine had already embraced militaristic values by the onset of civil war. They could build on the experience of their World War II veterans who were quite capable of adopting modern military methods and technologies.

Through the early months of 1948, the British occupation troops impeded military action by either side. The British government, however, intent on relinquishing the mandate, completed the withdrawal of its forces from Palestine by the established deadline of 14 May. With the British gone, the neighboring Arab states sent forces to save the Palestinian-Arab cause. Intervention by the League of Arab States (or Arab League, founded in 1945) had already been decided on 25 April. Their contribution to the war effort substantially improved the odds regarding military hardware and sheer numbers of combatants. However, except for the Arab Legion of Transjordan, the proficiency of the regular troops and officers was only slightly better than that of the irregulars of the Arab Army of Salvation and the Arab Liberation Army. The Jews, becoming Israelis at the declaration of statehood, retained a significant advantage in quality of manpower.

Although King (formerly amir) ʿAbdullah of Transjordan was chosen to be the head of the Arab Defense Council, operations in Palestine were not particularly well coordinated. The deployment of units of the Syrian, Lebanese, Iraqi, Transjordanian, and Egyptian armies presented the image of common purpose. Indeed, the Arab League had announced its dual aim of preventing the partition of Palestine and protecting Arab interests. Such declarations notwithstanding, some of the Arab states were probably prompted to action by mutual distrust. The following considerations were relevant. Palestine historically was a strategic area of interest for any governing power at Cairo or Damascus. As for the Amman regime, it had an historic tie to the original Palestine mandate and could make a plausible claim to Arab territory west of the Jordan River. Iraq was tied to Transjordan through the blood relation of their heads of state.

The Arab League invasion of 15 May brought security to most of the Arab-majority areas of Palestine. Part of western Galilee was taken by the Israelis, but the Negev, which the Partition Plan accorded to Israel, was occupied by Egyptian forces. Except for an unsuccessful effort to isolate the Jerusalem enclave, the Arab forces adopted a largely defensive stance during the summer of 1948. The Israelis, in contrast, pursued the offensive strategy that was necessary to hold the Tel Aviv–Jerusalem corridor and to seize strategically key areas, such as Lydda airport. They took advantage of two temporary truces to refit, reorganize, and expand their armed forces. By October, the Israelis had approximately 45,000 regulars and another 45,000 reservists under arms—almost double the strength of the Arabs. Operating along interior lines, they drove the Lebanese and Arab Liberation Army contingents out of the war and neutralized the other Arab contingents in the northern theater of operations. They then concentrated against the Egyptians in the south and drove them from the Negev.

When the United Nations brought an end to the fighting in early 1949, the Palestinian Arabs had no control of their political destiny. Hundreds of thousands of them were refugees in neighboring states. The areas that had been occupied by Arab Legion and Iraqi forces were united with Transjordan in a new state called the Hashemite Kingdom of Jordan. Although the Egyptian forces lost most of their initial gains in Palestine, they held on to the coastal enclave north of Rafaḥ, known as the Gaza Strip. By the armistice agreement, that territory came under Egyptian administration. The Israelis succumbed to international pressure and withdrew their forces from Egyptian territory in the Sinai. However, they risked a truce violation to establish a military presence at the Gulf of ʿAqaba.

The military failure against Israel led to political unrest in most of the Arab states that had gone to war. The public at large saw the paradox that tiny Israel had prevailed against several more populous states. Intellectuals explained this apparent anomaly as being due to the modernism of Israeli society and the stagnation of Arab society—the relative inadequacy of its government, economy, education, and culture in general.[5] The blame for such inadequacy fell on the governmental leaders, who happened to owe their status to the mandatory powers. They were discredited and eventually displaced by force. Three governmental coups took place in Syria in 1949 and further forceful takeovers occurred in 1951, 1954, and 1955. King ʿAbdullah of Jordan was assassinated in Jerusalem in July 1951. "Free officers" overthrew the monarchy in Egypt in 1952. There were uprisings in Iraq in 1952 and in Jordan in 1954.

Apart from justice for the Palestinians, the people of the Arab East demanded the progressive reform of society, and the military officer corps took on the role of champions of progress. The trend of military involvement in politics continued through the 1950s and 1960s. The number of coups d'état in Syria alone reached twenty-one before the rise of Assad (Ḥāfiẓ al-Assād) brought governmental stability in the early 1970s. Iraq went through a similar period of instability, with military officers being key power brokers from 1958 to 1968. There was also military coup plotting in Jordan in 1957, although the conspirators failed to displace the monarchy. Arab officers were seemingly inspired by the example of the armed forces of Turkey, which saved that country in the aftermath of World War I. However, the key factors in the Turkish experience were cohesion and discipline. The officers who followed Ataturk had common ideals and set themselves above factional politics. In contrast, the military officers in Syria and Iraq formed cliques that subscribed to one or another of the current competing ideologies of Arab resurgence. The incessant plotting to take or retake control of the government consumed energies that might have been applied to beneficial reforms and development programs.

The case of Egypt was somewhat different from that of Syria and Iraq. General Neguib (Najīb), the nominal leader of the cabal that overthrew the monarchy in 1952, was himself eased out of power in 1954. The famous Gamal Abdel Nasser (Jamāl ʿAbd al-Nāṣir) became the new leader and brought governmental stability, which, along with military involvement in policy-making, has continued to the present day. Regime stability notwithstanding, Nasser had to contend with various foreign relations crises. The sources for this period disagree about whether these crises were brought on by his own decisions or by circumstances beyond his control. The relevant circumstances were that Nasser was snubbed by the Western powers, the Arab-Israeli conflict was still unresolved, and Egypt was expected to lead the Arab cause. Nasser's reactive course of action included negotiation of a massive arms deal with Czechoslovakia, pursuance of confrontation with Israel and the West, and propagation of a Pan-Arab ideology throughout the Arab East. The consequent military buildup, nationalization of the Suez Canal Company, and strengthening of ties between Cairo and other Arab capitals brought on hostile countermoves.

For various reasons, Israel, Britain, and France conspired to invade Egypt and initiated offensive operations in late October 1956. In this so-called Sinai-Suez War, the Egyptian ground forces acquitted themselves well. However, they lost much equipment in the course of withdrawing before multiple-axis attacks. Egypt's air force fared much worse. Most of its combat planes were destroyed at the opening of hostilities. The war losses set Egypt further back on the road to progress. Despite the losses, Nasser's prestige was greatly enhanced by his defiance of Egypt's enemies. Besides, pressure from the United States brought an end to the fighting on terms favorable to Egypt. The invasion forces eventually evacuated Egyptian territory and relinquished control of the canal zone to the Cairo regime.

Nasser retained his great popularity and his hold on power even after the catastrophic defeat of June 1967. Unlike the situation in other Arab lands, Egypt's leadership was able to prevent factionalism within the officer corps, and Nasser was able to preserve consensus at the higher levels of government. His control of counterintelligence and special security organizations undoubtedly contributed to the relative stability of his regime. Such methods of governing, although abhorrent to Westerners, had some positive appeal within the context of Arab-Islamic tradition. Nasser might well have considered himself to be a modern-day Saladin.[6]

It is instructive to note that the governmental turbulence in Syria and Iraq came to an end with the emergence of strongmen, each of whom led his own faction to dominance over its rivals. To broaden their popular support, both Assad and Saddam Hussein (Ṣaddām Ḥusayn) more or less convincingly claimed the leadership of the militant, Pan-Arabist movement. Saddam, who had no military experience, assumed general officer rank to complement his status as head of state. This all indicates that Arab leaders were reverting to time-tested practices of government. Indeed, the pattern of coup d'état–junta rule–strongman rule had become prevalent throughout the so-called Third World.

Of course, Western scholars endeavored to make sense of this phenomenon of the military in politics. In some cases, preoccupation with social science methodology led to inconclusive studies. In others, predisposition to democratic process inhibited objective analysis. Western journalism and official propaganda went even further in creating a negative image of military rule. Nonetheless, the reality was that processes of voting and parliamentary debate had little value in lands where people were desperately longing for the progressive reform of society. As for interpretive theory, it may have been better served by a cultural-anthropological approach. It seems plausible that there was, and still is, some correlation between a people's acceptance of military rule and their espousal of a militaristic myth of origin.

The Sinai-Suez War of 1956 led the Arab states to dismiss the possibility of reconciliation with Israel. The various governments pursued armament programs and lent increasing material and moral support to Palestinian guerrilla groups (fedayeen), which had been intermittently raiding Israel since the 1949 armistice. However, the locus of major guerrilla activity shifted from the Egyptian-Israeli frontier to the northern borders of Israel. As the tempo of fedayeen raiding activity increased in the later months of 1966, Syria and Egypt reconciled their differences and established a joint military command. Israel was beginning to sense the emergence of a multifront threat.

Despite the severity of reprisal attacks, fedayeen raiding and other border violence continued. Damascus and Amman both berated Cairo for not actively supporting them against the Israelis. The Tel Aviv regime exacerbated the tension by making explicit threats against Damascus in early May 1967. Nasser's subsequent moves impelled Israel to consider a preemptive strike against both Syria and Egypt. In mid-May, Nasser officially demanded that the United Nations withdraw the Emergency Force, which had been stationed along the border and elsewhere in Egypt consequent to the 1956 war. It is significant that Israel had consistently refused to allow United Nations forces to deploy on its side of the border. At the same time, Nasser sent additional forces into the Sinai and declared a blockade of the Straits of Tīrān. The blockade, if enforced, would have interdicted the sea route between Israel and the Red Sea. The final impetus to war came in late May, when Jordan and Egypt, which had been estranged for some time, concluded a military pact.

Israel initiated hostilities on 5 June in much the same way that it had in the previous war. The Israeli air force struck by surprise and destroyed most of Egypt's combat aircraft on the ground. Reacting to the attack on Egypt, Syria and Jordan launched some ineffective air strikes against Israel. Their own small air forces were subsequently destroyed in turn. Iraq, which entered the war later in the day, also sustained some aircraft losses at its one airfield within range of Israel. Having attained control of the skies, Israel's air force provided critical support to ground force operations. Israeli aircraft pounded the strong points of enemy defenses, interdicted troop movements, and disrupted communications. Following a breakdown in command and control, the Egyptians' position in the Sinai quickly collapsed under pressure from Israel's ground offensive. Meanwhile the Jordanians' position in the West Bank territory became untenable, and they effected an orderly withdrawal to the east of the river. The Israelis quickly consolidated their hold on the areas evacuated by the Egyptians and Jordanians.

The Israeli army was now free to concentrate against Syria, except that the three Arab confrontation states had all accepted the United Nations' call for a cease-fire. The Israelis temporized and then, deciding to ignore the armistice, attacked the strategic Golan Heights, which dominate eastern Galilee. The Syrian government, perplexed by that action, withdrew its front-line units to establish a defensive line closer to Damascus. Israel effectively occupied the Golan Heights on 10 June. Having attained its last strategic objective, Tel Aviv agreed to the cease-fire the United Nations had been attempting to impose. The Arab states had already seen the futility of further combat. Egypt and Jordan had lost much of their armor and air forces in this Six Day War.

The quickness and completeness of the Israeli victory indicates that, despite their prewar propaganda, the Arab confrontation states were not militarily prepared for conflict. This recurrence of total defeat led to another outpouring of social criticism by Arab intellectuals. The critics had seen that Israel was able to defeat the Arab armies piecemeal because the Arabs lacked unity. However, they were unable or unwilling to perceive that disunity was a problem within states as well as between them.

Factiousness has been and remains prevalent among the Arab people. This tendency derives from an ethos in which kinship largely dictates one's identity, allegiance, obligations, efforts, and status in life. According to behavioral norms, loyalty to one's kin group (i.e., extended family) is a higher value than loyalty to one's country. Indeed, the idea of country or nation, let alone national institution, has yet to become fully intelligible in many parts of the Arab world. The consequence for the military establishment is that commissions, contracts, assignments, promotions, and certain benefits are often determined by kinship ties rather than by merit. Such practice has more or less adversely affected morale and organizational performance during both peace and war.

Another related problem which the Arab critics underrated was the politicizing of the military. One way that the ruling cliques in Cairo, Damascus, and elsewhere held on to power was by assigning politically trustworthy, but not necessarily competent, officers to key positions within the armed forces. This problem of military leadership might have become manifest through comparative historical study. The Egyptian army seemingly had a better combat record during the 19th century, when it was led by European officers. Similarly, the Jordanian Arab Legion seemingly had a better combat record in the 1948–1949 War, when it was led by John Bagot Glubb. However, largely because of ethnic pride, no Arab scholar was likely to pursue such a study openly. Apart from that issue, some intellectuals directed criticism toward governmental ideology, suggesting that secular Arab socialism was doomed to fail. They argued that Arab society was weak because the Arab people had abandoned their Islamic values. This thinking gave a boost to the Islamic movement (for social justice), which in one form or another had existed for some time and would eventually become a dominant, regional trend.

The Six Day War also had a significant impact on the Palestine liberation movement. With the Israeli occupation of the Gaza Strip and West Bank, over one million Palestinians found themselves subject to Tel Aviv's rule. Some 250,000 fled to Jordan to escape that fate, adding to the already large refugee population there. Although they established the Palestine Liberation Organization (PLO) in 1964, the Palestinians had been counting on the Arab confrontation states to further their cause. They now realized the necessity of expanding their own military capabilities. They strengthened their militias and increased the tempo of raiding activity over the winter of 1967–1968. They did not let up despite harsh reprisals. By March, the Israelis had resolved on launching a major cross-border operation to blunt the fedayeen threat from Jordan.

The Israelis struck on 21 March with a three-pronged tank-infantry attack, supported by air and artillery. Their main objective apparently was the town of Karāma (Keramah), where some 500 Palestinian militiamen were encamped. The Jordanian 1st Infantry Division was prepared for the Israeli incursion and effectively defended key terrain. However, the Israelis were able to land a heliborne paratroop battalion near al-Karāma and deploy some troops from their main column to link up with it. In the ensuing battle, the Israelis destroyed the town and inflicted about 200 casualties on the Palestinian fighters. They then promptly withdrew from Jordanian territory. Despite their losses, the Palestinians claimed that they were victors for having repelled the attack.

The mystique of al-Karāma brought increasing numbers of Palestinian refugees into the ranks of the various militias. The Palestinian guerrillas continued to raid Israel. However, they also became a threat to the Amman regime by contesting its authority in certain areas and failing to coordinate raids, which provoked reprisal attacks on Jordanian territory. Tensions led to sporadic clashes between Jordanian army troops and fedayeen units. Palestinian attempts to assassinate King Hussein finally impelled him to take drastic measures. In September 1970, he ordered his army to drive the Palestinian militias from their camps in and around Amman and other major cities. Syrian forces invaded Jordan to assist the Palestinians but were driven back. Regional tensions subsided temporarily. Nonetheless, King Hussein was unable to accommodate the Palestinian fighters who remained in Jordan, and he had to expel them as well; most of them fled to Lebanon. The Palestinian military presence there contributed to the collapse of the government, the outbreak of civil war in 1975, and the prolongation of that conflict.[7]

Meanwhile, the Israelis refused to evacuate the territory they captured during the Six Day War. The Egyptians, who received Soviet help in reconstituting their forces, continued to wage war across the new confrontation line of the Suez Canal. In March 1969, they determined to wear down the Israelis through sustained commando raids and artillery bombardments. However, Israeli counter moves eventually convinced the Cairo regime that it could not win this "war of attrition." The two belligerents accepted a U.S.–sponsored cease-fire in August 1970. President Nasser died of a heart attack the following month. His successor Sadat (Anwar al-Sādāt), honored the cease-fire, while he consolidated control of the governmental establishment. He saw, however, that continuance of the no-war no-peace situation was detrimental to Egypt's interests. Economic recovery largely depended on reopening the Suez Canal under Egyptian authority. Israel was not about to withdraw peacefully from the east bank.

In late November 1972, Sadat decided to resolve the impasse by force. Since Syria signaled its willingness to fight as well, the risks became less daunting. Egypt's newly appointed war minister directed the general staff to plan for a limited offensive to seize key terrain east of the canal and hold on until an armistice could be imposed. The Syrians similarly planned to retake the Golan Heights. The Arab war plans relied on deception and surprise and employment of surface-to-air missiles and antitank weapons to counter known Israeli advantages in mobilization, airpower, and armored warfare. The Arab allies chose to attack on the Jewish holy day of

Yom Kippur (6 October 1973), expecting that many Israeli soldiers would be excused from duty for the holiday. This date also fell within Ramaḍān—the Islamic month of fasting—which was traditionally a period of reduced military activity.

The Egyptians executed the initial phase of their campaign plan with near perfection. They stormed across the Suez Canal and established bridgeheads on the eastern side. The Syrians, being less aggressive, drove in the Israeli defenses but soon lost momentum. Through local, limited counterattacks, the Israelis were able to stabilize both fronts. With the rapid deployment of reserve units, they were able to go onto the offensive. The Arab campaign plan started to unravel when the Syrians were pushed back beyond their preattack positions. The Arabs had apparently waited too long to accept the inevitable UN calls for a cease-fire. Damascus urged Cairo to undertake some offensive action to draw Israeli pressure away from Syria. On 14 October, the Egyptians launched an armored attack on a wide front, which created the conditions conducive for an Israeli counterattack and exploitation. The famous Israeli thrust to the west side of the Suez Canal, which isolated half of the Egyptian Third Army, brought on the irresistible pressure of the two superpowers for a cease-fire.

This Yom Kippur–Ramaḍān War demonstrated that the Israeli military leadership had underestimated the capability of the Arab armed forces, while the Arab military leadership had underestimated the need for adaptability. Arab campaign planning was methodical, but only to a point; it failed to consider future operations. Studies of this conflict have mainly compared tactics and weaponry; however, the disparity in force reconstitution capability may have been the most decisive factor. Although the war ended as a military stalemate, the Arab people in general regained some pride in the performance of Arab arms, while Egypt regained strategic territory. These conditions gradually created an environment that was conducive to negotiation of differences.

Sadat, the habitual risk taker, was willing to make peace with Israel—especially since Egypt's economy could no longer sustain the continuation of large-scale armament programs. His attendance at the Camp David talks and signing of the resultant treaty in 1979 brought benefits for his country but cost him his life. Sadat's peace with Israel antagonized various groups—the Palestinians, other Arabs who upheld their cause, and radical Islamic fundamentalists, who were opposed to secular regimes like that of Egypt. Radical Islamist infiltration of the Egyptian armed forces led to Sadat's assassination in October 1981. That deed had little consequence, however, because Egypt's government remained stable. Meanwhile, the focal point of the Arab-Israeli conflict had shifted to Lebanon.

Fedayeen raids from Lebanese territory provoked reprisal attacks, as they had done on other fronts. Israel invaded Lebanon to establish a buffer zone in 1978, conducted extensive cross-border operations throughout

Map 7.1
The Arab-Israeli Conflict

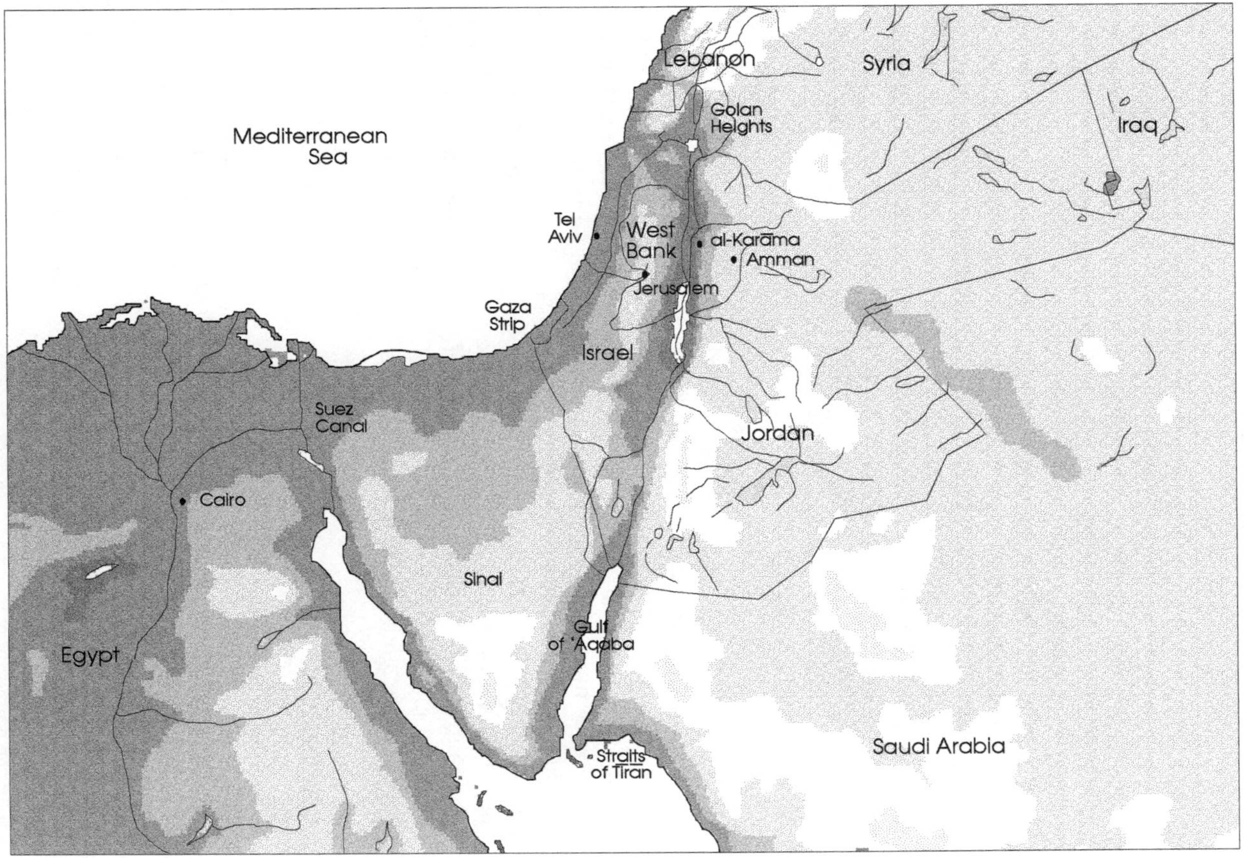

1980 and 1981, and launched a full-scale invasion in 1983. Israel's swift advance to Beirut led to the relocation of the PLO leadership and of many Palestinian fighters to Tunis. However, Lebanese Shiite and Druze and stay-behind Palestinian militias carried on a guerrilla war against the Israelis, who began to sustain unacceptable casualties. The Tel Aviv regime, reacting to domestic and international pressure, withdrew its forces from Lebanon during the spring of 1985. The Arab resistance forces claimed victory over Israel.

To the south, the Palestinians of the Israeli-Occupied Territories (West Bank and Gaza Strip) were watching the turn of events. They saw that the vaunted Israeli military machine was not so effective against a popular resistance movement. They had endured inferior status, limitation of rights, and harsh treatment for two decades. Such considerations undoubtedly persuaded local Palestinian leaders to initiate a popular uprising—*intifāḍa*. This insurrection became increasingly violent over the years, as Islamic extremist leaders challenged the traditional elite for dominant influence. The Israelis were worn down by domestic strife and eventually negotiated with the more moderate Palestinian power brokers for limited self-rule.

The *intifāḍa* is perhaps too recent an occurrence to assess fully its motives and consequences. Nonetheless, several efforts at interpretation have already been published. As with the Arab-Israeli conflict in general, the researcher must be attentive to both intentional and inadvertent bias in the literature. There is a multitude of sources on the Arab-Israeli wars, yet relatively few strive for objective analysis. Many pro-Israeli authors promote "David and Goliath" and "manifest destiny" themes, while many pro-Arab authors belabor the theory of American-Zionist conspiracy. With the maturing of a new generation of historians, there will hopefully appear more studies with balance.

NOTES

1. Notable exceptions were the Iraqi army's debacle at al-Ḥabbānīya in 1941 and the more positive experience of the Egyptian antiaircraft units which defended British lines of communication against German air attacks in 1941 and 1942.

2. My source was a native Palestinian who had lived through the first Arab-Israeli War, emigrated to Jordan, and subsequently took contract work in Saudi Arabia. His remarks were a commentary on the factiousness of the Arabs—who often hold their own immediate interests above those of the larger community.

3. See chapters 2 and 5 for a discussion of these four battles.

4. The volunteer fighters of the Muslim Brothers were evidently shocked when they encountered tenacious foes in their first engagements. See Richard P. Mitchell (Bibliog. 2), p. 57.

5. Raphael Patai has outlined the variant trends of this critical thought. See *The Arab Mind* (in chap. 2, Bibliog. 2), 258–67.

6. For background on this hero of the Islamic counter-Crusade, see chapter 5.
7. The subsequent Syrian-Israeli conflict over Lebanon is addressed in chapter 8.

BIBLIOGRAPHY

The following lists include only those sources that afford insights on Arab militarism and military practice. Works on regional politics and Israeli combat performance are omitted.

1. The Arab-Israeli Conflict, General

Amos, John W. *Arab-Israeli Military/Political Relations: Arab Perceptions and the Politics of Escalation.* New York: Pergamon Press, 1979.

Brooman, Josh. *Conflict in Palestine: Jews, Arabs, and the Middle East since 1900.* Longman 20th Century History Series. London: Longman, 1989.

Cordesman, Anthony. *The Arab-Israeli Military Balance and the Art of Operations: An Analysis of Military Lessons and Trends and Implications for Future Conflicts.* Washington, D.C.: American Enterprise Institute for Public Policy Research, 1987.

Downing, David, and Gary Herman. *War without End, Peace without Hope: Thirty Years of the Arab-Israeli Conflict.* London: New English Library, 1978.

Dupuy, Trevor N. *Elusive Victory: The Arab-Israeli Wars, 1947–1974.* Fairfax, Va.: Hero Books, 1984.

El-Edroos, S. A. *The Hashemite Arab Army, 1908–1979: An Appreciation and Analysis of Military Operations.* Amman, Jordan: Publishing Committee, 1980. See chaps. 6–11.

Herzog, Chaim. *The Arab-Israeli Wars: War and Peace in the Middle East.* New York: Random House, 1982.

Hirst, David. *The Gun and the Olive Branch: The Roots of Violence in the Middle East.* New York: Harcourt Brace Jovanovich, 1977.

Laffin, John, and Mike Chappell. *Arab Armies of the Middle East Wars 1948–73.* Men-at-Arms Series, no. 128. London: Osprey Publishing, 1982.

Lorch, Netanel. *One Long War: Arab versus Jew since 1920.* New York: Herzl Press, 1976.

Nicolle, David. "The Arab-Israeli East Air Wars." Five parts. *Illustrated Encyclopedia of World Aviation* (London) 9 (1983): 2041–44, 2061–64, 2081–84, 2101–4, 2121–25.

Rayyis, Riyad Najib, and Dunia Nahas. *Guerrillas for Palestine.* London: Croom Helm, 1976.

Rubinstein, Alvin Z., ed. *The Arab-Israeli Conflict: Perspectives.* New York: Praeger, 1984.

2. The Arab-Israeli Conflict through 1967

Bell, J. Bowyer. *The Long War: Israel and the Arabs since 1946.* Englewood Cliffs, N.J.: Prentice-Hall, 1969.

Bleaney, Heather, and Richard Lawless. *The First Day of the Six Day War*. Day That Made History Series. London: Dryad Press, 1990.

Chace, James, ed. *Conflict in the Middle East*. New York: H. W. Wilson, 1969.

Gawrych, George W. *Key to the Sinai: The Battles for Abu Ageila in the 1956 and 1967 Arab-Israeli Wars*. Washington, D.C.: U.S. Government Printing Office, 1990.

Hussein, King of Jordan. *My "War" with Israel*. Translated by June P. Wilson and Walter B. Michaels. New York: Morrow, 1969.

Kimche, D., and Dan Bawley. *The Sandstorm, the Arab-Israeli War of 1967: Prelude and Aftermath*. New York: Stein and Day, 1968.

Kosut, Hal, ed. *Israel and the Arabs: The June 1967 War*. New York: Facts on File, 1968.

Laffin, John. *Fedayeen: The Arab-Israeli Dilemma*. New York: Free Press, 1973.

Mitchell, Richard P. *The Society of the Muslim Brothers*. London: Oxford University Press, 1969. See subentries under Palestine in the index.

Mutawi, Samir A. *Jordan in the 1967 War*. Cambridge, England: Cambridge University Press, 1987.

Nicolle, David. "The Faluja Pocket (An Aspect of the 1947–8 Arab Israeli War)." *Army Quarterly and Defence Journal* 105, no. 4 (October 1975): 440–56; 106, no. 3 (July 1976): 333–50.

O'Ballance, Edgar. *The Arab-Israeli War, 1948*. New York: Praeger, 1957.

———. *The Third Arab-Israeli War*. Hamden, Conn.: Archon Books, 1972.

O'Neill, Bard E. *Armed Struggle in Palestine: A Political-Military Analysis*. Boulder, Colo.: Westview Press, 1978.

Safran, Nadav. *From War to War*. New York: Pegasus, 1969.

3. The Army in Politics

Abdel-Malek, Anwar. *Egypt: Military Society*. New York: Random House, 1968.

Be'eri, Eliezer. *Army Officers in Arab Politics and Society*. Translated by Dov Ben-Abba. New York: Praeger, 1970.

———. "On the History of the Free Officers." *The New East (Hamizrah Hehadash)* 13, no. 51 (1963): 247–68.

Berger, Morroe. "The Military Regimes in the Middle East." Mimeo. Congress for Cultural Freedom, Seminar, 1960.

Finer, S. E. *The Man on Horseback: The Role of the Military in Politics*. New York: Praeger, 1962.

Fisher, Sydney Nettleton., ed. *The Military in the Middle East: Problems in Society and Government*. Columbus: Ohio State University Press, 1963. See especially the following articles:

Campbell, John C. "The Role of the Military in the Middle East: Past Patterns and New Dimensions."

Khadduri, Majid. "The Role of the Military in Iraqi Society."

Kirk, George. "The Role of the Military in Society and Government: Egypt."

Rostow, Dankwart A. "The Military in Middle Eastern Society and Politics."

Torrey, Gordon H. "The Role of the Military in Society and Government in Syria and the Formation of the U.A.R."

Gutteridge, William Frank. *Military Institutions and Power in the New States*. New York: Praeger, 1965. See subentries under Egypt in the index.

Haddad, George M. *Revolutions and Military Rule in the Middle East.* New York: R. Speller, 1973. See Vols. 2 and 3.

Horowitz, Irving. *Beyond Empire and Revolution: Militarization and Consolidation in the Third World.* New York: Oxford University Press, 1982.

Hurewitz, J. C. *Middle East Politics: The Military Dimension.* New York: Praeger, 1969.

———. "Soldiers and Social Change in Plural Societies: The Contemporary Middle East." In *WTS.*

Kennedy, Gavin. *The Military in the Third World.* New York: Charles Scribner's Sons, 1974. See chap. 7.

Khadduri, Majid. "The Role of the Military in Middle Eastern Politics." *American Political Science Review* (June 1953): 511–24.

Lacouture, Jean, and Simmone Lacouture. *Egypt in Transition.* New York: Criterion Books, 1958.

Nasser, Gamal Abdel. *Egypt's Liberation: The Philosophy of the Revolution.* Washington, D.C.: Public Affairs Press, 1955.

Owen, Roger. "The Role of the Army in Middle Eastern Politics—A Critique of Existing Analyses." *Review of Middle East Studies* 3 (1978): 63–81.

Perlmutter, Amos. "The Arab Military Elite." *World Politics* 22, no. 2 (January 1970): 269–300.

———. *Egypt, the Praetorian State.* New Brunswick, N.J.: Transaction Books, 1974.

Rabinovitch, Itamar. *Syria under the Baath 1963–66: The Army-Party Symbiosis.* Jerusalem: Israel University Press, 1972.

al-Shawi, H. "L'Intervention des Militaires dans la Vie Politique de la Syrie, de l'Irak et de la Jourdanie—Un essai d'interpretation socio-politique." *Politique Étrangère* 39, no. 3 (1974): 343–74.

Torrey, Gordon H. *Syrian Politics and the Military, 1945–1958.* Columbus: Ohio State University Press, 1964.

Vatikiotis, P. J. *The Egyptian Army in Politics.* Bloomington: Indiana University Press, 1961.

———. "Politics and the Military in Jordan." In *The Military and Politics in Five Developing Countries,* edited by John P. Lovell. Kensington, Md.: Center for Research in Social Systems, 1970.

4. The '73 War, Prelude and Aftermath

Aker, Frank. *October 1973: The Arab-Israeli War.* Hamden, Conn.: Archon Books, 1985.

Aruri, Naseer, ed. *Middle East Crucible: Studies on the Arab-Israeli War of October 1973.* Willmett, Ill.: Medina University Press, 1975.

Badri, Magdoub and Mohammed Zohdy. *The Ramadan War, 1973.* New York: Hippocrene, 1974.

Bell, J. Bowyer. "National Character and Military Strategy: The Egyptian Experience, October 1973." *Parameters* 5, no. 1 (1975): 6–16.

Gawrych, George W. "Egyptian High Command in the 1973 War." *Armed Forces and Society* 13 (Summer 1987): 535–59.

Heikal, Mohamed. *The Road to Ramadan.* New York: Quadrangle New York Times Book Company, 1975.

Kelidar, Abbas. "The Palestine Guerrilla Movement." *World Today* (London) 20, no. 10 (October 1973): 412–20.

Lee, Eric. ''Infantry's Day against Tanks.'' *Military History* 7, no. 5 (March 1991): 34–38.

Lewis, Robert D. ''Ramadan War: Fire Support Egyptian Style.'' *Field Artillery* (August 1988): 32–36.

Lukacs, Yehuda, and Abdullah Battah, eds. *The Arab-Israeli Conflict: Two Decades of Change*. Boulder, Colo.: Westview Press, 1988.

Menshikov, Ivan. ''Hot Autumn of 1973 (the 1973 Arab-Israeli War).'' *Soviet Military Review* 2 (February 1989): 27–33.

Nicolle, David. ''The Assault on Mount Hermon: An Episode of the October War.'' *RUSI Journal* 120, no. 2 (June 1975): 43–46. Provides a rare view from the Syrian ranks.

O'Ballance, Edgar. *Arab Guerrilla Power 1967–1972*. Hamden, Conn.: Archon Books, 1974.

———. *The Electronic War in the Middle East, 1968–70*. Hamden, Conn.: Archon Books, 1974.

———. *No Victor, No Vanquished: The Yom Kippur War*. San Raphael, Calif.: Presidio Press, 1978.

Shazly, Saad. *The Crossing of the Suez*. San Francisco: American Mideast Research, 1980.

Tahtinen, Dale R. *The Arab-Israeli Military Balance since October 1973*. Washington, D.C.: American Enterprise Institute for Public Policy Research, 1974.

Williams, Louis, ed. *Military Aspects of the Israeli-Arab Conflict*. Tel Aviv: University Publishing Projects, 1975.

Yaacov, Bar Siman Tov. *The Israeli-Egyptian War of Attrition, 1969–1970*. New York: Colombia University Press, 1980.

5. The Palestinian Uprising

Dunn, Michael. ''Five Smooth Stones: Israel, the Palestinians, and the Intifada.'' *Defense and Foreign Affairs* 16 (June 1988): 15–20 ff.

Freedman, Robert O., ed. *The Intifada: Its Impact on Israel, the Arab World, and the Superpowers*. Miami: Florida International University Press, 1991. See pt. 1.

Hunter, Robert F. *The Palestinian Uprising: A War by Other Means*. Berkeley: University of California Press, 1991.

Lederman, Jim. ''Dateline West Bank: Interpreting the Intifada.'' *Foreign Policy* 72 (Fall 1988): 230–46.

Lockman, Zachary, and Beinin, Joel, eds. *Intifada: The Palestinian Uprising against Israeli Occupation*. Boston: South End Press, 1989. See pt. 2.

Peretz, Don. ''Intifadeh: The Palestinian Uprising.'' *Foreign Affairs* (Summer 1988): 965–80.

———. *Intifada: The Palestinian Uprising*. Boulder, Colo.: Westview Press, 1989.

———. ''Intifada and Middle East Peace.'' *Survival* 32, no. 5 (September–October 1990): 387–401.

Schniff, Ze'ev, and Ehud Ya'ari. *Intifada: The Palestinian Uprising—Israel's Third Front*. Edited and translated by Ina Friedman. New York: Simon and Schuster, 1989.

Shalev, Aryeh. *The Intifada: Causes and Effects*. Boulder, Colo.: Westview Press, 1991.

8

The Quest for Regional Dominance

The Arab-Israeli War of 1948–1949 led to the increasing militarization of the Middle East. The major Arab states pursued successive military expansion and modernization programs. Although this arms buildup was at first necessitated by conflict with Israel, it was not exclusively directed at Israel. The Arab states, despite the establishment of the Arab League, did not necessarily have the same interests or objectives relative to the regional balance of power. Rivalry was inevitable primarily because the political settlement of World War I left the Arab East with too many capitals.

Actually, the postwar political geography of the Arab East was illogical in many respects. The more developed societies were subjected to the rule of mandatory powers, while the less developed ones had full sovereignty. Historically enduring geographical concepts were treated inconsistently by the mandatory powers. In one case, the concept of Mesopotamia was taken as the basis for defining a country—modern Iraq. In another, the comparable concept of Syria was rejected. Moreover, the new division of that region ignored some traditional boundaries. The major coastal cities with their hinterlands often had distinct governmental status under the Ottomans, although they were more or less subordinate to Damascus. Thus, the *pashaliks* of Tripoli and Acre could be seen as precedents for the mandate states of Lebanon and Palestine. However, the Transjordan area was normally under the direct rule of Damascus, whereas northern

Syria was not. The boundaries set by the mandatory powers reversed this pattern of government.

Many Arab nationalist ideologues were natives of Syria. Prior to the imposition of mandate regimes, they had hoped to see a united Arab kingdom in place of Ottoman Arabistan. Having lost that hope, their intellectual heirs developed the concept of Greater Syria as a new symbol of unity. The relevant ideology had little appeal outside Syria proper, but over time it often complicated Syrian relations with Beirut, Amman, or the Palestine Liberation Organization (PLO). Moving beyond the theme of Greater Syria, Syrian intellectuals inspired the pan-Arab resurgence movement known as Baath (Arabic *Baʿth*). The Baath ideology appealed to many people throughout the Fertile Crescent (all of historical Syria and Mesopotamia). However, competition from parochial interests and Nasserist Pan-Arabism led to fragmentation of the movement. The outcome was the ascendancy of rival Baathist regimes in Damascus and Baghdad.

Iraq was perhaps destined to follow its own course. The country had inherited from its Ottoman past the ethos of a borderland that had separated rival Sunnite and Shiite dominions. With the cessation of Ottoman rule, Iraq remained a borderland, but the terms of confrontation changed. Iraq was to become the bastion of the Arab East against an aggressive Iran. The perception of an Iranian threat first emerged during the 1970s. At that time, the U.S. government looked to the shah's regime to act as the police power of the Gulf and accordingly assisted in upgrading Iran's military capabilities. That perception grew more compelling after the militant Islamists overthrew the shah in 1979 and called for an end to both secular and traditional rule in neighboring countries. Iranian propaganda disturbed many of the Arab governments.

As mentioned in chapter 7, military coups in 1949, 1952, and 1958 brought about the existence of secular, "revolutionary" regimes in Damascus, Cairo, and Baghdad. Through the same process, there emerged yet another such regime in Sanaa (al-Ṣanʿā'). This trend, however, did not affect the entire Arab East. It was seemingly limited to those states that had large populations relative to available land and other resources. Their experience differed from that of the smaller states, which retained traditional institutions of government. By coincidence, many of these sheikhdoms had prosperous economies as a result of the commercial exploitation of their petroleum reserves. There was thus an imbalance between population and resources within the Arab East. This imbalance was often the cause of friction between or among Arab states, which from the surface view appeared to derive from differences in political culture.

As with Iraq, Saudi Arabia also inherited one of the roles of the former Ottoman regime. By conquering the Hijaz in 1925, the Saudi regime became the servitor (or protector) of the two holy places of Islam.[1] Since the stronger Arab states eventually adopted secular ideologies, they have not contested possession of this honor. They have perhaps been more envious of the kingdom's oil wealth. The only contemporary challenge to the Saudis' claim to religious prestige came from the theocratic regime of Iran. Tehran's anti-Saudi propaganda exacerbated the strain in relations between Iran and the Arab East.

Various antagonisms impelled the Arab states to undertake military expansion and modernization programs. Except for Egypt, none of them possessed military industries of any significance. Thus, they had to rely on foreign sources of weapons and technology. The British and French had been providing military hardware and assistance to selective client states prior to the 1960s, when the United States and the Soviet Union became the major arms suppliers to the Middle East. The Arab-Israeli conflict afforded an opportunity for the two superpowers to test new weaponry and to continue their rivalry through surrogates. The Soviet Union generally supported the confrontation states; the United States supported Israel. The United States has also provided military assistance to a number of Arab states: Saudi Arabia, and, through Saudi Arabia, North Yemen; more recently, Egypt and the smaller Arab Gulf states.

Despite the scope and longevity of these armament programs, the Arab armed forces have been conspicuously slow to assimilate modern military techniques. Many instructors, advisors, and technicians have vented their frustration in written and oral reports. Officials and auditors of the recipient governments have similarly expressed dismay. A few studies alluding to the human factor of Arab military performance have surfaced. However, by and large, this issue of technology assimilation has yet to be adequately addressed. This may be because the efficacy of technology transfer has been taken for granted. Host governments assumed that their armed forces could fully assimilate modern military techniques. American military assistance teams assumed that they could "train to standards." Analysts and observers, lacking firsthand experience, assumed that technology transfer had taken place. One example of overestimation was their ascription of "combined arms capability" to certain Arab armies.

In reality, military assistance teams teach modern practices but do not inculcate the thought processes that underlie them. Combined arms warfare is ultimately predicated on the principle of cause and effect—conceived as relations of time, movement, and destructive power within two dimensions (surface and air). In traditional Arab thought, such considerations are irrelevant, if not impossible, because phenomenology is atomistic, not relational. That is, events or conditions are viewed as separate, individual occurrences, not as results of antecedent actions.[2] Without conception of cause and effect, there can be no integration of combat and combat support systems, which is the essence of modern warfare. Arab thought processes may be changing; however, they could never drastically change within one generation.

Other cultural factors have similarly made it difficult for Arab military leaders to adopt totally American, British, or Soviet war-fighting doctrine. As seen from the evidence of comparative military history, slight as it is, there appear to have been, and continue to be, distinct differences between Western and Near Eastern ways of war.[3] Western warfare has emphasized offensive action and shock effect, whereas Near Eastern warfare has emphasized standoff, attrition, deception, and surprise. It appears that this disparity not only has continued but has also complicated the military modernization efforts of the Arab states. To pursue this thesis, one would have to trace the continuity in military culture from at least medieval Islam through classical and late Ottoman times to the 20th-century Middle East—a daunting task perhaps. However, it can be shown that former Ottoman officers influenced military affairs in the successor states of Syria, Iraq, and North Yemen. Many veteran advisors can attest that the Arabs have been least compromising with their operational art.

The military assistance record in the combat service support arena has been similarly problematic. Nonetheless, many host nation officials have been willing to sponsor unending, redundant modernization programs because of their supposed coincidental benefit to society at large. In their thinking, military modernization compensates for the lack of a sophisticated private industrial sector by exposing native youth to modern techniques in many fields—medicine, veterinary science, computer applications, communications, and mechanical, electrical, and electronic maintenance. The time and expense of training are redeemed when officers and noncommissioned officers in technical occupations retire and take related civilian jobs in military and other governmental organizations. This phenomenon falls far short of mobilizing the whole nation for great socioeconomic advances, which was the promise of several free officer movements. However, it does contribute to the growth of defense industries in certain countries.

Apart from operational doctrine, some current attitudes within Arab military establishments are seemingly influenced by the practice of earlier times. The Arab Gulf States employ large numbers of expatriates within their armed services.[4] These are military retirees or seconded personnel, mainly from other Arab and Islamic countries, who serve on a contractual or set-term basis. They compensate for indigenous shortages of manpower and skill. They normally perform staff, training, and logistics-related functions, but, depending on host nation policy, they may serve in combat units as well. The potential for contracts or renewals often depends on the relations between the host country and home country. Host nation officials view the expatriates as servants of their state. Sometimes, they even view third-party defense contractors in the same way. They can probably justify the hiring of foreigners more easily, given that the employment of alien troops was prevalent in medieval and premodern Islam.

Martial traditions also seem to influence which military occupations or units are the most prestigious. Given a choice of career, the more advantaged of native inductees often opt to fly fighter planes. Among ground forces, commando units normally have high prestige. The relevant point is that fighter squadrons and commando units perform raid missions, and raiding activity has a high positive profile in Arabic-Islamic lore. Other high-prestige units are the elite guard formations (e.g., the Iraqi Republican Guards) which have responsibility for regime survival. These organizations have an historical precedent in the medieval *shurṭa*.[5] Apart from the culture of standing forces, the continuity of age-old patterns has been manifested in the role of militias in the civil wars of Yemen and Lebanon.

At the midpoint of this century, North Yemen was just beginning to make contact with the modern world community. The country had long been closed to foreign influence owing to the isolationist policies of Imām Yaḥyā. His xenophobic rule lasted from 1904 to 1948, when he was assassinated. His son and successor Aḥmad was at first reluctant to end Yemen's isolation. However, an unsuccessful coup attempt in 1955 brought to prominence the Crown Prince, Muḥammad al-Badr, who was favorably disposed to the modernization of his country. Under his influence, the Sanaa regime established ties and made agreements with a number of states, which led to the arrival of foreign missions in Yemen.

The Egyptian presence became the most pervasive; it consisted of hundreds of educators, doctors, administrators, and military instructors and advisors. Many of the Egyptians working in Yemen were spokesmen for Nasser's Pan-Arab revolutionary socialism. This ideology inspired many Yemenis and further encouraged the oppositionist Free Yemeni and Young Officer movements. When the reform-minded Muḥammad al-Badr succeeded his father in September 1962, opposition groups had already been plotting to eliminate the imamate altogether. They carried out a coup d'état shortly after his accession. The new masters of Sanaa set up a republican regime with Colonel ʿAbdallah al-Sallāl as its head and received immediate military backing from Egypt.

The quick arrival of Egyptian troops has been taken as evidence of Cairo's complicity in the coup. That issue notwithstanding, the change of regime did not progress smoothly. Muḥammad al-Badr escaped death and gradually made his way out of Yemen. He reached Najrān in Saudi Arabia, where some of his kinsmen had already established a royalist resistance movement. The republican regime retained fairly effective control of the area roughly bounded by the three axes: Ṣanʿā'-Ḥudayda, Ṣanʿā'-Taʿizz, and Taʿizz-Ḥudayda. With Egyptian support, republican forces contended against the royalist resistance for control of the outlying areas. The course of this war vacillated for six years, with Cairo committing large

Map 8.1
Northern Yemen

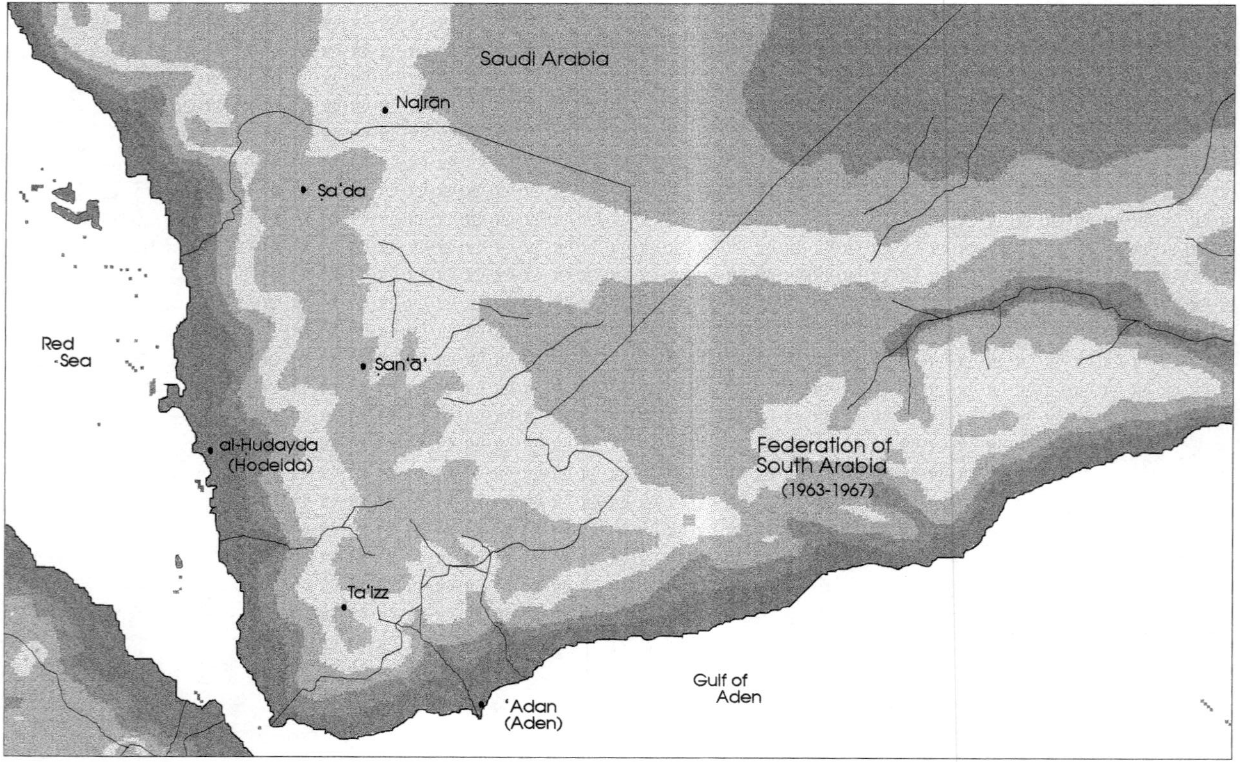

numbers of troops. However, the fighting did not receive much press coverage or historical treatment.

The royalists received financing and arms primarily from Saudi Arabia and occasionally from other countries. Yet, they had only about 5,000 regular troops under arms. To muster adequate forces, they appealed to traditionally loyal tribes as well as uncommitted ones to fight for their cause. The tribal warriors were influenced by payment of money, delivery of weapons, promises of booty, and other incentives. They were not particulary reliable unless they were defending their own homelands. The number of tribesmen willing to campaign probably numbered at most 50,000.[6] Over time, the royalist leadership was able to recruit disaffected former members or allies of the republican regime.

This makeshift army did not compare unfavorably with the republican army, which had 6 to 7 thousand regulars and used tribal auxiliaries to build up field forces. However, it is remarkable that the royalist fighters held out against the Egyptian Expeditionary Force, which at peak strength (summer 1965) numbered 70,000. They could rightfully boast of their martial deeds, although these mostly entailed the ambush and raid activity typical of guerrilla warfare. This struggle resembled the battle days (*ayyām*) of ancient Arabia in which free tribesmen defeated the professional troops of some king.[7] As the civil war progressed, the resistance effort was sustained more by anti-Egyptian motives than by proroyalist ones. After the Egyptian troops withdrew from Yemen, the royalist cause collapsed. The deeds of the resistance fighters were largely forgotten when republican rule eventually prevailed. Nonetheless, the guerrilla war in Yemen discredited Nasser's militaristic approach to unification of the Arab East.

Lebanon was another arena of conflict where native militiamen claimed victory over foreign soldiers. The problems there evolved from two factors. First, by 1970, the Shiites had become the most populous of the major indigenous sectarian groups, yet they lacked a proportional share of political power. Second, numerous Palestinian guerrilla units took refuge in Lebanon during the course of the Arab-Israeli conflict. As happened in Jordan, their activity began to jeopardize the security of the country. Governmental leaders held opposing views about dealing with the Palestinians, so the Lebanese army was not used against them. However, the leaders of the Maronites, the politically dominant Christian sect, mobilized their own militiamen to check the fedayeen and save Lebanon. This action precipitated the outbreak of civil war in April 1975. Many Lebanese Shiite and Druze clans sided with the Palestinians, forming the leftist opposition. The government collapsed, the armed forces fragmented, and rival clans rallied to opposing political blocs.[8]

The Palestinians and Lebanese Shiites were natural allies. They were both "dispossessed" people, albeit for different reasons. They both sustained the brunt of the Israeli reprisal attacks that followed fedayeen raids. The Palestinians often provided the Shiites with training, advice, and other support, as they organized themselves for militant action. As for the Druze, they sought to recoup some lost political power. They were by custom a militant people. When the leftist allies were on the verge of victory, Syria intervened on behalf of the Maronite-led bloc and occupied much of the country. The Syrian presence considerably reduced the internal strife but allowed the Palestinians to continue conducting cross-border raids. As mentioned in chapter 7, the Israelis solved this problem by invading south Lebanon in 1978.

Their forces advanced as far as the Litani River and made a buffer zone of the occupied territory. However, the fedayeen continued to strike from new strongholds. The Israelis eventually launched another, more massive invasion in 1982. Consequent to this campaign, the Shiite militias of south Lebanon initiated an intense guerrilla war against the occupation forces. (Druze and Palestinian militias also resumed active resistance.) The broken and close terrain severely constrained the Israelis' ability to employ their armored forces to advantage. By this time, the Shiites, particularly the Hizballah faction, were receiving extensive military assistance from the Khomeini regime in Iran, which was eager to have allies in the Arab World. Some of the Shiite tactics were denounced as terrorism by the Western press. However, such reporting was hardly impartial. The fact remains that Shiite Arab militias engaged the Israeli army in a conflict that it was ill-prepared to fight and ill-disposed to prolong. It was perhaps ironic—but only to Western observers—that militias had succeeded where standing forces had failed. In Arab tradition, the tribal warrior, or militiaman, seemingly has had higher prestige than the professional soldier.

While the guerrilla war was under way in Lebanon, the armies of Iraq and Iran were fighting to a standstill along their common border. Iraq initiated hostilities in September 1980 with the aim of attaining territorial and political concessions from Iran: full control of the Shaṭṭ al-ʿArab waterway, cessation of propaganda inciting the Shiite populations of Iraq and other Arab countries to rebel, and freedom of passage through the Straits of Hormuz (at the southern end of the Persian/Arab Gulf). With the last two issues, Iraq had the lead role in protecting the security interests of several Arab states. The Iraqi leadership assessed that it was then advantageous to resort to force since Tehran was estranged from both of the superpowers and Iran's once vaunted military establishment had been weakened and demoralized by revolutionary purges and organizational changes.

The Iraqi army invaded Iranian territory at several points along the border; the northernmost unit advanced toward Samandaj, and the southernmost struck at Abadan Island. The objective in the north was to seize and hold terrain critical to the defense of Iraq. The objective in the south was to capture the oil-rich province of Khuzistan. The Iraqi forces took Khorramshahr by assault but held up at the outskirts of Dezful, Ahvaz, and Abadan. Their momentum stalled, and the war became stalemated by the spring of 1981. To sustain the war effort, the Iraqi leadership recalled the archetypal struggle between the Muslim Arabs and Sassanid Persians and particularly the battle of al-Qādisīya.[9] The propagandists took the name al-Qādisīya as their war cry, and the Ministry of Defense made it the title of its official newspaper.

In the spring of 1982, Iran successfuly carried out a large-scale offensive. Its forces retook the city of Khorramshahr and recovered over 2,000 square miles of territory. Intraregional efforts were made to resolve the conflict by diplomacy, but these were derailed by the Israeli invasion of Lebanon. The Islamic Conference Organization subsequently appealed for an end to the fighting. The Baghdad regime responded by announcing a unilateral withdrawal of forces from Iranian territory. (Actually, the Iraqis did not relinquish all of their gains.) With momentum on its side, the Tehran regime chose to continue fighting and to take the war to Iraq.

Iranian forces conducted several cross-border offensives, attempting first to capture Basra and then to cut the strategic Baghdad-Basra highway. However, none of these operations succeeded. The Iraqis had become rigorous in their defensive methods. They established forward positions right at the border, entrenched and fortified them, and emplaced minefields and other barriers. They countered the Iranian assaults with massed artillery fire and strong counterattacks by forces held in reserve. Meanwhile, in 1984, the conflict took on a new dimension—attacks on port facilities and vessels in the Persian/Arab Gulf. The belligerents also resumed strikes against population centers, oil installations, and other industrial targets. With superior air and missile power, Iraq would prevail in these exchanges.

Tehran looked to attain victory through the ground war. Year after year, the Iranians attempted to break through the Iraqi defenses. They gained footholds inside Iraq at various points along the long border but sustained massive casualties in the process. The Tehran regime employed its Revolutionary Guard militiamen in infantry roles. When operating at night or in marshy or mountainous terrain, these irregulars were quite effective. However, when operating at day in open terrain, they did not hold up against Iraqi firepower. The rivalry between Iran's Revolutionary Guard establishment and its regular army often hindered operational coordination between the two forces. Iraq also employed irregular troops in this conflict—its Popular Army, otherwise known as the Baath militia. In the initial phases of the war, Baghdad deployed some Popular Army units at the front. Afterward, it used them more for rear area security and defense of key installations. In any case, militiamen could not have the same impact in conventional, positional warfare as they could in guerrilla warfare.

(لقد ذهب وولى الى غير رجعة ذلك الموقف الضعيف والآن لايقبل العرب بالقياسات المزدوجة ، وانما ينادون بقياس واحد في النظرة الانسانية وفي التصرف السياسي تجاه الامور ومنها القضايا المعلقة على حلول عادلة في المنطقة وفي مقدمتها قضية فلسطين)

الرئيس القائد
صدام حسين

جريدة يومية
سياسية عسكرية

تصدر عن وزارة الدفاع — مديرية التوجيه المعنوي

القادسية

رئيس التحرير: اللواء الركن منذر عبد الرحمن
نائب رئيس التحرير: أمير الحلو

AL_QADISSIYA Tuesday 4 - Des - 1990 [Vol . 11] No . 3448

١٢ صفحة ـ ٧٥ فلسا ـ العدد ٣٤٤٨ ـ السنة الحادية عشرة

الثلاثاء ١٦ جمادى الاولى ١٤١١ هـ ـ ٤ كانون الاول ١٩٩٠ م

الرئيس القائد صدام حسين يستقبل بعثة القناة الثانية للتلفزيون الفرنسي

الحوار المتكافئ لايقوم على اساس الشروط المسبقة

نحن أصحاب فكرة إجراء الحوار وليس الرئيس بوش

Plate 7. Masthead of *al-Qādisīya*, Iraqi political-military daily (courtesy of The Library of Congress). This newspaper promoted Iraqi militarism in the Iran-Iraq War and the Gulf War. The headline of this issue (4 December 1990) reads, "Even-handed talks are not based on preconditions. We know how to conduct talks. President Bush doesn't."

Map 8.2
The Persian/Arab Gulf Region

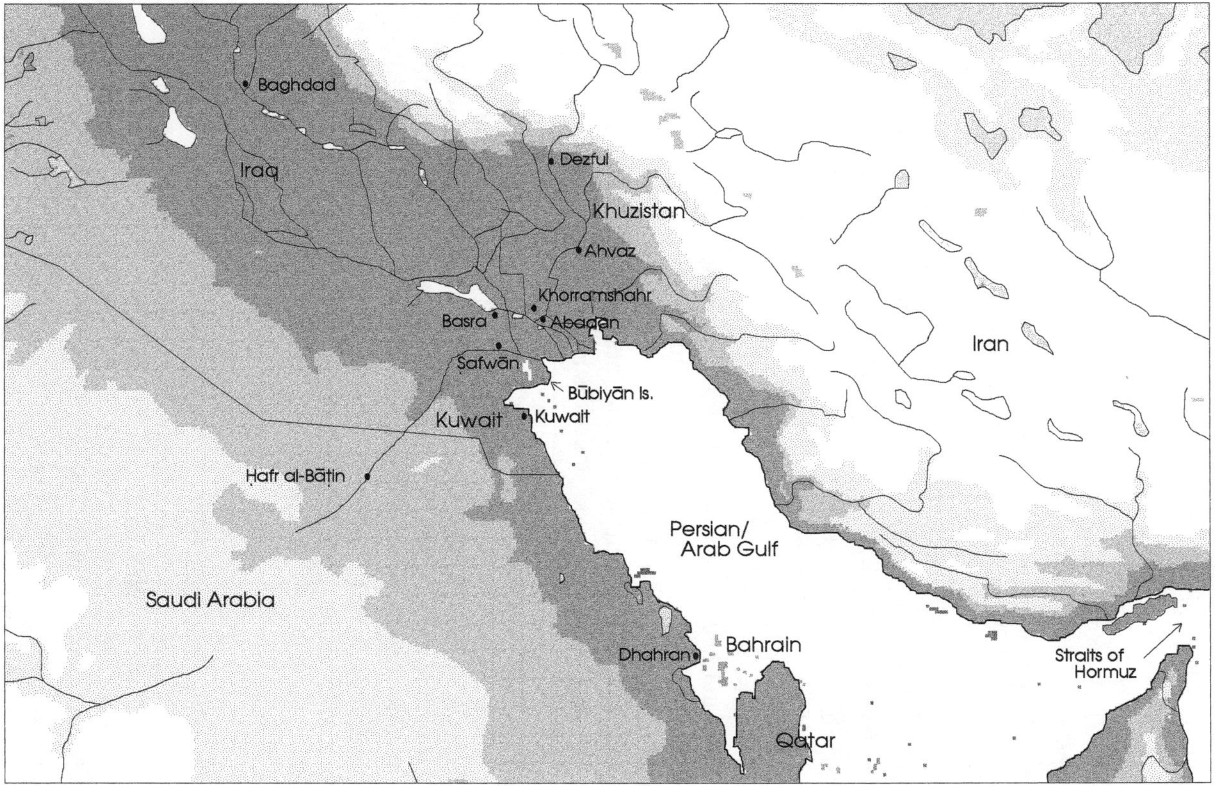

In the end, it was Iraq which achieved victory on the ground. Iran eventually had difficulty mobilizing enough troops to meet operational needs. It did not adequately weight its big offensive in the southern sector of the front in 1987, and it failed to launch any major offensive in 1988. As Iran was reevaluating its strategy for the war, Iraq seized the initiative. During the spring and summer of 1988, the Iraqi military carried out a series of limited-objective offensives, which annihilated much of Iran's ground force capability. This turn of events finally compelled Tehran to accept a United Nations–mediated cease-fire. The Iraqis had won their "second Qādisīya" in more than a symbolic sense. Despite differences in scope and duration of the two conflicts, the strategy reflected in Iraq's war plans for 1987 and 1988 was very similar to the one reflected in the Muslim Arabs' first great victory over Persia. In both conflicts, the victors relied on positional strength to blunt the enemies' attacks and then counterattacked at the decisive time. This experience of defensive victory had a profound influence on Baghdad's military thinking. As a consequence, the Iraqi high command was unduly predisposed to adopt a similar strategy during the next crisis.

Iraq finished the war with its army intact. It had the largest land force in the Middle East, which probably numbered over 750,000, including mobilized units of the Popular Army and border guards. Many original strength estimates were higher, but these were seemingly skewed because of secrecy, disinformation, journalistic zeal, faulty intelligence methods, and other factors.[10] For the same reasons, it has not been possible to reconstruct with surety various aspects of this long war, such as chemical weapons employment, clandestine arms transfers, and authorship of battle plans. Nonetheless, it is clear that Iraq did not attain victory solely through its own resources. Saudi Arabia and Kuwait expedited the import of weapons and supplies and contributed extensively to the financing of the war effort. Both countries sustained Iranian reprisal attacks for their assistance to Iraq. Volunteer soldiers from many Arab countries added to Iraq's military manpower. Similarly, foreign workers, primarily Egyptians, added to Iraq's labor force. Baghdad could claim with some reason to have led a pan-Arab effort to stop the spread of Iran's revolution.

Despite Baghdad's claim of victory, the war with Iran had demonstrated Iraq's strategic vulnerability with regard to the Persian/Arab Gulf. Given its restricted coastline of fifty-eight kilometers, it was all too easy for Iran to impose a maritime blockade or to sever access to the gulf by a land offensive. Besides, there was no room to develop a base large enough to support naval expansion. Faced with this territorial problem, Baghdad resurfaced the long-unresolved border claim vis-à-vis Kuwait. Kuwait refused to compromise on this issue and further rejected Iraq's fallback offer to lease Būbiyān and Warba islands. Relations between the former allies had already been deteriorating for other reasons. By the end of its war with Iran, Iraq had amassed a foreign debt of some $80 billion—perhaps as much as half owed to Saudi Arabia and Kuwait. The Baghdad regime thought that the Arab Gulf states should forego repayment in gratitude for Iraq's defeat of the common enemy. Kuwait did not agree. Moreover, the Baghdad regime was further perturbed that Kuwait and the United Arab Emirates were exceeding their OPEC-allotted quotas for petroleum sales, which depressed the market price for Iraq's main export commodity.

Spurning diplomatic efforts to reconcile differences, the Iraqi leadership resorted to military force. Iraqi troops invaded Kuwait on 2 August 1990 and proceeded to occupy the country. The following day, the United Nations Security Council, led by the United States, demanded the unconditional withdrawal of Iraq's forces. Baghdad saw its negotiating position undermined. War was inevitable since the Bush administration and the Saddam regime frequently misread each other's moves. The Iraqi leadership also erred in its plan to resist the U.S.–led coalition forces. The Iraqis deployed as if they were still facing the Iranians. They relied on a defensive strategy with the aim of inflicting higher casualties than the political leaders of the coalition could accept. Yet, the Iraqis lacked the air superiority and the natural terrain obstacles that were significant factors in the previous war.

In the end, Iraq's array of forces in static defense merely afforded targets for the most technologically sophisticated air and ground offensives the world had ever seen. Kuwait was liberated in 100 hours of ground combat, and an armistice was quickly signed. Certain defense analysts and publicists have since criticized the cease-fire decision, seeing that Iraq's military momentum was only temporarily checked. However, the United States was wise to forego continuance of hostilities, as they would have led to an untenable, counterinsurgency campaign in the land of the two rivers. Certainly, the Arabs' recent record of popular resistance struggles—North Yemen, Lebanon, and the Occupied Territories—has been far more impressive than their record in conventional warfare.

The larger issue of instability in the Gulf region remains to be resolved. There is likely to be further conflict. The Arab combatants will no doubt be influenced by their vision of the past. The chance that any state will achieve regional dominance probably depends on its people's ability to depart from traditionally subjective, atomistic thinking.

NOTES

1. Regarding the first use of this role as a symbol of prestige, see the account of Sultan Baybars' career in chapter 5 above.

2. In a religious sense, a situation exists because God wills it so, not because some set of external factors create or affect it. For further discussion of the at-

omistic nature of Arab thought, see H.A.R. Gibb, *Modern Trends in Islam* (Chicago: University of Chicago Press, 1947): 5–8.

3. The military history of the Near East has obviously not yet been written. Nonetheless, one gains an impression of this dichotomy from existing accounts of the wars between Greeks and Persians, Romans and Parthians, and Crusaders and Saracens.

4. Besides Saudi Arabia, the following countries used to or still employ hundreds of expatriates within their military establishments: Kuwait, Bahrain, United Arab Emirates, and Oman.

5. This institution is discussed in chapter 3.

6. See Edgar O'Ballance (Bibliog. 2), who is not at all empathetic toward the royalist fighters. See figures for royalist forces on pp. 109 and 191.

7. The topic of *ayyām* is addressed in chapter 1.

8. Contrary to the popular, journalistic view, there was no alignment of forces solely on the basis of religion. Christians fought alongside and against Muslims; they also fought other Christians.

9. The Arabs' historic victory at al-Qādisīya is discussed in chapter 2.

10. See, for example, Dilip Hiro (Bibliog. 4), p. 195. He asserts without question of plausibility that "the Baathist regime had put under arms nearly 1.6 million men in a country with a total of 2.7 million males aged 18 to 45."

BIBLIOGRAPHY

1. The Arms Buildup in the Middle East

Becker, Abraham Samuel. *Arms Transfers, Great Power Intervention, and Settlement of the Arab-Israeli Conflict*. Santa Monica, Calif.: Rand Corporation, 1977.

Bill, James. "The Military and Modernization in the Middle East." *Comparative Politics* 2, no. 1 (October 1969): 41–62.

Chubin, Shahram. "Hedging in the Gulf—Soviets Arm Both Sides." *International Defence Review* 20, no. 6 (1987) 731–35.

Cordesman, Anthony H. *The Gulf and the Search for Strategic Stability: Saudi Arabia, the Military Balance in the Gulf, and Trends in the Arab-Israeli Military Balance*. Boulder, Colo.: Westview Press; London: Mansell, 1984.

———. *Jordanian Arms and the Middle East Balance*. Washington, D.C.: Middle East Institute, 1983.

———. "No End of a Lesson? Iraq and the Issue of Arms Transfers." *RUSI Journal* 136, no. 1 (Spring 1991): 3–10.

DuPont, Pierre Samuel. *United States Arms Sales to the Persian Gulf: A Report of a Study Mission to Iran, Kuwait, and Saudi Arabia, May 22–31, 1975*. Washington, D.C.: U.S. Government Printing Office, 1975.

Gabriel, Richard A., ed. *Fighting Armies: Antagonists in the Middle East*. Westport, Conn.: Greenwood Press, 1983.

Glassman, John D. *Arms for the Arabs: The Soviet Union and War in the Middle East*. Baltimore: Johns Hopkins University Press, 1975.

Goodman, Hirsh, and W. Seth Carus. *The Future Battlefield and the Arab-Israeli Conflict*. New Brunswick, N.J.: Transaction Publishers, 1990.

Heller, Mark A. et al., eds. *The Middle East Military Balance, 1984*. Tel Aviv: Tel Aviv University, 1983.

Jabber, Paul. *Not by War Alone: Security and Arms Control in the Middle East*. Berkeley: University of California Press, 1981.

Karsh, Efraim. *Soviet Arms Transfers to the Middle East in the 1970s*. Tel Aviv: Tel Aviv University, 1983.

Katz, Samuel M., and Ron Volstad. *Arab Armies of the Middle East Wars*. Vol. 2. Men-at-Arms Series, no. 194. London: Osprey Publishing, 1988.

McCain, John. "Weapons Proliferation in the Middle East," *Military Engineer* 82, no. 538 (September–October 1990): 31–36.

Middle East Military Balance. Annual Report. Jerusalem: Jerusalem Post; Boulder, Colo.: Westview Press, 1983–1994.

Mottale, Morris Mehrdad. *The Arms Buildup in the Persian Gulf*. New York: University Press of America, 1986.

Navias, Martin S. "Conventional Arms Trade in the Middle East." *Army Quarterly and Defence Journal* 122, no. 2 (April 1992): 218–22.

Pascal, A., M. Kennedy, S. Rosen, et al. "Men and Arms in the Middle East: The Human Factor in Military Modernization." In *The Defense Policies of Nations*, edited by D. J. Murray and P. R. Viotti. Baltimore: Johns Hopkins University Press, 1982.

Privka, Otto Von. *Armies of the Middle East*. 1st American ed. New York: Mayflower Books, 1979.

Ra'anan, Uri. *The USSR Arms the Third World: Case Studies in Soviet Foreign Policy*. Cambridge, Mass.: MIT Press, 1969.

Rattinger, H. "From War to War: Arms Races in the Middle East." *International Studies Quarterly* 20, no. 4 (1976): 501–32.

Timmerman, Kenneth R. *The Death Lobby: How the West Armed Iraq*. Boston: Houghton Mifflin, 1991.

Zakheim, Dov S. "New Technologies and Third World Conflicts." *Defense* 86, no. 4 (July–August 1986): 7–19.

2. Egypt's Intervention in North Yemen

Badeeb, Saeed M. *The Saudi-Egyptian Conflict over North Yemen, 1962–1970*. Boulder, Colo.: Westview Press; Washington, D.C.: American Arab Affairs Council, 1986.

Dawisha, A. I. "Intervention in the Yemen: An Analysis of Egyptian Perceptions and Policies." *Middle East Journal* 29, no. 1 (Winter 1975): 47–63.

Kerr, Malcolm, H. *The Arab Cold War: Gamal 'Abd al-Nasir and His Rivals, 1958–1970*. 3d ed. London: Oxford University Press, 1971. See references to Yemen, civil war in the index.

McLean, Neil. "The Yemen War." *RUSI Journal* 111 (1966): 14–29.

O'Ballance, Edgar. *The War in the Yemen*. Hamden, Conn.: Archon Books, 1971.

Schmidt, Dana Adams. *Yemen: The Unknown War*. New York: Holt, Rhinehart, and Winston, 1968.

3. The War in Lebanon

Dupuy, Trevor N., and Paul Martell. *Flawed Victory: The Arab-Israeli Conflict and the 1982 War in Lebanon*. Fairfax, Va.: Hero Books, 1986.

Katz, Samuel M. et al. *Armies in Lebanon 1982–84*. Men-at-Arms Series, no. 165. London: Osprey Publishing, 1985.

Khalidi, Walid. *Conflict and Violence in Lebanon*. Cambridge, Mass.: Harvard Center for International Affairs, 1984.

Laffin, John. *The War of Desperation, Lebanon, 1982–85*. London: Osprey Publishing, 1985.

Rabinovitch, Itamar. *The War for Lebanon, 1970–1983*. Ithaca, N.Y.: Cornell University Press, 1984.

Richards, Martin. "The Israeli-Lebanon War of 1982." *Army Quarterly and Defence Journal* 113, no. 1 (January 1983): 9–19.

4. The Iran-Iraq War

Antal, John F. "Iraqi Army Forged in the (Other) Gulf War." *Military Review* 71, no. 2 (February 1991): 62–72.

Atkeson, Edward B. "Iraq's Arsenal: Tool of Ambition." *Army* 41, no. 3 (March 1991): 22–30.

Baram, Amatzia. *Culture, History, and Ideology in the Formation of Ba'thist Iraq, 1968–89*. New York: St. Martin's Press, 1991. The source is useful for tracing the honorific titles of Iraqi military units. See chap. 6.

Bergquist, Ronald E. *The Role of Airpower in the Iran-Iraq War*. Washington, D.C.: U.S. Government Printing Office, 1988.

Bigelow, Michael E. "The Faw Peninsula: A Battle Analysis." *Military Intelligence* 17, no. 2 (April–June 1991): 13–18.

Bulloch, John, and Harvey Morris. *The Gulf War: Its Origins, History, and Consequences*. London: Methuen, 1989.

Childs, Nick. *The Gulf War*. East Sussex, England: Wayland, 1989.

Chubin, Shahram, and Charles Tripp. *Iran and Iraq at War*. Boulder, Colo.: Westview Press, 1988.

Danis, Aaron A. "Iraqi Army Operations and Doctrine." *Military Intelligence* 17, no. 2 (April–June 1991): 6–12 ff.

———. "Military Analysis of Iraqi Army Operations." *Armor* 99, no. 6 (November–December 1990): 13–18.

Gardner, J. Anthony. *The Iran-Iraq War: A Bibliography*. London: Manse, 1988.

Grummon, Stephen R. *The Iran-Iraq War: Islam Embattled*. New York: Praeger, 1982.

Hiro, Dilip. *The Longest War: The Iran-Iraq Military Conflict*. London: Grafton, 1989.

Kamalu, Ngozi Caleb. "Regional Conflicts and Global Tensions: The Iran-Iraq War." *Conflict* 10, no. 4 (October–December 1990): 333–46.

Karsh, Efraim. *The Iran-Iraq War: A Military Analysis*. London: International Institute for Strategic Studies, 1987.

Khadduri, Majid. *The Gulf War: The Origins and Implications of the Iran-Iraq Conflict*. Oxford: Oxford University Press, 1988.

al-Lihaibi, Maedh Ayed. "An Analysis of the Iran-Iraq War: Military Strategy and Political Objectives." Maxwell AFB, Ala.: Air War College, 1989.

O'Ballance, Edgar. *The Gulf War*. London: Brassey's Defence Publications, 1988.

Pelletiere, Stephen C. et al. *Iraqi Power and U.S. Strategy in the Middle East*. Washington, D.C.: U.S. Government Printing Office, 1990.

Pelletiere, Stephen C., and Douglas V. Johnson. *Lessons-Learned: The Iran-Iraq War*. Washington, D.C.: U.S. Government Printing Office, 1991.

Rajaee, Farhang, ed. *The Iran-Iraq War: The Politics of Aggression*. Gainesville: University Press of Florida, 1993.

Rezun, Miron. *Saddam Hussein's Gulf Wars: Ambivalent Stakes in the Middle East*. Westport, Conn.: Praeger, 1992.

Sabin, Philip A. G., and Efraim Karsh. ''Escalation in the Iran-Iraq War.'' *Survival* 31 (May–June 1989): 241–54.

Segal, David. ''The Iran-Iraq War: A Military Analysis.'' *Foreign Affairs* 66, no. 5 (Summer 1988): 946–63.

Sterner, Michael. ''The Iran-Iraq War.'' *Foreign Affairs* 63, no. 1 (Fall 1984): 128–43.

Tahir-Kheli, Shirin, and Shaheen Ayubi, eds. *The Iran-Iraq War: New Weapons, Old Conflicts*. New York: Praeger, 1983.

Tucker, Anthony R. ''Armies of the Gulf War.'' *Armed Forces* 6 (July 1987): 319–23.

5. The Gulf War

Baram, Amatzia, and Barry M. Rubin, eds. *Iraq's Road to War*. New York: St. Martin's Press, 1993.

Bulloch, John, and Harvey Morris. *Saddam's War: The Origins of the Kuwait Conflict and the International Response*. Boston: Faber and Faber, 1991.

Eshel, David. ''Saddam Hussein's Spearhead—A Combat Assessment.'' *Military Technology* 15, no. 1 (January 1991): 251–56.

Hughes, D. P. ''Battle for Khafji: 29 Jan/1 Feb 1991.'' *Army Quarterly and Defence Journal* 124, no. 1 (January 1994): 13–21.

''Iraq and the Arab World.'' *Conflict* 11, no. 1 (January–March 1991): 1–15.

Jupa, Richard, and James Dingeman. ''Republican Guards: Loyal, Aggressive, Able.'' *Army* 41, no. 3 (March 1991): 54–58 ff.

Karsh, Efraim, and Inari Rautsi. ''Why Saddam Hussein Invaded Kuwait.'' *Survival* 33, no. 1 (January–February 1991): 18–30.

Rezun, Miron. *Saddam Hussein's Gulf Wars* (see Bibliog. 4).

Index

Abbasids: historiography, 5, 7–8, 55, 59–60; military campaigns, 5, 60; military establishment, 56–60
ʿAbdullah al-Baṭṭāl, 4–5, 13 nn.1, 2
ʿAbdullah ibn al-Zubayr, 37–38
Abū Jaʿfar al-Manṣūr, 5, 53–54
aḥdāth, al-, 59, 81 n.2. *See also* Militias
Ajnādayn: battalion, 107; battle, 22–24, 28 n.4
Aleppo, 61, 71, 78–79
ʿAlī ibn Abī Ṭālib, 7, 33–36
Amorium, expedition, 5, 60
ʿAmr ibn al-ʿĀṣ, 23, 28
Anatolia: Arab-Byzantine conflict, 3–9; Ottoman defeat, 94; Seljuk conquest, 61–63
Arab Army of Salvation, 106–7
Arab-Israeli Wars, 106–8, 110–16, 127–28; historiography, 116
Arab Legion (of Jordan), 100, 107–8, 112
Arab Liberation Army, 106–8
Arab Revolt, 98–99
Arabia, arena of war, 20–21, 37–38, 60, 90–92, 97–99
Archer of Islam. *See* Saʿd ibn Abī Waqqāṣ
Armenia: Arab conquest, 17, 43; Byzantine reconquest, 61; Seljuk conquest, 61
Armenian troops, 56–57
atabeg, 63, 71
ʿAyn Jālūt, battle, 76–77
Ayyām al-ʿArab. *See* Battle days, pre-Islamic

Badr: battle, 18, 20, 28 n.1; veterans of, 20
Baghdad, 53, 55–56, 61, 70
Bahrain, first Islamic influence, 21; tributary to Saudis, 97
Baḥrayn, al-. *See* Bahrain
Balādhurī, al-, 5, 10, 22–23
Baṣra, al-, 33
Battle days, pre-Islamic, 10, 36, 127
Baybars, 75–77
Bedouins: auxiliary troops, 11, 80–81,

About the Author

JOHN WALTER JANDORA, a Vietnam veteran who received his doctorate from the University of Chicago, spent five years with the Saudi Arabian National Guard Modernization Program. Being activated as a reserve officer during the Gulf War, he served at the Pentagon and with the U.S. Central Command Staff in Riyadh. He is the author of *The March from Medina: A Revisionist Study of the Arab Conquests* (1990).

ISBN 0-313-29370-8

90000>

EAN

9 780313 293702

HARDCOVER BAR CODE